The Dreamkeeper Messages

The Dreamkeeper Messages

by
Deborah Harmes, Ph.D.

Paper Paradigm Press

For information or clarification, contact the author at
dkhthedreamkeeper@yahoo.com.au

Third edition *(The Dreamkeeper Messages)*
published October 2009
Paper Paradigm Press
Central Victoria, Australia

Second edition (*The Dreamkeeper*)
published in August 2004
Paper Paradigm Press
Melbourne, Australia

First edition (*The Dreamkeeper*)
published in October 1999 by
Universal Publishers
Parkland, Florida USA

ISBN: 978-0-9751988-4-1

Cover art courtesy of NASA Archives
Cover design courtesy of Greg Calvert

Dedication

This book is dedicated with love to my husband, Mark Harmes, who has joyfully shared my work and my life.

CONTENTS

INTRODUCTION 9
Chapter One: ORIGINS 17
Chapter Two: HIERARCHY 35
Chapter Three: THE PLAYERS IN THE GAME 41
Chapter Four: THE AWAKENING 53
Chapter Five: HEALTH AND WELL BEING 61
Chapter Six: EXPRESSIONS OF THE ONENESS 75
Chapter Seven: EARTH CHANGES 85
Chapter Eight: ATLANTIS AGAIN: HAARP 97
Chapter Nine: CREATION TALE 105
Chapter Ten: THE CLEARINg 127
Chapter Eleven: CLEANSED AND REMADE 153
Chapter Twelve: IMAGINATION AND RENEWAL . . 169
Chapter Thirteen: QUESTIONS AND ANSWERS . . . 179
Chapter Fourteen: GOING HOME
(a Sept.11, 2001 message) 203
ENDNOTES AND ARTICLES 207
CONTACT INFORMATION 299

Acknowledgements

This book could never have been written without the support and encouragement of one person in particular and that person is my beloved husband, Mark Harmes. From the very first day that we met, he has believed implicitly in the importance of the Dreamkeeper messages and with his unconditional love, he has effectively created a safe space in which I may do this work. For that, and much more, I am profoundly grateful.

Additional thanks are offered to the dozens of people who have attended the Dreamkeeper sessions, both large and small, in the United States, Australia, Europe, and New Zealand.

For all of the readers of the Dreamkeeper web site on the Internet, I thank you for the many and varied questions which you have posed. I have devoted one entire chapter to answering a sample of these questions that we received from both you and the group session participants.

And finally, to the many kindhearted and curious people that I have been fortunate enough to meet because of this work, I thank you for your words of love and encouragement.

INTRODUCTION

The Dreamkeeper is not a new presence in my life and she did not suddenly arrive with the sweeping upsurge of interest in all things metaphysical from the 1980s onward. She has been with me since I was a small child, encouraging me and comforting me when I was having difficulties coping with being different.

From my earliest memory, I have been hearing voices, seeing people or objects that appeared and disappeared without warning, and watching visions of future events that unfolded in my head like a movie on a screen. But these were not acceptable subjects for discussion as a child growing up in the 1950s and 1960s and I learned very early on to fit in and stay out of trouble by keeping silent. Any manifestation of psychic phenomenon was considered bizarre back then and those who attempted to bring the topic into a conversation were frequently considered to be in the realm of the mentally disturbed. It was the reality of the time period, so I survived by blending in quietly.

When I refer to the Dreamkeeper from this point on as a she, I use that terminology because I always interpreted her gentle presence as being a female energy. I could feel her, sense her as a shimmering in the air shortly before she came into sight.

When I was small, I was able to visibly see her but she had to come in a form that I could relate to as a human child. So she appeared in the general shape of a human, clothed from head to toe in a hooded robe of shimmering shades of purple.

Where there should have been a face, there was a twinkling field of stars against a deep blue background. Where there should have been hands, there were smaller fields of swirling stars. I had no fear of her even when I was a tiny child and always felt safe in her presence. There was nothing intimidating or worrisome about this large being who came at night after the adults were asleep and stood at the foot of my bed. Children usually have excellent instincts about who is trustworthy and I always felt completely secure around her.

As I got older and was no longer able to see her visually, she continued to be present as a comforting voice in my head that gave me answers when I asked for them, but she did not begin to send me a consistent flow of information again until the 1980s. During times of stress or uncertainty in my life, I chose to switch off the voice so that I might have a more mainstream life as I raised my children. In retrospect, I know that it may have been a mistake to do that, but at the time it felt like the correct decision.

Beginning in the mid-1970s, although I was no longer in constant contact with her and had not asked for any assistance, the Dreamkeeper renewed the contact for a while and began sending me a series of movie-like dreams of what the future Earth would look like. I remember telling my husband and some friends about these visions. Their less than polite response was to tell me that I was nuts and that nothing like that could ever happen on this planet.

Twenty years went by. The children were grown and gone and I was divorcing my husband and working on my Master's degree when I unexpectedly reconnected with the Dreamkeeper. She picked a particularly inconvenient time to reappear since I was living alone in England and dealing with bouts of insecurity and loneliness, trying to stay on top of my graduate research in Spiritual Studies, and in general relearning to enjoy life and feel fine as just 'Deborah-alone' and not as half of a partnership.

We had some very bumpy and, on my part, angry periods as I coped with her sudden insistence that she had to be there and I had to just get used to it and get on with it.

Having just said that, though, let me clarify one point for the readers. The Dreamkeeper has always been firm in her assertion that doing this work was *my choice* and I had the right to simply say no. But what she wanted was commitment and not the back-and-forth wavering which I demonstrated in those earliest stages.

On a cold and gloomy November day in London in 1994, the voice-in-my-head of the Dreamkeeper, that had always been a familiar part of my life, suddenly manifested itself in automatic writing. I was working on an essay for school and had drifted off to sleep. But when I awakened, there were pages and pages of new material on the screen of my laptop computer that I had no memory of placing there.

I won't lie to you—it was a bit of a jolt. But once I was comfortable with being back in constant contact with her and with the new phenomenon of the automatic writing, there were some startling revelations. She explained that the Earth Changes, including drastic social changes, that I had seen decades earlier in the dreams and visions were to begin within five years and escalate with every year once we had passed the 21st Century marker. The Dreamkeeper emphasised that I was to be an instrument of peace and calmness in the stormy years ahead and I was told to expect a steady flow of information that was to be shared with the world.

Just when least expected, in the midst of all the chaos that I have described to you, the Universe sent me a lovely gift in the form of a friend named Mark who had travelled from Australia to visit his father in England and reconnect with the relatives in his birth country. We met over bowls of cereal and cups of tea in the breakfast room of our hotel in Chelsea in London.

For the next few months, this lovely man was my working-through-it sounding board on every subject from my evolving ideas for my thesis to my ongoing research in the paranormal and how that related to greater spirituality in some cases, to the spurts of information from the Dreamkeeper. He was funny and level-headed and he helped me stay grounded through this difficult yet exciting period. We found that we could talk for hours and never run out of things to say. We ended up driving all over Britain for almost a month in a wee little rental car, visiting ruins and abbeys, castles and stone circles, dolmens and prehistoric monuments. And somewhere in the middle of this adventure, we fell in love.

The Dreamkeeper came more and more often, but I was totally floored when she told me she wanted me to share this information in front of groups of people. What??? In all honesty, I was not happy with all the ideas that she was proposing. I had become used to doing the automatic writing and that didn't seem too intrusive, but the idea of standing up in front of an audience and discussing these concepts or of publishing entire books of her messages made me very uncomfortable. And then she began to hint at the idea that she'd like to speak through my voice. That made me even more nervous!

I allowed myself time to deal with these issues as I included some of her earliest messages in my Master's thesis at Goddard College in Vermont. I was pleasantly surprised when I was not regarded as a total lunatic for my beliefs and discovered that there was a great deal of interest in what the Dreamkeeper had to say when I was on campus during residency periods. That level of acceptance enabled me to feel safer about sharing the work in public.

As the reader may have guessed by now, the friend in London named Mark is the husband Mark that this book is dedicated to. A little less than two years after we met, we were married in a medieval registry hall in Norfolk, England. Shortly after that, we moved to Brisbane, Australia for two years and during that time, the Dreamkeeper did indeed begin to speak through my voice.

I was initially hesitant about the intrusiveness of it since my consciousness was 'placed in a waiting room,' so to speak, while she spoke through me. But through trial and error and much encouragement by friends and loved ones, I came to appreciate this communication with the Dreamkeeper as a gift to the world.

Some of these messages were shared with groups in several countries in the mid-1990s and were always greeted with great affection and respect. The bulk of this book, however, was received between the years 1997 and 1999 and includes many chapters written specifically for the book. One entirely new chapter was added during the 2004 revision.

I have chosen to not add any new material to this late-2009 3rd edition since there is a new book coming out within a few weeks that discusses new visions from the Dreamkeeper as well as a series of dreams and visions that I have received that are quite separate yet complementary to the Dreamkeeper work.

The original version of this book was published more than ten years ago in October of 1999 and for an entire year after the 2004 revision, it was the number 28 best-selling book of its subject matter at the world's largest internet book retailer, Amazon.com.

These particular visions may have been received a decade ago, but the information is even more crucial and timely now since NOW is when they are all unfolding. They were shared with the world a decade ago in a spirit of service so that people could prepare themselves mentally and spiritually for the times ahead. But those times have now arrived and the contents of this book may now be viewed both as a series of warnings and as a set of timely spiritual messages.

As a personal aside, my working relationship with the Dreamkeeper has reached a place where the material flows quickly and easily and is no longer a stress on my body as it was in those earlier days. Thankfully, there is no longer a need for me to be in a trance or even a semi-trance state to receive the visions.

I now live in Australia and when any of my books are printed in future, they will contain the Australian spelling of words. So if you are reading this in the USA, color is spelled colour, honor is spelled honour, etc.

There is a new book in the works with *totally new information for the second decade of the 21st Century* but for the new readers of the Dreamkeeper material, this first book is being re-issued so that you may know more about the events that are *unfolding right now.*

NOTE from Deborah, October 2009: This is the 3rd Edition of this book and a slight change must be noted. Due to a conflict in names on the Amazon website, and to avoid confusion with a similarly named children's book that apparently received an ISBN number without noting that there had already been another book with the same name for over a decade, I have altered the name of this book. The contents remain virtually the same but the new name is now *The Dreamkeeper Messages.*

Chapter One

ORIGINS

We are Dreamkeeper, a keeper of the collective dreams that bind all dimensional, interdimensional, and non-dimensional existence together, and a creator being. We too are creations of the Oneness that is known to you as God. We are true equals with you in our source of creation and in our soul essence and all of us, even those that humans have called enlightened beings or masters, are equal in the sight of the Oneness that is God.

When the Oneness created all beings with a thought, all souls as sparks of the Light that is around, part of, and encompasses the Oneness, we were given different roles to play.

Our role was to create the races of beings that, after their own time span of evolution, eventually came to your planet to create you in human form. The race known as Dreamkeepers are not the only creator beings, but all of us have one thing in common and that is that we have been here since the origins of what you term time. We have watched as the races that we made then went on to make other races, and those included the human race. For the most part, once our role as creator was complete, we maintained a hands-off status so that you were free to grow and develop at your own very human pace.

You may then be wondering why we have begun to speak through this woman called Deborah and share our thoughts with humankind, if they choose to receive them. It is because you, on this planet and in your surrounding solar system, are moving into the biggest period of transition in terms of spiritual growth since your first movements as life forms on the surface of this world. It is your time of destiny—the fulfilment of this latest cycle of evolution—and although the specific time is in flux due to several ever-changing earth-world conditions, the general timeframe is approaching and the stirrings of knowing are beginning to create a buzz in your humans with visionary abilities.

There are many of us here now—beings from other worlds, other planets, other planes of existence—and we will talk more about that later. But we have come to watch and encourage as you make those first tentative steps back to your true state of Light Consciousness, and the reunion with the soul-beings you have known in between your incarnation into solid matter. It is an exciting time, but it is not without challenges. That is why we are here to share information with you that may help you on the journey ahead.

We cannot do the work for you. We cannot rescue you from the years of upheaval ahead. You must, as an individual and as a species, do the growing and struggling and discovering for yourself. We will not hold your hands to give you a false sense of security or make promises except to say that it is a journey well worth taking if you have the courage.

Now we will answer some of the questions that people ask us when we speak to public groups or that you may have sent to Deborah through the communication form called Internet.

What do you look like?

We have been coming to Deborah since she was born and she remembers us from a very early age. To make a visual interpretation that could be understood, we appeared to her as we had done to many civilisations in past times, as a tall being dressed in a hooded purple gown. The pieces of body that should have been visible, the face and hands, were instead seen as stars, which is actually part of our true nature and appearance.

We have been asked why we picked that style of dress and colour of robe. It was chosen initially in times long past to fit into the culture that was then in existence. The hooded robe protected the humans of the time from the sudden gusty storms and fluctuating temperatures in these earliest colonies on the emerging planet-world.

In some kind of group-consciousness decision throughout the far flung and remotely populated regions of this planet, the colour purple was chosen again and again by the people of those earliest civilised-human periods to signify spiritual leadership. This was of great interest to us since it implied that you, as a species, had not completely abandoned your ability to communicate across the time-space barriers in a group-psychic fashion. And it also signalled to us that you 'remembered' the significance of certain colours and their spiritual energy.

When we suddenly appeared then in the midst of these early humans, it was slightly less disturbing to them if we had at least the familiar shape of a human and the coverings that they wore. We have, at select times in the past and in the company of those who are especially fearful, overlaid a projection of a human face and hands over the starry fields we described above, and have found that a gradual transition to our true appearance was then much less disturbing to them.

In the case of the infant Deborah, she had known us in her prior-to-incarnation state as a being of light and at that time she recognised the starry field as a normal state of being. But the human child Deborah had also been conditioned from the day of birth-entrance to accept human shape as normal, so we encompassed that into our appearance for her sake.

We have never been incarnated into a physical body. That was not necessary since we were fully developed in every sense from the moment of our creation. If you were able to see us as we really are, you would see a shimmering mass of pulsing light that can change shape and move instantaneously from one place to another with a thought.

Deborah has placed an image of us on canvas—that being she knew in childhood—all dressed in glistening shades of purple. And when she takes that painting to our discussion sessions and public meetings, she finds that often people are better able to relate to that image than they are to the idea of a ball of light. That is fine. We understand the human need to have a form that is more familiar to use as a reference or starting point.

Why do you call yourself we?

You will notice that we mainly use the term *we* when referring to ourselves. It is because we are a dual consciousness that communicates through this body known as Deborah. We have no sexual orientation and are not divided into female and male beings as you are. Deborah calls us a She because that is the portion of our essence that she strongly relates to—the more feminine-feeling aspect of our dual self—and which she feels at ease in allowing to flow through, or channel through, her body. This feminine aspect is the one that gives her most of the information about spiritual growth, psychic truth, relationships with humans and other forms of life, how to relate to the Mother Earth, and stories from civilisations long past.

She is comfortable with all of this. But there are other times when we are sending her more technical information regarding mathematical or scientific issues and she instantly equates that as the other aspect and her present-life-self interprets that energy as being male energy.

The Dreamkeeper energy signature is the same in both cases, but there is a subtle difference in what she calls the male aspect. Deborah has difficulty finding the technical information to be as interesting or relevant and therefore is less inclined to have it hold her interest. We have adjusted to that, although there is much information we would like to share that does not 'translate' simply due to Deborah's lack of scientific or mathematical understanding of the subjects.

How many Dreamkeepers are there?

There are only two of us left now residing as a joint consciousness. It was the nature of our race of beings to merge into a one-group-consciousness for large periods of what humans would interpret as time and then to separate off during other periods. The rejoining process took micro-fragments of a second, as you have come to know that increment of time, so constant joining-separating-joining was the norm.

People frequently ask us when we departed, why did we leave, and where did we go. The answer is quite simple. We went back to the Light—to the Oneness—which is the ultimate goal of all creations of the Oneness, to be reunited with that source of all. We regard all time as a simultaneous event, so we cannot give you dates that would relate to you. As to the why, we tell you that many races of beings have come and gone, many living for hundreds of times or, in the case of those of us without bodies, so many times that amount that it would be unfathomable to you. We come for our time, do what is our work, and then move to the next realm quite gladly.

Yes, we as a race did many things throughout time, created many races of beings, created unseen barriers or gates that protected your particular part of space and time from intrusions from other dimensions and times until you were sufficiently evolved and prepared to understand the concept of simultaneous life co-existing with you in interdimensional space-time. This has been a hard concept for many of you to grasp when you thought that this planet and time was a place that you and you alone were residing in.

One by one, the Dreamkeepers, as had many other species and creator-beings who had fulfilled their purpose, went back to the Light. That is your human goal when you talk about reaching Heaven, is it not? That is the goal of the Dreamkeepers also. Although our vision of Heaven is not as limited and reliant on concrete imagery as yours is, the goal for all of us is essentially the same—a reunion with the source of creation—the Oneness. You must realise that we have been here in a constant state since the first creation. We do not come in and out of a series of incarnational lifetimes as you have done. We have simply always been here. How we have longed for the complete rejoining of energy to the source of all, the Oneness. Is it any wonder then that one after another, the others of the Dreamkeeper race left in a joyous burst of starlight to go back for that ultimate reunion? They are still living—just not in a form that interacts with humankind.

Why are you still here, and why are you speaking through Deborah?

Quite simply, we have stayed because there was more to do and a promise to keep. Earth was one of our primary areas of creation and we have watched with interest the steps forward and backward that you have made as a species.

Deborah had remembered us from both childhood and pre-incarnational visitations. But she also had memories of an interaction with us in a past-life human incarnation. This was a very rare event when many of the Dreamkeepers interceded on behalf of a race of beings on another humanoid-inhabited planet that was facing complete extinction due to an imminent catastrophe. The group decision was made to assist in the rescue of the children of that planet. We knew, from the timelines we are able to read, that these children had a part in the future of civilisations not yet in existence on other worlds. It was essential for those children to survive. We took this unusual measure and the story of this race of beings will be told later in this book.

We had been trying to reconnect with Deborah for many adult years, but she had her own reasons for not listening when we called. We understood her actions during that period of her life and she will tell you about those reasons in her own words. Without a conscious awareness or memory of the decision, she has given us prior permission to return precisely at this time for a 'jump-start' into a life of service to others. It is certainly not what she thought she would be doing with her life.

Your entire planet and all species of life residing on it are on the verge of a massive transition to a new form of being. There is an awakening on the planet that is necessary before you move into the transition period, and the information that we are giving you can make both the awakening and the transition easier, if you chose to read it. It is free will at all times. You can embrace or reject the information that we give you through this woman, but know that it will continue to be freely given with love.

We state this quite firmly. Everyone, every single living being, is destined to make the transition and no one will be left behind. You may trust in the truth of that. The Oneness that is God is not judgmental in the manner of humans and sees the original beauty in each piece of soul-light.

For some it will be smoother and for some it will be a bit of a jolt to look around and see the world through different dimensional eyes. You are going to be quite amazed when you see what you have *not* been seeing!

What does it feel like to use a human body?

When we first returned to Deborah, we were a set of two-way conversations in her head. Deborah would mentally ask us a question and then she would turn to Mark and say, "The Dreamkeeper just said..." This was a transition period as Deborah became accustomed to having our energy, which is very different from human energy patterns, in her body for short periods of time.

The next means of communication was through automatic writing. This was much more efficient since we didn't have to 'move into' her body as fully for this. We could operate like a broadcast signal and send the pictures into her brain which then translated the signals into words on the computer screen. We were now able to send her large volumes of information in a much more logical manner. Deborah's own brain does the editing of the signals and creates words that correspond to the concepts. This method also incorporates the vocabulary that she has available, and if there is a picture or idea that does not match up to any known concept in Deborah's memory, it will not translate into anything recognisable. All of these things are issues that we have had to work through.

Finally, we began speaking through her voice. But this was the hardest adjustment for both Deborah and for us. She balked. She found it extremely intrusive to be shoved aside, as she put it, while we came into her and used her body. And how she fought with us about this!

At the same time, we were having difficulty 'sliding into' her small body space. We are not referring to the physical body of Deborah, but rather to the life-essence and aura-surround area that is the reality of who you are. Our life essence is in a constant state of expansion and contraction and is much larger than a human being's life essence. It was not a comfortable fit.

We had never used human language before our contact with Deborah since all of the Dreamkeepers, and most other off-Earth life forms, are telepathic even when they do have a spoken language or some type of sound communication. That was a great obstacle for both Deborah and for us as we learned to find words to match the pictures we were sending into her head. She would listen to the tapes of our early channelling through her voice and sometimes even she was having a hard time understanding what it was we were trying to communicate.

If you wonder why this difficulty does not occur when we are transmitting though automatic writing, it is because we are not taking over her consciousness. We broadcast something like a radio signal and Deborah's own brain acts as a decoding mechanism and looks for the appropriate word for the image.

She is always partially aware and in a semiconscious state while we are doing automatic writing. But when we do a voice transmission and move her consciousness aside to use her body to speak through, then we are responsible for finding the correct words. It is as if we have a computer bank full of information and vocabulary and we have to scan it until we find the right words for the ideas we are attempting to communicate. If Deborah does not have a word to use for that concept, or in the case of the mathematical and physics information, if she does not have a technical knowledge and vocabulary that applies to the images we are sending, we are unable to pass this information on.

In spite of some of the obstacles we have encountered though, we are fortunate since Deborah has a lot of words in her head. All of her years of study have served us well since she had more concepts available for us to expand on and many more words to tap into than she would have had when we first spoke to her when she was very young.

What sensations does Deborah get when you are sharing her body?

We try not to stay in her body for more than an hour or so at a time. When we are speaking to a group, we take a break part of the way through the session so that we are not in Deborah for too long. She finds that, depending on the subject matter of the discussion, she is either extremely tired and barely able to stay awake, or she is over-stimulated. The over-stimulation is also a form of fatigue, but she has greater difficulty accommodating that energy than the simple fatigue.

After we have been in her body for a while, the temperature of her extremities begins to drop. When we leave her body, she almost always has ice-cold hands and feet. But then she finds that she is flushed and overheated within minutes after our departure as her own body tries to stabilise itself. The coldness is usually accompanied by a tingling sensation in her limbs, at the back of the neck and top of the scalp, and across the bridge of the nose.

How easy is it now for both you and Deborah to do the channelling?

We have reached a good place with this. She is quite comfortable and we are easily able to slide in and out of her consciousness throughout the day if the need arises. She has agreed to make this her primary work for now, and her acceptance allows the transmissions to flow in an uninterrupted way.

We have learned when it is not appropriate to be there. There are times when she is too tired, is ill, or when her personal life is too stressed for us to be "knocking in her head" as she calls it. So we try to wait and return at a later time. However, if we feel a sense of impending personal danger for either Deborah or Mark, we will just arrive in her head whether she expects us to or not. We have saved her life on several occasions in this manner.

What are the timelines you refer to?

We will make this as simple as possible by giving you a reference from a human perspective. It will be easiest to explain the concept of timelines if you are able to picture us as sitting on top of a mountain. From our vantage point, we can see far off to the left, for example, the past—then directly in front of us is the present—and off to the right is the future. The timelines are the ribbons of time, like parallel highways running along below us.

We can see the past, present, and future running simultaneously as it truly is. You are hampered somewhat by your third-dimensional disability to be able to visualise all time as operating in a simultaneous space. We are pleased that there are now computer simulations of this simultaneous time available in embryonic form and in use by your physicists and philosophers.

What we want to emphasise to you is that none of the events we see happening in your present and future are firmly set and unchangeable. One of the reasons that we come to speak to you is to give you indications of areas that may need attention so that you may correct a potentially difficult outcome by your own action and intent.

Sometimes the timelines are changed by events beyond your control and, although it may leave you with a sensation of being powerless, we think that it is fair to be honest with you about that. The leaders of a country, for example, may be taking some kind of unethical or dangerous action that changes the entire future of that country that they rule and as a result it affects the future of the other countries that they interact with. But do you have face-to-face access to that leader to give your input or opinion? That is unlikely.

Unknown variables like these are always able to shift the timeline and its corresponding impact on your life.

But you, as an individual, are also able to have a positive impact on your own timeline. The awakening that you are undergoing, the seeking of knowledge of a spiritual life beyond the highly limited reality of what you see and sense around you, can truly alter your own timeline. The fact that many of you are doing your 'inner work' to resolve any past life and present life difficulties that you have had so you don't keep dragging them around like a necklace of stones is also allowing you to move to a more positive place in your individual timeline in spite of the less than positive actions of others around you.

The present and future is yours to create and we want you to truly believe that. Surely each of you can think of someone you know who has prospered even when everything else seemed to be collapsing around them, including world events. This person is manifesting that life of change in their own personal timeline and lessening the impact of the perhaps less positive group or planetary timeline. Would it not be better to walk through life thinking that you are making your life happen—rather than thinking that life is happening to you?

The necklace of stones of past life and present life difficulties can truly be cast aside and the real and lighter you, the being of the light of the Oneness that you may sometimes forget that you are, will be allowed to walk away from that dusty and perhaps depressing road you had been plodding along.

We will say one last thing about time. It is not a straight line from one point to another. It bends and flexes and loops back upon itself. When you have an episode of deja-vu or a strong sense of personal history repeating itself, you are encountering one of these time drifts. Time is like a handful of shimmering ribbons, wafting back and forth through the universe. If you are able to visualise time as these ribbons that you can blow gentle breaths of change upon, they will sway into a new direction. You will then be less likely to believe society's teachings that history and social reality is one particular way and cannot be radically altered in the space of one breath.

And what of those occasions when you feel that you are observing or hearing something that belongs in another time period—either past or present? We know that most of you have seen a child's toy called a slinky and it is constructed of a tightly coiled wire tunnel that slips and slides and moves with the slightest amount of input from the person holding it.

If you can picture each ring of that coil as being a segment of time-history, then you can see how time might be 'bridged' when the individual coils are pressed tightly against one another and perhaps, just for a moment, your current time may be in contact with the past or the present. This is part of how Deborah is able to do time-bridging when she tunes in to historic locations for research purposes.

What does it mean when metaphysical teachers say that some people are 'old souls' and some are not?

This is both humorous and incorrect, but we believe that these people mean well when they say such things. It is quite likely that people mean it in a generous way when they call a person an 'old soul' and they think that they are giving that person a compliment.

However, since all souls were created at the same time and in the same burst of creation by the Oneness, you are and we are all technically the same age. Those who are referred to as 'old souls' have simply had more human incarnations on *this* planet, and therefore they have more experience in Earth life.

Likewise, there are many souls who have chosen not to incarnate on Earth over and over and have had other work to do in other worlds. That work in those other locations was equally as important as an Earth incarnation. We hope that you understand that since your world-planet is not the only world, so called 'old soul' knowledge on Earth would not necessarily translate into wisdom in a different planetary culture or in another type of interdimensional life space.

What is the point of the Dreamkeeper being here?
Why have you come to Earth right now?

We are here to give you love and encouragement, share ideas and concepts and history that is pertinent to your current evolutionary phase, and to cheer you on as you each, and as a species, make your own progress and discoveries and thus move closer to the great light of the Oneness.

We are not here to change you, to tell you how to live, to make any grand gestures or physical displays. We are not looking for converts or believers. We are simply asking you to do the spiritual work for yourselves, if that is appropriate for you and is your personal choice.

That is our biggest message—responsibility and free choice. You need to make your own choices and not give your decision-making process over to someone else, whether from this planet or from another source. You must go within and decide what is right and true for you—what sounds a gong of truth in your heart—and then make your own choices without the weight of someone else's ideas of how to live life pressuring you.

Deborah tells every group, and we restate it here, that you will be the ultimate source of truth in your own life and your truth is not necessarily the same as that of society in general or even of your own friends, family, and other loved ones. You do not need gurus and teachers to move you towards enlightenment. You need yourselves, an inquiring mind, and an honest and open heart.

We will share information with you. We will give you a piece of the Great Puzzle of Life. But then it is up to you to go out and find the other pieces of the puzzle for yourself. We may be a stepping stone for you, and a road marker at an intersection of life perhaps, but you have to find the road back to the Oneness through a spiritual search that will be unique for each and every one of you.

You must each learn to make responsible decisions about what road to take. It is all too easy to turn the navigation of your life and your spiritual essence over to someone else, someone who tells you that they know all of the steps that you need to make so that all you have to do to be 'saved' is to listen to them. These frequently include family members, friends, or work colleagues who pressure you to conform, well meaning religions and so-called 'Masters of Enlightenment' who spring up and attract large followings. Does that feel right to you?

Yes it can be warm and fuzzy and easy if someone says to you, "I will be the loving teacher or parent figure. You just do whatever I say and everything will be fine." But what have you learned from that? Have you learned to think independently? Have you learned to practice discernment about what is truth and what is being sold as truth, but in actuality is falsehood? Have you experienced the thrill of discovery when you get just enough pieces of the puzzle to begin to see the formation of an image?

This is a matter of concern for us when, after hundreds of years of so-called civilisation, we see so much aggression against one another and see so many of you obediently following the belief system of your culture or family or nation without questioning the validity of this belief system for you as an individual. We would like to see more waking up in the world, but it is a personal choice that each of you must make for yourselves. However, we hope that through our words, perhaps a little shaking up will occur and new ideas will either sift into your realm of thinking or percolate up through your own levels of consciousness.

We have no agenda for humankind. We have no wish to see you follow any path of development other than your own as individuals and as a species. We simply hope for your success in these most exciting and simultaneously difficult days. We are glad to be with you at this time.

Chapter Two

HIERARCHY

When we speak to groups, we have noticed that a concept frequently arises for discussion—that of the hierarchy of what you call heaven or creation. We are asked where you, as humans, fit into this scheme.

First we must tell you that there is no such thing as hierarchy in the realms beyond this world or even in the temporary reality of this Earth-based life. It is a creation of the minds of humankind. But why? And for what purpose?

Would you feel more empowered if you knew, truly knew in every part of your being, that you were the equal of every living thing or being that was ever created on this Earth—or that you were an equal of the angels—that you were an equal of the other races of beings from other planets or dimensions, no matter how technologically advanced they may be—or that you were a true and complete equal of the teachers such as Jesus or Buddha—or were equals of the creator beings?

We all have equality in our soul-light state which is our true state. We simply have different job assignments that are given to us. In our particular case, our assignment was given by the Oneness at the time of creation, as was the assignment of the angels.

We were specifically created to act as creator beings of other races. The angels were a race of beings that were specifically created as helpers and guardians over humans, animals, plants, minerals, and many other life forms throughout the universe. That is the nature of their soul-life path through ALL of time and their work is not done on this planet alone.

We will poke some gentle fun now. We think that it is humorous that some of you have developed a belief system that includes the idea that when you die from human life, you turn into angels. Please let us assure you now that this is not the case.

When you leave this particular life, some of you might choose the role of a spiritual guide to other humans who are still in active human incarnation, but you will not evolve into angels. They are life-form creations that are quite unique and separate from human life forms. It is an interestingly human desire to attain the status of a being which you consider to be loftier and somehow more advanced than you think that you are. But the truth is, you have an equally interesting and important job assignment in your human state of learning and evolving.

However, if you have been programmed, so to speak, by the input of generations of organised religions who proclaim as truth that there is a hierarchy in God's realm of creation and that angels are superior to humankind, it is not then so surprising that you have this curious belief system.

When you are in a between-incarnation state and are able to choose the place to go or life experience to have next, you make your own assignment regarding where to go. But on a soul level, when you examine the *inner light,* which is what you all are in reality, all forms of creation are equal.

You are all size-shifting and pulsing masses of light, pieces of the great light of the Oneness, underneath the 'clothes' of bodies that you temporarily wear during each incarnation. If you had been allowed to have this knowledge all along, why would it then be necessary for you to believe that there is a hierarchy in heaven or on Earth?

It is an artificial means of control that has been created here on Earth and not in the heavens or in the mind of the Oneness. You will find that this is an area that we return to over and over throughout this book—control—and how to regain control of your own life and disallow the control of others over your life and your own unique destiny. Later in this book, we will examine in greater depth these controlling influences and who the people are who maintain this rigourous measure of control over humankind.

Would you believe in the necessity of a big building for worship and a once a week ceremony as your means of contacting the Oneness that is God if you thought you were an equal of all other forms of creation? We think not! We think that then you would remember that it is just as easy to have a genuine and direct conversation with God, the plants and animals, and with other life-forms, seen and unseen, in any setting that felt comfortable to you and you would not feel that you are required to be in a special building built just for the purpose of worship. Being in those buildings would then be a choice, not a necessity.

If you felt that you were the true equal of those who claimed to be 'in power' in your world, would you allow yourself to be bullied into following illogical and human-invented laws that are designed not for the creation of order and harmony among society, but for the control of your free-thinking abilities? We think not!

Just because other beings and their vehicles from other planets and dimensions are now being glimpsed in greater numbers and these beings apparently have more advanced machinery or technical abilities than you, does this then make them more spiritually advanced than you? Would you believe that they are higher or more evolved or more worthy than you? We think not.

If the mechanisms of control were suddenly released from humankind, would you instead learn to recognise the sacredness of all life and all choices of how to live that life, whether on this planet or dimension or on another? Would you allow the feeling of oneness with all creation to seep into you, fill you with love, and empower you? Would you reject all further efforts to make you feel small and weak and controlled in any fashion? We would sincerely hope so!

If there is no hierarchy, then you may ask if there is any structure which defines this universe and all others. Yes—*it is the spiral.* The ancient peoples of your planet knew this and drew it or carved it on many structures that survive to this day. The creation energy that is a part of each of you is expressed with that signature symbolism, the spiral, in the formation of your DNA. The spiral, the ever-moving flow, connects you to both the celestial energy and that of the planet Earth that you reside on. Your passage through current incarnational life and previously incarnated lives is in a continual spiral moving back, back, deeper *inward* towards the source of all movement, the centre of the spiral, the Oneness.

The movements that you make in various incarnations, or in personal growth in this lifetime, are not steps upward towards the Oneness who supposedly resides in some heaven-in-the-sky illusion. There is no up! Rather, it is a spiralling closer and closer to the centre. To believe in stepping up is to believe that someone or something else is always above you, over you, or behind you, rather than being beside you and around you.

This is part of why we have come at this time—to help tear down these artificial illusions such as hierarchy and to allow you to grow unhampered. It all begins with the acts that you, as free-willed individuals, must do and the steps that you must take. The starting point is the belief in the truth that is hidden behind the many veils of illusion that are dropped in front of your outer and inner eyes.

And who determines what is truth? The wise inner self—the spark of the Oneness that has never left your consciousness—links you straight back to the Truth.

Chapter Three

The Players in the Game

At this point, we think it is appropriate to discuss the other participants in this time of transformation—the other players in the game.

Angels

Let's begin with the angelic realms. Angels are not a more highly developed form of human consciousness. You do not 'graduate' to angel status when you die after an earthly incarnation. This is a mistaken impression that many of you unfortunately have.

Angels are a very separate race of beings, created by the Oneness at the same moment of creation as that of all life. Their very purpose for being is to interact with humans and other life-forms and to be of assistance and encouragement. They are very powerful, loving, and are more consistent in their emotional approach to life due to their lifelong connectedness with the Oneness. They have never been forced to wander in the doubt and despair that humankind has.

When we say this next thing, we truly mean it. Angelic intervention and help is there and waiting for all of you, but only if you ask for it. There are rare occasions when an angel will seemingly spontaneously intervene in a human life, but these are not mere random occurrences. If the human in question had a larger mission to accomplish in their life and some unforeseen act was about to harm or even take the life of that human, thus preventing them from fulfilling their mission to help humankind, then an angel might be assigned to 'rescue' the human.

However, this type of intervention is not the norm. For the angels to step in and prevent you from making errors in your life, even errors that might cause physical pain or death, would be interfering with your progression on a soul level. Sometimes the lessons that make the largest impression on you are the ones that are the hardest or most painful to learn.

Nonetheless, if you need and ask for assistance from the angels, they are there. In every instance, they react with the maximum level of *appropriate* response. It may be that you suddenly feel not so alone with a problem and that there is a way out of the darkness that has descended over you. Or it may be that they physically protect you from harm. In whatever manner the angels offer you help, it is essential for you to complete the circuit of contact by remembering to acknowledge their help and by being grateful.

Is that too much to ask? We are amazed by the lack of gratitude that you as humans display to those beings who offer you assistance with the greatest of love and devotion, and with no demands for thanks. But we say this to you—do you think that the universe will continue to send you encouragement and assistance if you forget to express gratitude? It is something to remember to do each and every day of your lives. No matter how badly you think your day has gone, someone else's has gone much worse than yours. So remember to say thank you for the blessings that you do have instead of focusing on what you may think you still require.

Spirit Essence

Who else is out there in a non-incarnational form working for your benefit? Those loved ones who have surrounded you during your earthly existence, but who have preceded you in their departure from life, are still with you to some extent. Although their soul essence has passed on to the Oneness and into the light, and they may be either in the resting phase between lives or even in a new human incarnation, a piece of their essence is able to reach you when you need help.

It is as if a radio-wave projection of their loving thoughts is broadcast back to you, and thus they are able to be with you. No life-form, whether in an incarnated form or in spirit essence, is ever completely separated from the greater Oneness. There is always a piece of each individual residing in the heart of the Oneness. So that piece of the loved one is what is accessed when you ask, for instance, for a departed relative to give you help and hope in times of trouble. You are never alone.

Spirit Guides

Many of you have asked us what spirit guides are. In some cases, they are the spirit essence of a formerly incarnated human who has chosen not to reincarnate, but rather has chosen to work from the 'other side' through psychic contact with humans who are presently residing on this planet. In other cases, the spirit guide is a being who may or may not have ever been incarnated as a human and who has attained such a state of enlightenment that they could rejoin the Oneness for all of eternity if they chose to do that. But again, in the spirit of love for humankind, they have stayed in spirit essence to give assistance to humans by contact on a psychic or soul level.

This does not mean that these spirit guides are ghosts. That which you call ghosts are the soul essences of humans who are trapped in a beyond third-dimensional state and who have forgotten or have chosen to ignore the way back to the light and the Oneness.

If a human is killed unexpectedly, for example, they may not realise that they are dead to this life and may not understand that it is no longer appropriate for them to be inhabiting this Earth plane. These soul essences may need to be contacted and made to understand that they have more work to do in another place, and that they need to walk into the light and move on.

In the case of those who have left feeling that either their loved ones cannot go on without them or that they have left certain earthly tasks undone, these beings may also remain in a ghostly form and occasionally be seen. There are many variations on these reasons. But whatever they may be, it is best for them if they are gently brought to the realisation that they need to go forward to the light, rather than remain in a space where they are no longer progressing on an earthly level or a soul level.

Other than the ghosts that we have mentioned above, any of the guides who are meant to be assisting humankind may reach you in several ways. You may get direct contact such as Deborah gets through channelling. This channelling may be through voice or writing or a series of what you may think are inspired thoughts that you then begin to realise are not originating from you.

Sometimes the guides reach you through your dreams. For this reason, we would encourage you to keep a writing implement and paper by your bed to write down your dreams as soon as you awaken each morning. When you review these notes, you will find that great wisdom is being given to you in your dream state. Most of the time this information is literally slipping out of your mind as soon as you awaken and move, but if you make a conscious effort to begin recording it, you will soon find that you have triggered a process of increased memory.

Guides may also be entities—life forms—who have never been in any type of physical form but who know that their role is to assist in the development of life forms in many universes through messages of love and encouragement.

Some of them are like ourselves, creation beings who are best described as a mass of glowing light from which a conscious energy-intelligence originates. But we will be honest with you, there are very few of us who choose to attempt to burrow through the layers of human consciousness that normally prevent any such psychic contact. And this is why.

With each incarnation you have had in human form, you have accumulated more and more layers of 'psychic pollution' and social programming that has removed your ability to see with clarity—to remember that you are part of the Oneness, and not some isolated life-form trapped and alone in your life-state.

Societal conditioning plus past-life accumulated 'pollution' makes it most difficult to reach you. That is why most of us who are the original creation beings, and most of the angelic race, prefer to maintain a position of watchful observation and allow our creations—the beings from the skies, the interdimensional entities, and the spirit echoes of human life—to be the ones who actually communicate with you directly through channelling, thought, and inspiration.

The guides may also be off-planetary life-forms who are soon to be in direct contact with humankind. This is where it gets a bit difficult because we have told you that not all off-planetary or interdimensional entities wish you well. True, most of them have only your best interests in mind, but you must rely on your inner heart sensing—your personal judgement—to determine if the information that you are receiving, or which is being shared with you by another person, is correct and appropriate for you.

Aliens and Other Entities

Let us very briefly discuss the beings from the skies—what you call aliens—and the interdimensional entities. Just as we, acting on behalf of the Oneness who created the soul essence of us all, were responsible for the creation of these many and varied beings, they were then responsible for the creation of humankind.

You do not look exactly like anyone else in the universe—did you know that? You look a little like several other life-forms since you were the result of a combination of genetic material from several races of beings. We must warn you that when they arrive, none of them will look exactly like you do.

Also, your final appearance, the one that you have now, is the result of much trial and error. The creatures that you have seen in mythology that were half man and half animal were earlier efforts at refining your final form. These creatures were not mythology in that respect—they are all that remains in pictorial form of long gone prototypes of humankind.

We must give a slight caution at this point. Some of the beings from the skies will arrive and visually be very beautiful to behold. But do they have beauty in their message? Conversely, some of the beings that you will encounter may be disconcerting to you at first in their appearance since they will be so radically different from human form. Yet some of what you will call the ugliest will have the most beautiful and pure of messages.

Do not be deceived by humankind's obsession with physical beauty and listen only to messages that may not be for the true benefit of humankind. When the beings from the skies and the beings from other dimensional states arrive and make contact, you must once again listen with your heart, not your eyes, and not your mind which can be easily manipulated.

Most of these off planetary and interdimensional beings have been watching and patiently waiting for many millennia until you reached a developmental stage where you could accept their existence without giving them the status of gods. This is essential to remember—they are simply at a different stage of development, but that does not make them superior to you.

Technological advancement is simply a matter of possessing bigger toys—but it does not necessarily mean that they are any more spiritually developed than you are. You are meant to meet them as equals and not assign them the role of gods. Your primitive ancestors may have looked at these visitors in that manner and worshipped them as gods, but you are meant to meet in a state of equality.

Many of you have asked us why there is a sudden burst of UFO activity in all of the skies of your world. In spite of the lack of reporting in your media about these events, these craft are being seen in each and every country. You are being mentally prepared for the new reality of coexistence with beings that are very different from yourselves, but it only appears to be escalating because you, as a species, have quite recently reached an evolutionary stage where you are able to cope with this knowledge. As you absorb what we have just said, ask yourselves why you are being prevented from knowing just how many of these beings from the skies and interdimensional beings have made contact with the scientists of your world in times long past and continue to do so at this present time. If you are now ready for this knowledge, why is it being kept from you?

We must now explain about filters. Your eyes perceive the world around you and send information to your brain based on the spectrum of colours and dimensions that are visible as you look through the filters in your eyes. But what if we told you that the world is quite different from what you are currently seeing and that as you move into 4th- and then 5th-and-beyond dimensional states, your filters will change and you will be able to see the surrounding colours and other beings that have been there all along, but which you were unable to see through third-dimensional filters.

This is an exciting time for humankind. You are regaining part of your heritage and will soon be able to say that you really DO see reality.

What else can you expect to see as you move closer towards the 4th dimension. Some of you have already begun to experience these changes, although only in unpredictable and sporadic occurrences. If you are able to fleetingly see the movement of a body shape from the sides of your eyes, and then when you turn your head and look at that area face on, you find that there is nothing there, then know that you are beginning to notice what human writers have called the tearing of the veils between dimensions and you are glimpsing other dimensional life-forms who are actually coexisting in the same space as you are.

This is not something to be alarmed about, but it does require some adjustment on your part when you realise that you are never truly alone in a room!

Some of you have told us that you are seeing blocks of colours or rapidly moving streams of colours out of the corner of your eyes, but then they disappear when you turn your head. Again, this is another form of life, a form that exists between dimensions and that has no body shape that would seem familiar to you. But it is a life-form all the same.

The key to being able to observe these sightings for more than a fragment of time is to resist the natural human urge to turn and look at them. The sensing mechanism in your human eye is currently only able to see these things from the side. But as soon as you face the object head-on, you are looking through a different sensing part of the eyeball and that part is unable to detect the other-dimensional object or movement. If you truly want to see these things, you must be able to relax and train yourselves to look at them through your peripheral vision only.

For many years, Deborah has been seeing a flow of geometric symbols, numbers, and mathematical formulas streaming by in her waking vision—as if a clear screen was overlaid onto her normal vision and these additional objects were being projected onto the overlay. When she has shared this information in group sessions, she has seen many hands shoot up into the air to acknowledge that they had also seen similar things in the last few years.

This stream of numbers and symbols is a dual-purpose concept. You are being 'fed' information by those of us who are attempting to awaken you to your full potential. And this information is also your own unconscious awakening of long dormant soul memories regarding the true nature of the universe and all creation.

The beings from the skies and the interdimensional beings will be able to communicate with you telepathically. From one species to another, that is the true form of communication that you are meant to have had all along. We will speak more of this later.

However, the true language of creation—of the stars and celestial objects as well as the various life-forms that are scattered throughout creation—is mathematics. Are you surprised at that? You will find that when you begin to venture farther and farther away from your planet of origin in this lifetime and begin to interact with other life-forms among the stars, the language that you will all have in common is mathematics. If you were truly able to remove your mental blocks, as some of your prominent physicists are able to partially do, you would see creation and the Oneness revealed in all of its perfection through numbers.

This is why we tell you that although you may not understand what you are seeing when these numbers and symbols stream by in your waking or dream state, be assured that the knowledge that you need is subtly being reawakened in you and will soon seem like second nature when you move beyond the limitations of third-dimensional living.

Another topic to mention is the tones that are being heard by many of you inside your head. Again, this is nothing to be alarmed about. On worlds past, and on many worlds in other galaxies, rather than using the spoken word (which is an artificial means of communication when compared to the more natural method of telepathy), beings recognised one another by means of a tone given off from their body.

It was like a signature sound for each individual, and no two tones were exactly the same. In some cases, families or tribal groups had similar sounding tones and that was a means of identifying a group. But the individual sounds were still separate.

Sound carries a vibration, and vibration can be reduced to a mathematical formula. Do you see what we are telling you? It still comes down to the numbers, the mathematics that are the basis for all creation.

You may be hearing these tones in your waking state, but many more of you are sensing them in those fragmentary moments between the waking and sleeping state. Relax and flow into the sound. It too is a tool for your awakening consciousness and you will find that as you acknowledge, become accustomed to, and then embrace these sounds, and numbers, and visions, you will be cognisant of realms of possibility beyond your previous imagining.

This is an appropriate place to mention the crop circles that are being left in many places around your planet. They also have a multidimensional purpose. The beings from the skies and the interdimensional entities are leaving them as symbols to awaken your slumbering consciousness to long-forgotten truths. Your scientists have discovered that the mathematical calculations of the lengths, angles and curves in each crop circle have yielded a surprising result. They are musical tones!

Once again, the symbolism is intended to register a series of tones in your cellular makeup that releases the stream of numbers.

The symbols and numbers and tones are all working in harmony to assist in your awakening.

But the crop circles serve one further purpose—they are a time marker. You have noticed that as the years have progressed, the designs have become more and more elaborate. The increasingly complex symbolism serves to further awaken you. But it also serves as a dating method for the various forms of time travellers who are able to bend and flex time and space and can pop back and forth into Earth's atmosphere at various periods in time. The crop circles act as a time 'beacon' that allows them to pinpoint what period they have arrived in. This may sound illogical to you since you may assume that beings who have the technology to travel through time and space are always able to arrive precisely where and when they expect to with pinpoint accuracy.

However, as we told you in an earlier chapter, timelines move. And all of time is like ribbons slowly swaying in the great cosmic space. So there is no such thing as 100% accuracy in the arrival time of these time travellers from other worlds. No matter how sophisticated their instruments may be, there is no such thing as a hard and fixed time and they have learned to be flexible with this issue.

The other purpose of the time-marker-patterns is to determine which of the beings have left the 'artwork' to be admired in the fields. It is not one race of beings along who enjoys this method of awakening or this form of 'planetary painting.'

This is an amazing time in your Earth history. Can you feel the truth of that? It has been many millennia since humankind was able to interact with beings from so many levels of consciousness and so many types of creation. It is a long-lost gift returning. And it is just the beginning of an ever-increasing level of interaction, so prepare yourself for an interesting next few decades as what you had always considered to be reality changes into *something completely different* before your newly awakened eyes!

Chapter Four

THE AWAKENING

You have found us at this time in your lives for a reason. You are responding to an inner awakening that will soon be shared by all of the inhabitants of this planet, whether they think they want to be awakened or not!

We are hearing from so many of you that you feel *compelled* to make immediate changes in your lives and these may include a change of jobs, a move to a new location, the severing of ties to relationships that are no longer viable, and perhaps the deeper exploration of spiritual paths that are radically different from what was previously your norm. A healing process is beginning, a healing of the previously severed parts of your soul that you are now reconnecting to your more whole self. This healing frequently prompts many of you to begin your journey 'on the path' by exploring alternative healing methods and we are not surprised that the first thing we hear from many of you is that you have just taken a class in one of the many methods of manipulating and correcting energy imbalances in the body.

Many of you would have laughed at the idea that you were an artist a mere few years ago, yet we now hear that you freely give joyful expression to many varieties of artistic pursuits. This too is a kind of healing, is it not? This is a liberation of blocked creation energy. All of these healing modes reconnect you to the source of the ultimate creation—the Oneness—and your individual role in creation.

What you are answering is your own inner voice, your own awakening soul-self. Please understand and believe, you are not being 'programmed' by outside forces to suddenly make these changes in your lives. But when you awaken to the lack of authenticity in your way of living and interacting with other beings, then, and only then, is a doorway opened for us to begin to communicate with you. It is against the laws of creation for us to force ourselves upon you and we are concerned that some of you come to us in fear after having heard some religious leader state as a fact that all of these kinds of alternative belief systems are the work of some dark force.

Can you really believe that all of these creative avenues, which change so many lives for the better and reconnect you with the Oneness in a more authentic manner than you may have felt in a building known as church, are evil? Only you know what is best for you!

But you must be the one to open the door and invite us in and many of you are beginning to do that on both conscious and unconscious levels.

There are many of us who have come to awaken from your long slumber and it is not only those who do channelling, such as Deborah does, who are responding. You may be internally 'hearing' some of the messengers and not knowing what you are responding to.

We may speak to you through thoughts that are suddenly in your waking consciousness, and you may find yourself thinking, "Where did this thought come from? I wasn't thinking about anything like that."

Some of you may find us in dreams. Have you awakened in recent times with the feeling that you are not as well rested as you would like to be because you were very active, very busy, in your dreaming state? This is not your imagination! You are interacting with many of us in your unconscious dream state when your human barriers of fear and suspicion are removed and we may more easily reach you for two-way communication. There is much learning and interacting going on in your dream states.

There is a sensation of impending change that is now pulsating in the atmosphere of your planet and is being recognised by the ever-increasing number of you who are sensitive to such vibrational change. We are pleased at this and encourage you to continue your exploration of the changes and the new knowledge that accompanies it, even in the face of disapproval by family or friends who may not understand this new passion of yours. They will reach the same awakening eventually, but this period of change comes to all of you in very individual timeframes.

When you have heard people state in the past that the vibrational rate of the planet is increasing, it may have sounded silly to you. But those people, who may have made those statements for decades with only a total faith in their convictions but no scientific evidence to stand behind, have now been vindicated. Your scientists are now able to confirm that the vibratory rate of your planet has indeed increased dramatically in the last few decades. And this increase is playing havoc with navigational instruments and human body functioning.

Why does an increase in vibration cause difficulty?

If you look at a table, for example, it is a group of molecules vibrating together to form the image of a table. And you are each a group of molecules vibrating together to form a person. If the Earth is increasing in vibration, then all of the beings and objects living on that surface are also increasing their vibratory rate.

From the beginnings of history on this planet, there have never been this many creatures living on the surface of the Earth at the same time. And just as Earth has a vibration of her own, each of you has a vibration. This is contributing to an overall large and ever-rising tremor in your atmosphere.

The Earth is easily able to sustain a certain level of population, but you have vastly exceeded that number and are continuing to grow in numbers with each passing year. You are literally shaking her apart!

The evidence for the Earth Changes is there for you to see in your daily news. The weather patterns you have observed in the last few years are not the weather patterns of a mere decade ago. Can you ever remember a time when there were so many floods and droughts, tornadoes and hurricanes, earthquakes and volcanoes all happening in the same year? The Earth is attempting to give you an advanced warning of what is coming when she shakes off some of the energy build-up through an increasing number of seismic and weather events.

But there is soon to be a time when you will look back on the current situation and realise that these were merely minor energy releases. These will no longer be sufficient to relieve the stress on the planet, and the Earth will toss and roll and forever change the appearance of her surface as we now know it.

The waters of the ocean will rise as your Earth continues to warm and polar caps melt. Large centres of population on coastal areas will need to relocate due to these rising waters that will wash over and submerge these towns and cities.

But this is nothing to be afraid of. Think of yourselves as participants in the process of rebirth. You can help her in this transition by being loving and effective midwives as the Earth is reborn into a new kind of existence.

You, who are reading this book or who have been awakened to these truths already, are by those very acts better able to handle the ever-increasing vibrational rate and the exciting changes that accompany all this activity. You know what is happening and make mental and physical compensations for it most of the time. But what of the people of the world who do not know about this? Do they think they are going mad when they feel this surging energy that creates a list of symptoms and they don't know where the buzzing in their head or the crawling sensation on their skin is coming from?

It is *a sound that has no sound* and at times is like a silent set of fingernails scraping on a blackboard with that screeching sound, that disruptive vibration in the atmosphere, going into every molecule of the body and disturbing it. Is it any wonder then that there is an ever-increasing level of violence in your world? If there is a constant disruptive 'sound' making you feel rattled, keeping you from getting a good night's sleep, and generally tearing away at your sense of well-being, you can understand why so many people are going seemingly mad and committing random and unexpected acts of violence against themselves and others. It is a means of escape from that vibration.

Please do not think that you have no options regarding these physical disturbances. We would urge you now to begin to imagine or re-image the world in the form and state of being that you want it to be. Meditation and prayer and intention are powerful acts that create powerful results. They are a statement to the universe around you and to the Oneness that you are willing to participate and make a difference, that you are willing to create an alternative life to the one that may be around you, that you are not willing to just take whatever is available with no say in your own destiny. You must have faith—you must fully believe in the power of this intent—and it will come to pass.

We must explain that until the Mother Earth does her cleansing 'dance' of renewal, the vibrations will continue to step up and up. But there are ways to cope with it. Your coping mechanisms will involve everything from meditation and prayer, to a changed attitude towards food and health, to learning to just flow through the vibrations until your body-level matches it and becomes calm again.

Physical Symptoms of Transformation

Many of you have written and asked about aches, pains, and other bodily sensations that you are experiencing. We will address these symptoms of the global awakening.

Some of the questions we have been asked are concerning extreme insomnia, aching in the joints at night, and a sensation like electrical impulses moving through your bodies. In the daytime, there may be difficulty maintaining a consistent level of mental concentration. And many of you are reporting a not-unpleasant but persistent ringing in the ears all throughout the day. Those of you who report a feeling of rocking back and forth, as if on the deck of a ship, are simply noticing the instability of the magnetic fields that surround your planetary alignment.

All of these sensations are related to the flexing and stretching of the Earth as she releases some of her tension. These big movements and severe weather began in earnest in 1998 and will escalate with each passing year. The more you are able to flow into these sensations without seizing up or becoming fearful, the easier it will be on your bodies. As your bodies are attempting to adjust to these changes however, you may feel some aching as you go through these growing pains of awakening consciousness. Ask your guides, angels, and other helpers for assistance when you are having trouble concentrating or staying on top of your physical discomfort. Help is always at hand—if you ask!

We will speak in a later chapter about the HAARP project and other secret energy-weapon work that is being done by the misguided governments of your world. Irresponsible pulsing of energy waves into the planet is being answered by a return pulse from the Earth and that echoed pulse is causing a range of answer-back effects from violent weather to power failures and seismic activity. Your scientists are well aware that they cannot alter the natural order of a planet without repercussions of some kind, but they are persisting in these dangerous experiments that are recreating the same early pole shift and destruction that was created in Atlantis.

You will begin to read tiny and uncomplicated reports in your newspapers that will introduce you to the idea of magnetic shifts, strange patterns in magnetic energy, or magnetic storms in space that effect the technology of Earth. This is a means for preparing the population of the planet for what the scientists know is already an irreversible activity. [1,2,3]

The time of remembering is now unfolding and many of you are eagerly reconnecting with the gifts that the Oneness gave you at the time of creation—telepathy, psychic abilities of all kinds, and creation through intention of all that you need. You are not helpless observers of events. Trust and believe in that. The future is yours to create, as long as you are truly willing to be a responsible and ethical participant in the act of creation.

Chapter Five

HEALTH AND WELL-BEING

We would like to discuss ways to prepare your bodies, minds, and spirits for the changes that you are moving into.

Sound and Vibration

When there is no peace, when there is no complete and soothing silence at any time of the day or night in your cities, the vibrations of these sounds are absorbed into your body and your mind and they begin to wear you down. All through your day, and even as you sleep or meditate, there are sounds seeping into you and crumbling your body's resistance to illness and this is a serious issue that is often overlooked when health and well-being are discussed. We would prefer to have each of you live with large daily periods of silence, except for the sounds of the birds and movement of the trees—but we know that it may not be an option for you. [4]

For that reason, we would suggest that you have harmonious music to play in your homes to mask the sounds of traffic, neighbours, animals, and more. And if you are able to further distance yourself from the noise at night by placing soft earplugs in your ears, you will find that the soothing sound of your own heartbeat will give you more restful sleep and dreams. If it is feasible, remove yourself from your normal surroundings at least once in each of your weeks and find a peaceful spot, surrounded by nature. Simply sitting in silence in such a place can provide refreshment to your mind and body that will recharge you for a time and allow you to cope with the stresses of your daily lives in an easier fashion.

We will also mention other sources of sound and vibration. If your homes and offices have lights that are fluorescent, they give off an unpleasant background hum that has cumulative effects on your overall health. We are aware that you may have no choices about the types of lighting used in your work places, but you can limit your exposure to these lights in your homes. You will find that being under or near them for too long will cause you to feel agitated and edgy, drained, and you may notice that you have an accelerated heartbeat that immediately returns to normal when these lights are turned off. [5]

Also, some of you are spending many hours in front of electronic machines such as this computer that Deborah is using. We would also like to mention that the vibration that is given off by any machine of this type will contribute to the wear and tear on your body. We are pleased that this medium is being utilised for the spreading of information about the many issues you are concerned with. But we are also aware that some of you are so lost in your contacts with the 'computer world' that you may, in varying degrees, have turned your back on human contact.

Use these things as tools in limited contact, if that is possible, and network with one another on a face-to-face basis at least some of the time. You will find that you notice a distinct increase in your sense of well-being when you remove yourself from this type of constant vibration. [6]

Radiation

We now address a subject that many of you are experiencing, questioning, and worrying about. It is the state of 'offness' that you are sensing in the world—the sense that things are not what they should be. You have not imagined this. Your minds are not mentally disturbed for having a knowing that there is something skewed in your world and for feeling a sense of agitation about this.

As we sit in front of this computer machine and use the hands of the woman Deborah, there are birds singing at full volume outside, and the hour is just past three in the morning of your time. It is now the deepest part of the winter. When all is dark and all such creatures should be resting prior to their dawn chorus, they too sense the 'offness' of the atmosphere and cannot rest. Is it any wonder then that if the animals are already sounding the alarm, you too are feeling a sensation of discomfort?

Many of you write to the woman Deborah and share information regarding your own lives including the facts of lack of sleep in spite of profound fatigue and a sense of disorientation on more and more days as if you were walking in circles and forgetful of what you are meant to be doing. None of these things are imaginary. The song of the bird has turned into a shrieking sound and the meaning is multi-level. We shall explain.

If you are outside for any period of time now, especially in the direct sunlight, you will notice that you feel a sometimes life-threatening draining of your energy reserves.

We would ask you to pay attention to these sensations and limit your period of outdoor exposure. Your planet is being bombarded with large amounts of radiation from your sun and it is having a strong effect on all life forms on this Earth. The bodies of all beings, from animals, to plants, to microscopic organisms, to human bodies, are impacted by this incoming radiation. It is a painful, in some cases, beginning step to an evolutionary leap you are about to make and there are accompanying sensations of discomfort. The bird does not know why it feels compelled to sing through the night instead of the day. Humans do not know why they are unable to sleep through the night and instead are barely awake during the hours of sunlight. [7]

In the years to come, you will find that as the radiation level progresses, the working and waking hours of this planet will reverse themselves from what seems like the norm right now. You will find that being in the sun puts you to sleep, much as the darkness has always done prior to this time throughout your life. Can you understand the wisdom of this?

You will be less oriented towards the sun for your nourishment in the physical and spiritual world. You will instead be moving into a time of inner contemplation, calm, quiet, spiritual renewal and reconnection with the Oneness that is God. All of these things are greatly assisted by the coolness and subtlety of the darkness. You are becoming true beings of the stars—beings of the *inner light,* not the outer light that is represented by your sun. This time of spiritual reflection and change in body is part of your transformation as a species and is not an area of major concern.

Now we will discuss the effects that this increased radiation is having on your physical bodies and your mental state of being. This is an area of great concern for many of you since you do not have the ability to reverse your working hours and function fully at night.

Some of what we will tell you today may lessen the harshness of the transition period that you are just entering. Know that you as humans have lived in the light of your sun for as many thousands of years as you have resided in this place—this feels normal to you. It will be generations ahead before you are fully assimilated into a state where your bodies do not constantly crave the sun for energy.

When we have told the woman Deborah that we are about to discuss the similarity between eyes and feet—she laughed and did not understand. What part of your feet is the toughest and the most resistant to outside pressures? It is the bottom of your feet which is, by necessity, the thickest part.

The tissue in your eyes is also being affected by this increase in radiation and will thicken up to accommodate the changes in your atmosphere. This will result in a lessening of what you are eventually able to see. Deborah has just asked—are we referring to cataracts? No, that too is a side effect of the increased radiation and sunlight spectrum. What we are referring to is a loss of subtle tones and shades of colours—that which makes vision a joy—not a loss of sight.

Your eyes are such a gift, are they not? Your senses dance with pleasure at visual elements that are introduced to your brain. Is it not then worth protecting them through the simple measures of avoidance of direct incoming light and wearing of protection over the eyes?

Some of you may already find that your eyes are extremely sensitive to bright light and that you work and function better in muted lighting situations. You may have felt the effects sooner than the general population of the planet and have already adjusted to this life of general avoidance of brightness of the sun.

Please understand—we are not telling you that the sun is now your enemy in any way. The sun is evolving—just as you are. And as it evolves, it gives off more bursts of radiation. This radiation is what we are concerned about.

Now we will discuss your internal organs. One of the side effects of increased radiation in your general atmosphere is a lessening of your internal organs, in most cases, to function at their optimum ability. For this reason, we ask you to increase the amount of filtered water that you are drinking each day to soften the impact of this radiation, specifically the effect on your kidneys, liver, and intestines.

Understand now about the energy depletion. When you are exposed to a burst of radiation being broadcast from your sun, you are not feeling replenished by the warmth and light of the sun, as you may have been in the past, but are instead left feeling drained and weakened. This is truth and you are not imagining it when you feel barely able to move after being in the sun for a long period of time. Your life essence is forced to work overtime to compensate for the drain caused by the radiation. To recover from this energy drain, your body may require a much greater amount of sleep and operate at a less than optimum level for several days afterwards. We would suggest that moderation in exposure is the better path.

What of the wakefulness at all hours of the night when you would formerly be sleeping deeply? What of the sensation of 'floating' through the daylight hours when you are operating with an insufficient amount of sleep due to nightly disturbance in your sleep patterns?

We would suggest that you do the following. If you are able to take short naps in the daytime, please do that to refresh yourselves. If this is not an option for you, try to find a quiet place for a few moments and do a short meditation to ground yourself and relieve the 'floaty' feeling.

Picture yourself as a strong and healthy tree with roots going deeper and deeper into the Mother Earth and you will notice a feeling of safety and 'anchoring' right away.

Avoidance of the television box will also help to relieve the fatigue since the programming-to-be-agitated that is in it simply elevates both your stress and fatigue levels.

Understand again what we have stated earlier—this is an evolutionary period for humankind and *you will not see this stage of completion in your lifetimes.* Your species is in a bridging period and unfortunately you are feeling the effect of the transition in your bodies. The consistent practice of common-sense preventative measures may keep you in a safer and healthier state and also allow you to notice the signs of danger in those around you.

Food

You have chosen wisely if you have begun to limit your food choices to mostly fruits, vegetables, non-manipulated protein (containing no medicines, steroids, or chemicals) and grains. But even in these choices, care must be taken.

We will state this strongly—unless you grow your food yourself and oversee each and every step along the way, you have no idea of what substances you are actually ingesting. All of your commercially grown products, and even most of what is grown on small farms, is pumped full of chemicals from the planting stage to the harvesting stage. Even your grain products such as bread, cereal, and pasta are saturated with chemical by-products.

Much of your food is being dosed with radiation before it reaches your stores so that it will last for longer on the shelves. Your doctors and scientists have disregarded your concerns that you are poisoning yourselves and your children with your food choices. [8]

Nearly all commercially available food products contain both agricultural chemicals and other additives placed in the food during processing and the combinations of chemicals are diminishing your bodies' ability to fight off even the most basic illness such as a cold.

When you are exposed to both the newly discovered and already known illnesses of the world in this state of diminished immunity, you will find that you have less and less ability to fight off illness with each passing year.

In some cases, this is an intentionally caused situation. There are populations in almost every country that are being used as 'lab animals' by unethical governments and scientists so that a study can be made of the lasting effects of these various chemicals.

Have you wondered why there is an overabundance of antibiotic use in your society? It is cheaper for both humans and animals to be saturated with antibiotics than to address a more natural and balanced lifestyle.

Physicians are able to move you quickly through their examining rooms if they give you these drugs rather than delving deeper into the root causes of your illnesses. And the farming industry is happy with the increased profits from 'healthier' animals. In the over-prescribing of these drugs to humans, and the placement of these drugs in the feed of animals, an immunity has been created that may soon be the ruin of your species as the new versions of plagues continue to surface.[9]

You may think that you are safe from antibiotic abuse if you simply don't take them when your medical doctor offers them, but unless you purchase from strictly organic sources, these antibiotics are in every bit of dairy product that you consume and every piece of meat that you eat if you are living in the United States.[10]

The hormones that are pumped into poultry and meat are now in the tissues of your bodies, giving you fertility problems, encouraging cancer cells to grow, and causing new diseases through bonding with other artificial substances already in your body.

Blockers

If consumed in excess amounts, the animal products that you call dairy will also cause a slow build-up of congestion in your heart area that has more implications than simply the serious problem of heart disease.

If you choose to consume dairy products as a dietary requirement, we would urge you to either lessen the amount of these products that you ingest or move towards soy-based products that give you the same appearance and taste as dairy. Blockages in the heart area, sometimes caused by excess dairy products, will prevent you from getting clear signals regarding psychic or intuitive heart judgement.

The substance called caffeine may be causing damage to both your third eye reception and your heart reception. We realise that, even if you cut out all consumption of these products, you may each encounter these substances on occasion in situations outside of your own home. Try to limit or avoid them as much as possible since they will impair your blossoming individual abilities.

You may be aware that your bodies are vibrating essences that are crystalline in nature. If you removed all the liquid in your body, you would be a handful of crystalline minerals. We have discussed in previous sessions the distress that some of you are feeling from the increasing vibration of the planet and your bodies as you are all being remade in an awakened state.

But you are contributing to the agitation in your bodies when you consume the crystalline substance called sugar. It reacts with the already agitated cells in your body and is one of the reasons that you are having difficulties in staying calm and focused and grounded.

Seafood

The Earth is pushing and pulsing with geological movements and the toxic substances that mankind has placed in the oceans and on or under the surface of the planet are returning to you as the Earth vents through holes under the sea and by cracks and eruptions on the surface of the land.

These toxins are combining with the Earth's own ancient substances that are harmful to mankind, and this combination is spewing forth from the vents in the ocean floors. This deadly mix is being absorbed by even the smallest form of sea life, yet it is rarely poisonous to them. But as this chemical mix enters the food chain that you consume, the number of deaths, illnesses, or impaired health from the consumption of seafood is increasing. This is a serious health problem that has not been addressed by your medical or scientific authorities.

Good Food Choices

We are aware that many of you do not have access to food that is grown with no chemicals—organically. But for those who do, we suggest that you choose these fruits, vegetables, and grains.

If you are able to grow your own food and herbs, that is an even better option since you are in control of all stages of development. There are many written resources that will teach you how to do these things.

If your only source of food is the local grocery store, we would ask you to consider doing several things:

1. Reduce or eliminate your reliance on prepared and packaged foods and eat only fresh food. There is a little more time and effort involved in this, but you have been asking us for ways to improve the quality of your lives. Fresh food is one of those ways. This reduction/elimination extends to prepared cereals at breakfast time.
2. Your bodies are, in part, made up of a solution of salt water. This is a direct reflection of your earliest planetary origins as creatures of the sea. Therefore, we would ask you to soak your commercially purchased fruits and vegetables in a solution of fresh water and salt from the sea for a few minutes when you bring them home from the store. This will partially alleviate the chemical substances and will restore a healthy balance to the food.
3. Although the chemicals we have spoken of are added to each and every stage of growth, the greatest concentration is in the outer layers or skins of the vegetables. We would suggest that you remove this

outer layer before cooking or consuming these fruits and vegetables that are non-organically grown. It is unfortunate that we must suggest this since many of the vital nutrients are in the outer layer or skin, but it is essential that you begin to lessen the amount of chemical build-up in your bodies.

4. In some cultures, it is still a common practice to pray over the food that is about to be eaten. In our opinion, it is a sign of respect and gratitude to the planet and energy forces that provide you with sustenance. But are you aware that you can also alter the chemical and cellular composition of food through mental interaction with it? We are not stating that all of the harmful, residual material in your food will be eliminated in this fashion, but you ARE able to bond with the food through mental contact and ask that it provide you with positive life-force and nourishment and less residual toxin.
5. Consuming meat is an individual choice that you must make according to your own belief systems. Some of you feel very uncomfortable with the idea of eating the flesh of another creature, and we honour your choices. In cultures of the past, those who were about to kill an animal for food first 'communed' with the spirit of the animal and honoured the life-force that was being given to the human to survive. There is very little of that practice left since the sterile atmosphere of the store where you purchase your food bears very little resemblance to a field or forest and you are not the one doing the slaying of the animal that provides you with sustenance. We must also

emphasise though that there has been a not-so-subtle change in the pressures of the planetary energy on your bodies in the last few years and as you head into the next few decades, you may need to ingest meat as a means of allowing your body and brain to function clearly and rapidly through this transition period.

For that reason, we ask that you look at the point we made in item #4 if you are now consuming meat. Place your hands in a cupped fashion over the plate of food, allow energy to flow from the centre of your hands that will transmute any residual energy in the food that would harm your body, and then send a blessing to the animal that gave its life to you so that you may continue to survive.

6. You each need to be consuming twice the amount of pure water that you are currently consuming. This liquid is the basis for your life essence and will both refresh you and allow the psychic transmissions that are being sent to you to be more clearly received. You are able to hold a greater amount of light in your body, both in meditation and throughout the day, when you are more liquid and therefore lighter and less dense.

Be aware that many of you are ingesting chemicals in the water that comes into your homes. These chemicals are adding to the mix of 'toxic soup' that is in your bodies from the agricultural products, antibiotics and hormones in dairy products and meat, and the toxins from the ocean. You are each so saturated with this chemical mix that it will take you many years to undo the damage—but the damage can partially be undone! Start by drinking water that is filtered to remove as much chemical residue as possible and follow up by mentally stating the intention that this fluid will nourish you and not harm you.

Body and Mind Strength

You may need to get more exercise, in a quantity that is sufficient to maintain the energy reserves that you will soon need. It takes discipline, but it will help you to set aside time each day to do breathing and strength building exercises. You will find that this physical release gives you a more peaceful state of mind and refreshing, deep sleep.

We have suggested that you will be more peaceful, grounded, and focused if you are able to pray or meditate or consciously intend-for-good during your day. This reconnection to the Oneness that created us all will allow you to remember that you are part of the great family of creation. You are never alone with your problems or pain. Help is always at hand, but you must ask for intervention and assistance. It is rarely given unasked-for since the assistance might interfere with your own spiritual and soul development.

The many loving beings that surround each of you are always on call for love, guidance, and tangible assistance. Begin to feel your own part in this great drama called life by reconnecting with the Oneness in this fashion.

Finally, take time to play. Remove yourself from the pressures of your life as often as possible. You will find that an amazing amount of information flows into you easily at these times, even when you are not consciously asking for it. A relaxed mind assimilates the energy and information more easily. So try to maintain a relaxed and fluid state of being as much as possible. It will benefit your life on many levels.

Chapter Six

Expressions of the Oneness

We have spoken to you in a previous chapter of the awakening that is now occurring on your planet. Many of you are reconnecting to that sense of completeness that encompasses you when you acknowledge that the Oneness is in you and with you at all times. You are never alone.

How curious it is to us then to listen to the stories that you tell us and absorb the information that Deborah reads or listens to regarding different religious groups and their approach to life on this planet.

If all religions were formulated to accommodate different versions of reality, that would be understandable. But truth is truth and it is just that simple. And the truth of creation and your universe is the same for all humankind. Why then do you create these artificial differences?

How can one particular religion or belief system completely ignore or deny the validity of another religion or belief system simply because it is not identical to their own? This makes no sense, does it? This rigid thinking pattern is the same in many places around the world and may be the undoing of you as a species if you are not careful.

Why is this not examined with greater seriousness in your society since it is such a crucial issue? Why are you now, at the end of this period in history, going backward into religious persecution and a small-minded attitude when such forward progress had been made for much of this century?

When we speak to groups, we have sometimes heard gasps and sometimes heard laughs when we have called the book you know as the Bible a nice fairy tale book meant as a teaching guideline. We have not intended then, nor do we now, to hurt feelings when we are this blunt. But this book that many of you claim is the complete and literal word of the Oneness *is not.*

It is a human interpretation of the societal rules and lessons that different people have considered appropriate for you to know at various stages throughout your history. Although it relates stories and mythology from various periods of history, these are what they are for the most part—stories—not literal truth. Yes, some of the characters in this book did exist and have lives similar to what is portrayed, but each story about them is like a cartoon compared to the real flesh-and-blood person.

The writers of this book, and there are many, gave their *own personal interpretations* of the people or incidents they were describing.

If in today's time period you read a book about a famous person, would that book give you the same 'feel' and information as any other book about that very same person? No, they would all have the impressions of that person *as interpreted* by the writer. This is exactly what has happened in the Bible.

How then can any religious group claim that this one book is *the* definitive book of God's will and thoughts about humankind when it is written through many people and filtered through their opinions and ideas? What about the other books of religious thought that have been inspired or channelled from the Oneness? Why are they not regarded as equally valid? Is it logical that God would speak in the same way to all people? No, an individual approach to individual groups is in fact what has happened historically.

Yet if you are a Christian, in many parts of the world, you are told that the only valid book of truth is the Bible and that it is to be taken as literal truth. This is silly and nonsensical thinking since the Bible is not only a teaching tool and moral guideline of what the early Christians thought was appropriate, it has also been watered down to only reflect the masculine thinking and not the feminine reality of both the time period of the Old Testament, but also the life of the person Jesus. The man who was Jesus was inclusive of women and there were women in his inner circle, yet those important women have, for the most part, been edited out so that you only know about the male disciples. How is that then to present you with a valid and true version of history?

What you are receiving in what is called the New Testament is a public relations version of the 'highlights' of the life of Jesus and it is not a true reflection of the fullness of his rather complex incarnational experience.

Contrary to what the followers of Christianity may tell you, Jesus is not God. Jesus is a reflection of the Oneness that is God and came to Earth (and many other planets) as part of a specific 'job assignment.'

A certain type of *signature energy* is recognisable in the man Jesus and the other great teachers who have been sent to this planet throughout time. This energy of love and service and devotion to teaching in spite of great odds is now being called, somewhat incorrectly, the *christ energy.* It does not apply to the person of Jesus only, but in some cases, specific religions are disallowing the recognition of this energy in others who were sent by the Oneness and they are only acknowledging its validity in the person of Jesus.

We must be truthful here and state that this type of thinking is limiting your ability to expand and grow into your next evolutionary stage, yet many of you have been coerced into thinking that the only valid path back to a reunion with the Oneness of God is through the person Jesus.

This narrowly focused thinking negates the validity of other choices including those religions who choose not to view Jesus as the one-and-only saviour of the world, but rather as a teacher of goodness and love. These other religious choices are equally valid, fulfilling, and wise.

Regarding the being known as Jesus, his enlightened soul, having already reached a reunion with the God essence and needing no further life lessons through a further incarnational state of being, chose to move back into a body and offer assistance to humankind through a life of service, teaching, and acts that would seem political in nature. Yet he became hampered by the fact that he was in human form. This was not his first incarnation as a master-teacher, but once within the body of a human, he too was suffused with the 'forgetfulness' of other lifetimes and other 'teaching assignments' and he had no memory of the many, many times that a piece of his essence had come to this planet, sometimes as a man, sometimes as a woman.

You now have scientists in your world who are recognising that your body-circuitry, the 'wiring up' of all of your functions, has somehow been incomplete. This disconnected wiring, related to your not-fully-functioning DNA strands, has been explored in depth in other books and we would urge you to read further on this subject. Why have we brought this up? It is to point out that the nature of human bodies contains faulty wiring and incomplete memories of who you are in creation and what magical creation abilities you have. Jesus fell into this human body trap from the moment he incarnated into a body and was immediately subject to limitations and emotions such as doubt and fear that do not exist in a non-incarnational form.

Jesus may have been sent to Earth with a specific assignment of waking and shaking you up, but from his first breath at birth, he was as human as the rest of the population and subject to serious depression and doubt about his ability to complete the task. None of these things are adequately addressed in the presentation of the life of Jesus in your Bibles. If you are able to read about the lives of the other great teachers who have this so-called *christ energy* vibration, you will find that they too struggled with their humanity while temporarily trapped in human form. Each of them incarnated with a partial memory of why they came and what they were meant to do, but it was only after a series of mental, physical, and spiritual trials that they were able to move beyond the human body limitations and fulfil their assignment.

In the recorded time of your current version of humankind on this planet, the Oneness has also sent the Buddha and the Mohammed and all the other names of the great teachers of any religion. There were many women, such as Hildegard in Germany, Juliana in England, and Brigid in Ireland, who were sent as great teachers and leaders. Yet their incarnation is only regarded as holy or special if they have been nominated to what your churches call sainthood and so many more of them have been overlooked or lost in history because they did not meet the requirements for sainthood or were not known to any major religion.

Many of these women were also what your churches would call pagan since they lived in a time that was pre-Christian or they followed a belief system that did not include the man Jesus. Yet they too were true incarnations of the *christ energy* essence and they came in that same sense of teaching and service. In their system of ancient religious beliefs, they were frequently referred to as 'goddess' due to their level of healing, teaching, and visionary abilities in comparison with everyday humans.

The very young woman who was Mary, the mother of the man Jesus, was also a divine being who struggled with her humanity. Yet the official religious leaders of your world have all too frequently forgotten her 'goddess' role and have instead relegated her to a secondary position due to their need to revere male divinity only.

All of these 'divine' women were also perfectly developed souls who had no further need for human incarnation but who willingly accepted that assignment from the Oneness of God. Why then are there still only small pockets of people who revere the female teachers or 'goddesses' sent by the Oneness?

To continue with the man called Jesus, he was much more human than his portrayals, yet his generous nature and open heart seems to be accurately chronicled. You ask us how we know these things? It is because we have been in the presence of this being, and the other *christ energy* teachers, on many occasions. There is much humour present in the out of incarnational body state and these so-called 'divine ones' find it quite amusing to see how later generations of humans have translated their messages and embellished the facts of their lives.

Jesus was indeed able to create many miracles that were meant to be shared. We would note at this point that the ability to heal and transmute matter with energy from his hands is only just now being rediscovered on this planet. This is unfortunate since it was a legacy that he left for you all. These skills originally were meant to be included in a book of his teachings that was later manipulated, edited, and amended until they were almost unrecognisable.

The men in power after Jesus' death were upset by the possibility that everyone might have access to this information and believed that allowing the 'common man' to have such powerful knowledge would lessen their grip on the populations. The information mysteriously disappeared and is known in full to only a handful of people on this planet.

There has been much of this kind of knowledge given through each of these divine ones—these beings with what you call *christ energy*. Yet in every case, those who followed have disregarded the wishes of the divine messenger-teachers and have instead jealously guarded this information for their small and elite inner groups that reside within the larger religious group. What kind of world would this have been right now had you been able to access this ability to heal without potentially harmful chemicals or unnecessary surgical intrusion? What if the passionate displays of weather on this planet could be soothed into a calmer and less destructive version? All these things would have been possible with the teachings that were left behind.

The ancient knowledge, which was your rightful legacy, has been lost to you both through suppression by those who longed to keep the power in their hands and by the annihilation of civilisations with a more highly developed technology and social order than you can imagine.

There have been many teachers—male *and* female—who had the *christ energy* and even now there are the remnants of ancient sects and orders throughout the world who have carefully kept these scrolls, tablets, or other written records in secret places known only to a handful of their followers in each century.

This was meant to be a legacy for all of you that would have radically altered your understanding of love, wholeness, and the interconnectedness of all life forms on this planet. But we must ask you in truth—if you had all of this knowledge available to you, would it be used correctly and for the good of all life-forms?

We do not see a majority of earth's citizens who are in a frame of thinking that would think first of the common good before thinking of the individual gain that could be made by controlling this new power.

When we are looking at the most likely possibility for your future on the timeline that you are currently occupying, we see great chaos ahead for the world where religious issues are concerned. We are concerned that you will not reach your evolutionary pivot point in the next 15 years but will instead regress even further into these religious and doctrinal wars.

UPDATE from Deborah: The statement above was dictated in 1999 and although she hoped for the best possible outcome for us, the world has indeed become further mired in both global and regional aggression and in intolerance for the spiritual belief systems of others. We have certainly not become a more tolerant and loving species.

This was not what we had hoped for you after all this time, but humankind has always had free will in the ordering of its destiny and, just as we did not step in during past ages, we will not interfere if you decide to destroy your potential selves. There will always be an isolated few of you who do not follow the movements of the greater population and who choose to embrace a loving and inclusive lifestyle, but these will be small pockets of people compared to the greater picture of chaos and destruction.

Do you truly think that where you live is immune from this type of violence and repression? We can view the world through Deborah's eyes and ears and we see that there is a rising level of rigid religious doctrine versus freedom of choice. If there is a revolution in places like the United States in the next few years, it may be a war over your right to freedom of thought and belief.

Yet for those of you in quieter and calmer parts of the world, you too must be vigilant regarding these issues. What is now unfolding in other countries could duplicate itself on your doorstep if you fail to pay attention to these potentialities.

The Oneness that is God gave each of you an open mind and heart, free choice, inner knowledge, all the tools to be successful humans. But what we are seeing is that some of you turn these beautiful gifts and the power to control your lives over to those who claim to know what is best for you or who 'persuade' you to follow their teachings. We ask you to seriously assess what is happening in your world rather than turning a blind eye to it. Your actions today will shape the future world you occupy.

All expressions of the Oneness that is God are valid. All belief systems are meant to be honoured and respected.

Chapter Seven

Earth Changes

We have spoken several times in the last few chapters about Earth Changes. We will now give a more complete explanation of these events but we would like to also emphasise one thing—the Earth Changes that so many of you are worried about are a natural progression on this planet. These types of events have happened in cycles that have been repeated many times in ages long past.

Yes, a percentage of the population of Earth's human occupants will not survive in their physical form as a result of these upheavals, but they are merely a small part of the many challenges that you will be facing in the next few decades. Your treatment of one another, the Earth herself, and the companion species on this planet should be your primary interest, not whether or not the weather and geological events will claim you or where the 'safe zones' are. However, we will now discuss what lies ahead.

The Earth's vibrations are increasing with each passing day and that these vibrational increases are due to both the sheer number of beings living and vibrating on her surface and from the burden of the pollution and damage of all kinds that has been done to her in the name of progress.

Some of you have asked on occasion why we call your planet the Mother Earth. Do not many of you refer to her in that way? Is she not the source of your lives and essence in this incarnation? She too is a living entity and deserves respect for the essential role that she plays in your lives. We honour her nature when we use the terminology of your more awakened and sympathetic humans.

Understand also then that she has an important role in your lives but it is all too frequently an under-appreciated role. Yet the Mother Earth too is part of the fabric of the creation of the Oneness

There are other factors at work in the upcoming events. When you looked into your night skies as children, you saw familiar things such as the moon and various constellations.

But the skies that you are looking at now, the space that they are contained in, is not the same space as that of your childhood. Yes, the same planets and constellations are there, but now they are joined by new planets and new stars.

Each month in your news media, there are excited announcements of the discovery of previously unknown stars or planets. Yes, we are aware that your exploration instruments are more sophisticated with each year, but is it likely that something as large as these planets would not have been discovered prior to this time? In some cases, these discoveries are truly due to the new technology and the greater number of satellites and tracking vehicles that humans have launched into space.

But less well known and most likely completely denied by your Earth scientists is the additional truth that these discoveries are also being made at this time because your solar system and its occupants are in a new position in space. These 'new' stars and planets are only new to your world because you have only recently moved into a position in space where your scientists could find them.

If you think of your solar system as a mass travelling group, it is as if a large city had been lifted up and transported, familiar surroundings and solar system occupants included, to a new location.

This travel through the universe that you are making is exerting different gravitational and magnetic effects on your planet and all of its occupants—including you!

Can you ever remember a time in your life when there were so many comets being discovered? These too have quite a distinct effect on you.

You have known since childhood that the Moon affects the tidal flow on your planet Earth, and that this includes the 'tidal flow' of women's monthly body cycles. If that one planetary object has such a profound effect on you and your world, imagine the immense differences when you are suddenly introduced to new celestial bodies, each exerting their own set of pulls and tugs on the body of the Earth and its occupants.

And if you picture the core of the Earth as the large liquid-metal sphere that it is, the magnetic pull of these celestial objects is increasing the instability of the Earth's rotation. This tugging sensation is also causing more flux in the magnetic atmosphere of the planet with each passing year.

The comets, the sun, and other celestial objects are not only affecting your gravitational and magnetic fields, but they are influencing your weather patterns. Look for periods of great weather instability during any period of prolonged exposure to objects such as the comets we have just mentioned or forces such as magnetic storms.

You will find more and more evidence of severe weather that suddenly appears without warning and causes great loss of life and property. Your weather predictors are only now beginning to understand that the patterns of weather that they had always been able to predict in the past are no longer valid.

This is due in part to the influence of these celestial objects passing in the vicinity of your 'Earth aura.' The Earth has an energy field that surrounds and protects it just as you humans do. When her aura is invaded with external energy, she reacts with strong weather. All of this should make perfect sense to you.

Another reason for the gradual but continuous unbalancing of the planet Earth is the movement of her natural reserves. If the Earth is naturally balanced by the amount of liquid placed in specific sites around the surface of the planet and by the amount of different heavy elements buried within her surface, what do you suppose is the effect of removing water or petroleum from one part of the Earth and pumping it to another?

What do you think happens to the balance of the planet when mining removes certain elements from her body and that balance is not replaced? Try to picture a spinning gyroscope with weights on different parts of it to correctly balance the sphere. If you remove some of the weights and move them to a different spot on the sphere, it will suddenly wobble and spin out of control. This is what has been done to the planet by the mining of the Earth and the redistribution of the liquid masses. She is now wobbling on her axis and this is threatening to throw her off balance to the point that she spins out of control—much like the gyroscope we have described above.

This potential to alter the lives of humankind should be examined in the light of the greater damage which is the harm to a living being, the Earth herself. Each redistribution of her balance weights causes her pain. It is as if someone were gouging flesh out of your human bodies. That is a harsh image, is it not? Then please think of that when you allow this level of destruction to continue on this planet without speaking out for the rights of the living entity called Earth.

You are all aware of the phenomenon termed Global Warming. But some of this is being created by means other than the use of specific chemicals and the burning of fossil fuels. It is also created by man-made devices such as electromagnetic pulse weapons and the activation of HAARP which excite the molecules in the protective upper atmosphere of the Earth and allows the atmosphere itself to 'cook' and warm up. We will discuss the folly of this in a later chapter.

The Mother Earth herself is creating some of this warming and although it is not directly man-made, it is a result of her interaction with humankind and the celestial objects around her. She is pushing and thrusting and releasing some of her pain through earthquake activity and, ever more frequently, through volcanic activity. The inner and outer self of the planet is increasing in temperature and that is the reason for the melt-off of the polar ice caps and the rising level of the oceans throughout the world.

This is an easily verifiable fact and the change is measurable. There are no beaches anywhere on the planet that have not been strongly affected by this rising water and this will escalate with each year. [11]

Part of this can be looked on as a cyclical event. Any geologist can tell you that the positions of the North and South poles have moved many times in ages past and when it happened, it was so sudden that it brought on events such as the Ice Age or the sinking of large landmasses or the melting of polar caps within the span of a day. As the surface of the planet 'peels away' and then slides into a new position before becoming stable again, the shifting of the magnetic poles will confuse both humans and animals alike as cellular-memory migration patterns no longer prove to be accurate. [12]

We will deal now with the proliferation of diseases on your planet that seem to have no precedent and for which there are no cures. This is only the beginning of mass plagues that will sweep your world, so you are well advised to be prepared for this type of event to be reported in your news media in the near future. If you are mentally prepared ahead of time, it will not have such a severe psychic impact on you.

Mother Earth is fighting back and releasing back to humankind all of the toxic substances that have been placed in her body for many years. Long forgotten organisms that thrived in the pre-human developmental stages of the earliest Earth are rising into your air and moving into your lungs with each volcanic eruption and earthquake that tears apart the outer surface of the planet. These ancient organisms have lingered under the protective skin of the planet.

From the deepest crevices in the ocean floor, toxic-to-human substances that are part of the natural makeup of the planet are seeping out and being absorbed into the plant life and then into the sea life. These substances are combining with the human-created residues in your oceans to produce an even more deadly final product.

When this toxicity travels far enough through the chain of life, it is then presented to you in the food that you ingest.

You are beginning to contribute to your own potential extinction as a species.

This toxic leaking is also appearing in the soils in which you grow your food and in the bodies of fresh water from which you draw your drinking water and additional fish life. Humankind has soiled its own 'living room' for so many generations that you are now being forced to face this inevitable feedback.

Another area to be informed of is the increasing amount of solar storms. You may have noticed that there is an occasional reference to the amount of solar activity in your news—usually to explain the increased difficulty in launching satellites and space probes or the interference with radio, cellular phone, or television reception. We must tell you that these solar magnetic storms will increase with each new year and they will be the likely cause of wild outbursts of destructive weather events, even when your devices and technology are not impaired by them. The concept of what is normal weather will have to be rewritten.

Your scientists and specialists are reluctant to let you know these facts because they have no solutions to offer. The world will soon be a very different place for you as you cope with unpredictable weather that causes the loss of life and property and gradually deprives you of the benefits of technology that you now take for granted. [13]

In some parts of your society, the prophecies that have always been part of the native tribal culture regarding the Earth Changes are now suddenly of interest to non-native people. And you are presented with many diluted versions of what to expect in the years to come through television documentaries and books of prophecy. We, and anyone else who is a responsible 'prophet' of the times, are not telling you these things to create fear and panic but rather so you may be in a better state of mental and spiritual preparedness. [14]

This Great Cleansing that is coming is a natural and cyclical event for the Mother Earth, but this time there are many more life-forms on her surface. The Earth must save herself, renew herself, and unfortunately that will mean the physical body deaths of some of her inhabitants including some of humankind.

We encourage you to prepare and do the personal spiritual cleansing that will allow you to be at peace if you are not in a so-called 'safe place' during the great shifts ahead. If you can remember that the body that you are wearing now is simply a suit of clothes for this particular lifetime, perhaps you would be less likely to hang on to it with such ferocity.

We shall be sharing many types of information with you in this book, but one of the most important subjects is spiritual growth. This is why you have incarnated onto the planet. You have not come just for another ride on the merry-go-round of emotions that you call human life, but for the growth experience, the inward movement on the spiral of all consciousness, the spiral that moves you ever closer to the Oneness.

For this reason, we would suggest that you may want to look at your life as a living legacy to the planet. We are not speaking of being famous or well-known, but rather of leaving a legacy of goodness and love. What difference can you make to the world with your life? What legacy for good can you leave behind? Will you be able to depart from this incarnation in the firm belief that you have made a positive statement by your actions and words? What will you be remembered for?

These are the important issues to deal with now, not whether or not your temporary suit of physical 'clothes' survives any upheavals that are on the way. If it is your time to depart this Earth, would it not be better to depart in peace, knowing that you had created an outpouring of love and goodness that made a positive difference, rather than leaving in a panic over the loss of your body or with a sense of regret at things left undone or unsaid.

Many of you have asked in our group sessions if you have the power to change the ever-increasing Earth Changes in any way.

The answer is a firm YES!

Many examinations have been done on the power of intention, the power of prayer, the power of thought, and the genuine results that are achieved through these means. But think of the power when it is multiplied.

If one person, in a persistent effort to exert change for the highest good of all, combines their thoughts and prayers and intentions with another and another and another, then the strength of that intention multiplies by more than the actual number of those participating and sends a powerful message out into the vast consciousness of the Oneness and the fabric of all life-essence. The statement is made that this is what these people are hoping and wishing for. And in many cases, the hopes and wishes are answered.

All of you know of some example of this kind of group intention or prayer that has worked. In some religious traditions, the results are called a miracle and in other traditions they are referred to as a response to mass intent. Whatever you choose to call it, if enough people focus their energy on a specific outcome, seemingly final outcomes *can change.*

We are not implying that the Earth is not going to change and move and 'dance' herself into transformation, but we are stating with firmness that these movements can be softened, can be surrounded with imagined clouds of love and hope and goodness, and that the loss of life will then be reduced.

But these events can only come to pass if enough of humankind awakens to the potential for change and takes the necessary action. We are not talking about a random prayer or an occasional meditation. We are referring to consistent actions of this type that reinforce to the universal consciousness that this IS what you are asking for.

Repetition is what is required—but repetition in a spirit of love and change-for good—not in a sense of desperation or fear.

The Mother Earth is a living entity herself and is able to feel these intentions that are aimed at her well-being. She is also able to gratefully absorb any healing energy that is directed towards her. In several places around the world, groups meet each month to send healing energy into the planet to help her cope with her pain. But how much better would it be, and how much more effective, if the number of these groups was multiplied.

Yes, the water is going to rise around the planet due to the warming of your atmosphere and the melting of your polar caps. We cannot say that these things will be reversed since they are already well under way. But the strength and severity of the storms, earthquakes, and volcanic eruptions can be softened through the sending of healing energy into the planet. The question is though, are you willing to make the commitment to help in this way?

It is also necessary to heal the planet with direct action. You must state clearly to those who have polluted the air, water and soil and to those who perpetrate abusive mining practices that these things will not be tolerated and must be repaired now, not five or ten years from now. You may feel that you cannot make a difference as one lone voice, but if you join together with other voices that refuse to see the planet placed in such peril, you can then create a unified power for positive change.

We are in a place beyond what you call time, so we are able to look upon your Earth and see several possible outcomes for your near future. In many cases, we see very few members of humankind left after the chaos of Earth Changes, political and religious wars, and plagues. But none of these visions of your timelines are what you call written in stone. They are probable outcomes at different points of examination—but they are not the only choice for your future.

It is time to focus less on the potential outcomes of various landmasses and more on the spiritual growth that will save the planet and save yourselves also. Do you have the strength of character and belief to stop spinning in circles and waiting for a rescuer or a guru or a teacher to tell you what to do and how to live your life?

It is quite simple. It is time to begin making concrete and positive changes for good and for individual and collective spiritual growth—and no one can do these things for you. The Earth Changes can then be regarded as a catalyst for the uplifting of the spiritual lives of the occupants of the planet.

And is that not a better potential outcome?

CHAPTER EIGHT

Atlantis Again: HAARP

(Originally posted on the Internet on August 27, 1996)

We have much to talk about that is of seriousness today—but please keep it in your heart as you read our words—we have come to make you prepared, not to leave you in fear.

We will speak of the energy movement through the planet that you call HAARP. In the time long past, during the civilisation of Atlantis, the original motivation of those who colonised this Earth location was to assist in the development of the primitive species that was already resident on the planet as a result of earlier genetic experiments. But by the time that several thousand years had passed, the residents of Atlantis had, for the most part, forgotten their original spiritual purpose and had devolved into greed and a longing for power and control. That desire for power led to the misuse of the crystal technology that was controlled by a select group on Atlantis.

The crystals were huge life-forms that interacted with the humans and the resultant crystal generators had multiple purposes. They provided the power source for the cities and villages and they controlled the weather, keeping it at a perfectly balanced stage at all times with no extremes of temperatures or conditions. The crystals were part of the sending and receiving mechanism for contacting the home world of Ah-ta-lan. But they also began to be used for mind control of the masses and could generate powerful waves of destructive energy that could destroy populations on the far side of the planet in an instant.

We will not give you the entire history of Atlantis in this chapter, but will warn you that those long ago events could become active once again in your lifetimes. In their greed and hunger for power, those who were responsible for the maintenance of the crystal energy pushed the life-form crystals beyond viable control and created the destruction of their own colony as a result.

The energy from the huge polished crystals began to remain in the atmosphere instead of being dissipated after discharge and that energy began to tear apart the physical reality of their world. They knew what irreversible destruction they had created, so they sent portions of the population away to be saved by colonising in other places such as South America, Egypt, Greece, the far north of Canada and Russia, and Britain.

The island trembled and shook the cities apart for many decades before the final artificially created pole shift and the resultant sinking of the landmass into the ocean. These out-of-control scientists are back in a current incarnation—and they are recreating the very scenario that they once created on Atlantis with disastrous results.

The technology that is called HAARP is only the most visible tip of what is a mountain of destruction and deception. This technology is being used to alter the patterns of the weather on this planet. But it is also being used to aim powerful beams of energy through the very core of the planet and trigger specifically targeted geological and weather changes in innocent countries that are confused as to why the planet is becoming even more unstable in such a rapid fashion. [15, 16]

If the populations of a country are in fear and chaos due to fire and flood and earthquake and volcanic eruption, is this not an excuse for officials to come in and take control in what they claim is the best interests of the people?

We have stated above that one of the other uses of this technology was mind control of the masses. This is happening once again through images and sounds that are overlaid in low frequency waves that are being emitted from these generators. We will describe what many of you are feeling and you will now know that there is a concrete reason for this and, although you may be angry that you are being unwillingly manipulated in this fashion, just having the knowledge of what is creating these problems in your bodies will give you some peace of mind. [17]

Aching—you may be feeling an aching in all of your joints and bones and an extreme heaviness in your limbs. There may be a numbness or stiffness and pain at the base of your neck. You may be feeling a tingling sensation in your limbs like small electrical shocks. And you may find yourself washed over with nausea at unexpected moments throughout your day.

Your sleep, if you are able to get to sleep, is disturbed and 'busy.' And some of you do not feel safe sleeping during the hours of darkness and may only get the rest you need during the daylight hours. This is extremely problematic from our point of view because you are having these sensations for two completely different reasons.

Many of you are aware that the bodies of your human species are being slowly changed in preparation for your transition into a new type of dimensional reality. Much of that change is happening when your conscious state is unhooked from third-dimensional sensations. So the 'remaking' is happening as you sleep.

Knowing that, the sensations that we have just described may be partly attributable to that. But how will you feel when we tell you that those who are operating these generators are well aware that you are already expecting these symptoms, so they are layering their mind control INTO the same symptoms! [18]

You must be extremely discerning about what you are feeling and learn to distinguish between the two different sets of sensations. We tell you in truth, this differentiation will be difficult. Some of you have known for years that the minor inconvenience of having your bodies 'remade' while you slept also involved some of these types of symptoms listed above. But you also knew that you had a sense of playfulness in the morning after such episodes and you were easily able to shake it off in the knowledge that you were doing a good job at 'school' as you slept.

This is *not* the case for the low energy wave programming that now leaves you feeling depleted, sad, angry, and confused as you walk about through your days, knowing that something is happening to you but being unable to define just what it is.

Some of you are finding that you are unexpectedly angry with the people around you or are filled with a generalised rage for no specific reason. Or you may feel the opposite end of the spectrum and be washed over with physical and sexual desire to be close to and bond with another.

This is your unconscious or higher-self pointing out the lightness/darkness, love/hate duality that you have had to cope with during your incarnation on this planet. It is bubbling to the surface in increasing strength and we are laughing as we say this, but we would rather have you send waves of love and healing/creative sexual energy into the atmosphere than to see you succumb to the anger and hatred that they are trying to promote.

You are being prepared for crowd control and you must try to avoid any further programming if you can.

Turn OFF your television sets that send programming into your minds through images and sounds that are layered into what you watch. Disconnecting it entirely is even better since it is able to send these images and sounds into your household atmosphere even when it is turned off. For those of you who feel that you must have this in your homes so that you are aware of the events in the world, please limit your contact with television to a short time each day and you will immediately notice how much lighter you feel! [19]

The Oneness has created many variables of the time line for you to participate in during the next few years. But we are seeing you moving into one of the least desirable of these timelines unless you awaken. You have unlimited power in your ability to visualise and create. Do not surrender your power to others who may seem to be creating a 'better world' through technology. Question everything that you hear and see and go within for heart guidance that is connected to the Oneness and which is your most accurate source of truth.

Do not give in to the programming. Tell yourself that you *will* be strong and whole and purposeful. Love one another, even in the face of those who seem to be the most unlovable. Hold each other and cherish every life and every breath and pray or meditate or intend as one being of light or in a group. Then watch as the world begins to change when they realise that they cannot defeat or alter your connection to the Oneness and the light.

Note from Deborah: On Wednesday June 23, 1999, the television show 20/20 presented a startling report from military officers who felt that they had to 'go public' with the fact that the Russians have apparently developed new energy-pulse weapons and laser weapons that our United States government has no current means of defending ourselves against.

Journalist Diane Sawyer interviewed an American scientist who demonstrated his own current inventions that can neutralise the ability of any electronic-ignition automobile to operate and can 'fry' the circuitry in any computer large and small.

The point of these demonstrations was to illustrate that a weapon of this kind could immobilise control systems for everything from personal computers to corporate operations computers, from banking records to all governmental records and security operations, from the systems that keep hospitals able to monitor patient life functions to aircraft flying overhead.

The navy pilots that were interviewed described a laser beam that had hit them both and caused them to lose part of their eyesight. But even more chilling was the revelation that these laser weapons can be used to simply disrupt all functions of a human's internal organs, thereby dropping them in their tracks. This type of weapon could be used in a targeted pass over large populations to render all of those who were 'pulsed' immobile. [20]

As I read the posted transcript of this show, I was chilled by every description and the Dreamkeeper said in the back of my head, "This is a primitive version of the energy weapons that the ancient-and-returned Atlantean's use for control of populations. You have the potential to destroy yourselves with these devices, yet there is nowhere to hide from them."

One of the subjects who was interviewed also stated that whether it was an energy-pulse weapon or a laser weapon, it would penetrate a building as if it were paper and that simply being indoors is no protection. I have passed this on to you so that you may stay apprised of the facts.

These things are here now and are no longer simply predictions for the future!

Chapter Nine

Creation Tale

Shall we give you a story, a Once Upon A Time?

We believe that this 'fairy tale' that we now share, which is part of the true history of Earth that may never be available to historians and archaeologists, will both give you hope for your future selves and perhaps help you to not make the same errors.

Do you think that you are the first humans that have lived upon this planet? Do you believe the words of your scientists who firmly tell you that the age of the Earth is so-many million years old, yet they continue to revise the number higher and higher when they discover new evidence? We will tell you now that you were not the first humans but were, at that time, the second wave of humans to reside in this place. You are currently in the eighth version of humankind to have lived on this planet.

When you as a species think back to what you consider to be the highest evolutionary period of humankind in all fields from art to technology, you hold in your cellular and species memory what you considered to be the pinnacle—Atlantis. But even before the brilliant but flawed Atlantean's—many versions of humans prior to that time—there was another set of occupants.

Your scientists have correctly told you that you have arrived at your current physical appearance and ability level through evolution, but these humans that we will now tell you about came as colonisers to your planet from a star system many light years away. These were survivors of a dying solar system where their sun was about to collapse and destroy them all.

Their location in space would sound to you like a series of unpronounceable letters and their true race name would be equally difficult for your word-sounds to convey. For ease of identification, we shall call their star system Xlng and their race, the Olm. If you are able to say these words, then you are close to what they were called throughout the universe at that time.

Before we tell you of the disaster that befell them, let us relate their way of life so that you may understand the contrasts they were about to encounter.

The Olm Home World

The colours of their world might seem quite strange to some of you—gold and yellow and multiple shades of red with occasional sprinklings of purple—not the greens and blues that are predominant on the Earth. Their grasses were in shades of yellow and gold and the foliage on their trees was reddish or dark golden. Their water reflected the colours of their sky, a darker purple version of the delicate violet sky.

The Olm themselves were lovely to look at by human standards—tall and slender with skin the colour of toasted almonds. Their hair was uniformly wavy and thick and ranged in colour from light to dark brown with occasional streaks of reddish-gold. In temperament they were serene. Having long moved away from a need to display emotions, they were a tranquil and kind-natured people. They had evolved past the stage of requiring intrigue or danger, violence or anger, extremes of passion that were damaging to themselves individually or as a whole.

Do they sound boring to you? Let us assure you that their serenity did not negate their passion. And since they had no need to display this in an aggressive or forceful way, it was turned inward—towards intellectual, artistic, and spiritual pursuits. In these areas the Olm retained and displayed passion, but always in private. It was in the arts and in intellectual matters that they shared and debated.

Personal spiritual beliefs were just that—personal. And each of the Olm had reached a place of understanding regarding these matters following a five-year period known as Transition during adolescence. As their bodies were changing, each member of Olm society was taught to channel this bubbling cauldron of emotions and urges into a deep and serene examination of their place in the creation of all worlds by the Oneness. This channelled spirituality continued to ripen throughout adulthood as each of the Olm explored his or her own inner truths.

Upon completion of Transition, each of the Olm was allowed to make a personal choice about what areas of art or academics to pursue. And at this point, they moved out of the home of their biological family and into a community of study in their chosen area. The finest minds in each field of study offered their services as teachers and mentors to these special children and thus they were loved and parented and guided to wisdom by both their birth parents and by Olm society as a whole.

This specialised education did not cease when the Olm reached their early twenties but continued well past their 40th year since this was still considered early adulthood to those who lived 200 years or more. With none of the distractions of today's Earth such as war, violence, hunger, disease, or aggression of any kind, the Olm children and young adults were able to fully concentrate their energies on expanding their intellects and spiritual natures. These same lovingly guided children flowered into the long-lived adults that created an aggression-free, disease-free, bias-free society.

And what did their homes and cities look like? For those of you who are reading this from a large metropolitan area, it might look surprisingly rural. Their homes were all of natural materials provided by the planet.

Technology was kept to the barest minimum in the Olm houses so that time with family or in solitude was uninterrupted. And their cities never contained a population that exceeded 15,000 people. They considered that to be a manageable number of people to be sharing physical and psychic space.

There were large masses of grassland or orchard space all around so that a short walk from the centre of the community took you into an undisturbed place in nature.

The houses were low, smooth-edged, organic in feel, and those same qualities were found in the public buildings as well. A great percentage of the buildings were rounded, either in proportion or at the edges so that sharp edges were never visible.

This smooth-not-sharp philosophy extended to the furniture that they utilised and the objects that they used.

Sharpness was dramatic—and the Olm were not dramatic people. These qualities of 'sharpness' were occasionally found in works of art where some kind of statement was being made, but even in their art, music, and literature, smoothness and organic wholeness was valued over dramatic statement.

All Olm communities, whether they were a handful of people or a city, were constructed in a generally circular shape and were completely surrounded by a stone or earthen wall that encompassed all of the occupants and their homes and businesses. This method of construction was partly left over as a racial memory from their earlier days as warring tribal societies. But more importantly, it was discovered that a circular surround seemed to keep their psychic and spiritual energy focused in a spiral and creative way. For this reason, it was decided by the Elder Council that this tradition would be continued for the good of the whole.

For those who lived outside of the city or village walls and who maintained individual farms, their house and barn complex was always surrounded by a small-scale version of the city wall so that they too might derive the maximum benefit from the circular energy.

In every town or village, there was a round central plaza where the people could congregate and it was an important setting for a daily ritual shared by all the Olm. Although they had moved beyond the need to have central locations for worship and had done sufficient inner spiritual evolution to enable each of them to summon up an inner sacred space at any time through meditative practice, they maintained one important remnant of their past.

The Olm would stream out of their houses and public buildings to gather each evening in the central plaza and, just as the sun would set and drape the sky with brilliant sheets of colour, they would sound a tone in unison. This tone would vary from individual to individual and the combined sound would reverberate through the circular plaza and the circular village, sending a wave of sound around and around until it rose in a spiral towards the sky.

This was the Olm society's way of paying respect to the Oneness and of acknowledging their active participation and reverence for life. It was all the more special because the tone was not given off by their voices, but by the energy of their individual bodies.

The Olm had long before ceased to use vocal sound once they evolved into the use of telepathic communication. External sound was reserved for sacred or spiritual expression or for works of art such as music, which the Olm also believed was an expression of their spiritual natures. The peacefulness and quietness of their daily lives made the evening ceremony all the more special for the dramatic effect it had on their full beings.

NOTE from Deborah: Several years after this book was written, a scene similar to this was in the movie *City of Angels.*

Their great works of literature had been long ago transcribed into the central information data bank that could be accessed at any home or building throughout the planet. Books, in the physical form that you are familiar with, had not been a tangible or touchable reality, except in their cultural museums, for many millennia.

All expressions of art, whether written or visual or heard, were known to be part of the fully evolved spiritual essence of the Olm individual and society. Therefore, each and every member of their society was an artist in some sense of the word and it was not always regarded as a separate occupation. Every Olm was able to create these works of art to varying degrees of competency. It was simply regarded as an essential part of a well-rounded life.

Although each Olm was educated in a cross-section of all of their arts and sciences and mysteries, some chose to take this education a step further and were apprenticed to a specialised school upon completion of their Transition. It was like a cross between your Earth forms of apprenticeship and your university education. But in the case of the young Olm apprentices, once their general education was complete, their learning was focused on those subject areas that they would spend their life pursuing, mastering, and refining for future generations. The most highly sought positions were in the Living-Mystery Schools, which encompassed spiritual studies, metaphysics, science, and philosophy, and in the Healing Schools that emphasised various methods of energy healing and natural plant supplements.

We called this last thing supplements because the Olm had created a disease-free society and they did not require medication except in the case of injury. This was the focus of the Healing Schools—the repair of damage to the body that was not disease related. An interest in these schools did not guarantee acceptance into their rigourous programs, however. The applicant had to pass a series of intellectual *and* spiritual tests to assure that they were suitable.

More general schools of science and art and philosophy also existed and were attended freely by any Olm who wished to pursue these areas. Only the Living-Mystery School and Healing School had specific admission standards.

There was no want, there was no need, there was no inequality, there was no difficulty of any kind to keep the

Olm from pursuing lives of peaceful intellectual and artistic pleasures. Their weather and atmospherics were perfectly balanced and maintained by the robotics, their homes and public buildings were created through the labour of the robotics, and their farms were maintained by the robotics. It was as close to idyllic as you could get in an incarnational form of life.

The Crisis

This advanced race had great technology and the ability to travel through space as easily as you traverse your globe, yet they had felt no pressing need to do that for centuries. But when it was determined that their sun would soon be wiping out all traces of their population and culture, they were forced to deal with the fact that they had a very short time to create a limited number of interstellar vehicles to remove their people from danger. There was insufficient time to create enough additional vehicles to safely transport their total planetary population of less than 900,000 people. It was thus decided that, in order to hopefully save a portion of their race, they should concentrate their efforts on saving the children.

In their carefully ordered life on the lovely but small-scale home-world, the Olm lived long lives by current human standards and felt only the occasional desire to reproduce themselves. It was a very conscious act to create another life and one that was prefaced by special ceremonies and counselling sessions with the elders of the Council. Each child was thus considered a sacred addition to their society and was treated with tenderness and reverence.

The total number of children on the Olm home-world at the time of this disaster was less than 200,000 including those who were in or past adolescence. Yet only a fraction of those would fit into the ships that were being hurriedly prepared. In the end, the tiniest percentage of those children were evacuated in the waves of ships that took off into an unknown future.

Those were desperate hours for the Olm. They knew from earlier explorations in centuries long past that your planet had the potential to support life, but other races had begun developing prototype 'baby races' of both humanoids and work beasts on the chosen planet during those elapsed centuries and the Olm were uncertain what or who would be there to greet the arriving ships. On the Olm home world, any place on the tiny planet that was not filled with clear and pure lake water was covered with gently rolling plains that were sprinkled with cultivated orchards and occasional forests. It was not a challenging landscape.

But the evolving planet that they would be arriving on was, at last examination, densely forested with few open areas for cultivation and a great percentage of the surface was covered with salty water, a strange concept for the Olm who knew only fresh and highly oxygenated water above ground. The salt-filled bodies of water were confined to underground oceans in the world of the Olm.

Without the climate control mechanisms of their home world, the air quality on this new planet was strange to them also—filled with mould particles and perpetually smelling almost rotten to their sensitive noses. All of these facts had been documented by Olm explorers many centuries past and the adults of Olm perused this information with a combination of apprehension and resignation.

Their choices were limited to just this planet, known to you now as Earth, and one other possibility even further beyond their home world. In their own solar system, the Olm inhabited the single planet that did not have a hostile environment to their particular human bodies in either temperature, geological stability, or breathing atmosphere. In their region of space, each tiny planet that could sustain life of any kind was occupied by a single race of beings who, although interacting with one another in a mostly hospitable fashion, did not choose to freely welcome waves of refugees from another planet.

It was decided in the Council Hall that the children would be evacuated to the new home world, accompanied by teachers, healers, and counsellors of all kinds. The robotic creations that were the work force on the Olm home world would both pilot and navigate the ships through space.

All of the human occupants on the voyage were to be placed into a deep sleep state for the duration, and since the robotics did not require rest or nutrition, they would not feel the physical effects or passage of time on the long journey. But what of the possibility of emergencies that might arise or decision making that required a non-robotic pattern of thinking? This was where the Dreamkeepers entered the story.

We were known to the Olm from millennia long past and were part of their creation mythology. We had interacted with their developing species and made ourselves visible to them dressed in the purple hooded-gown form that was our first appearance to all new humanoid races. None of the Olm had physically seen us for many generations, yet they truly believed and remembered our part in their beginnings.

Although the Dreamkeepers are not beings that have emotions as you know them, we had a sensation of satisfaction when we viewed the evolution of the Olm. They had matured in an admirable way and had long since moved beyond negativity and aggression into peaceful, productive, and serene beings.

It was not difficult for them to access us since their daily lives so fully incorporated the spiritual and psychic that they knew full well how to contact us in a state of non-body reality.

When we had listened to their proposal, we agreed that a collapsing sun should not mean the total eradication of this race. So to each departing ship full of sleeping children and adult teachers, a Dreamkeeper was added to accompany them on the journey. Since we were not corporeal beings, we too, like the robotic pilots and navigators, needed no food or rest.

As the time for selection commenced, many families withdrew their requests for the evacuation of their children, choosing instead to meet the coming crisis together. And of the remaining candidates, a cross section of ages, abilities, and an equal number of female and male were chosen. In the end, there were less than 10,000 made ready for the voyage. But there was no dissent and there was no panic. There was simply an acceptance and a preparation for the spiritual journey back to the Oneness when the physical bodies had ceased to be. Yes, we were proud of these creations.

We shall describe the vehicles that carried the Olm on their long journey. Each of the vehicles carried slightly more than one thousand passengers. They were rounded, spheroid ships that glided smoothly through the occasionally harsh currents of space energy. Shielded with a magnetic energy barrier and also propelled by means of magnetism, the interior was divided into circular passages spiralling towards a central control room where the robotics and the Dreamkeepers passed the long journey.

The central control room was surrounded by a round outer chamber, the walls of which were honeycombed with sleeping chambers containing the children and handful of adults. Clear windows placed throughout the walls of the central control room allowed the Dreamkeepers and the robotics to see the walls of slumbering passengers at all times. Yet these windows were completely unnecessary. The Dreamkeepers could sense in an instant if a passenger was ill or in need of attention.

Each of the honeycomb segments contained a sleeping capsule made of a clear material that was stronger than any substance you currently have on your planet. In these capsules were systems that monitored the life signs of the passenger and regulated their nutritional needs. One by one the lids would be closed on the capsules and it would fill with the colourless sleeping gas that lowered all the body functions and conserved bodily energy. A Dreamkeeper closed each and every one of the capsules, and many of the children had one last memory of a twinkling face seemingly smiling at them as they drifted away into a thick and comforting blanket of darkness.

Deborah remembers this. She remembers placing her five-year-old right hand against the inside of the clear lid and feeling the warmth of the Dreamkeeper as she 'touched' her back in spite of the barrier. "Sleep. Sleep. Dream peacefully." Those were the last things she heard in her head.

Deeper and deeper into space they travelled, passing through and around many star systems on their way to a new but unknown home. Years passed, yet the Dreamkeepers and the robotics did not notice the passing of time, and the children had aged a mere few months by the time they reached their destination and the sleep-gas was turned off, one section of passengers at a time.

As the ships slowly entered the inner atmosphere of the new planet, the passengers were allowed to move to the outermost of the circular passages—the ones directly against the outer wall of the ship. From these passages, which were lined with windows to the outside world, they had their first glimpse of the new world that was to be their home. If there was any sensation of fear or insecurity, it was rarely seen or expressed.

Instead, as if given a command in unison, the children and adults spontaneously linked hands as they stared out the windows at the foreign landscape.

The New Olm World

How dark and dense it looked—and such strange colours were painted across this planet. The ships were slowly descending in locations scattered all over the large single-island continent of this new world. It was as if a giant hand had taken a handful of seeds and sprinkled them randomly.

No ships had been lost during the long voyage and each of the passengers had awakened in good health. The ships were used as living and meeting places while the transition was made from temporary shelters to more permanent buildings. The robotics that were not part of the ship's crew had been placed in an inactive state during the trip, but they were now awakened and put to work with construction and clearing of the deeply wooded sites.

As soon as the Dreamkeepers had determined that the adult companions to the children had the rebuilding and settling in under way, they dissolved before the eyes of the gathered groups as quickly as they had materialised on the Olm world. Their time of direct interaction had passed.

Yet problems arose almost immediately in each of the colonies sprinkled around the planet. The level of moisture in the air and the bacteria that had never been previously encountered made many of the children and some of the adults quite ill. Depending on where their ships had landed, some of them were coping with extremes of heat while others were wondering how to live with snow and ice. The central weather control machines on their planet had been left there since human life was deemed more valuable to evacuate than machinery. Many began to wonder if their elder adults would be able to recreate this seeming necessity with the assistance of the robotics. It was never to be.

Over the decades to come, the numbers of the children and adults was dramatically reduced by illness caused by weather and unknown diseases, fatal accidents due to their lack of familiarity with the terrain, and by attack from the animals that were already resident on the planet.

They chose from the very beginning to not interact with the primitive potential-human creatures that were still in their earliest evolutionary stages, so no loss of life resulted in that fashion. The primitive, fur-covered beings were still more animal than human, walking on four padded feet, standing upright only when startled, and making strange guttural sounds that were harsh to the ears of the Olm.

Their observations of this evolving set of beings convinced the elders that the primitives might not reach an understanding of how to interact with the Olm for many millennia and that it would be irresponsible for the Olm to interfere with the natural order of their evolution. In their deepest racial memories, the Olm knew that they too had once been at this level of development. They also knew that this species might never move past this stage of evolution and they would be interfering with the nature of the species to scientifically introduce Olm-like thinking patterns and intellect into them. To maintain the integrity of the primitives, it was decided that all contact with them should be avoided.

By the time a century had passed, almost all of the adults who had accompanied the children were dead and serious divisions were beginning to arise in their little communities. Without the stabilising influence of the mass numbers of elders who had kept the highly evolved Olm society on track, they began to fight with each other and revert to a more aggressive state. Some of the colonies simply ceased to be a few years later from a combination of disaster and apathy.

The consumption of food, which had seemed completely incidental to the Olm on their home world, now became a highly pleasurable activity. And sexual union was now frequent and unregulated by birth control. It became another pleasurable activity like the consumption of quantities of food, but the resultant prolific production of offspring failed to offer the spiritual and social status of their home world parents' decisions when bringing them into life.

A great percentage of the Olm were regressing and there was less and less interest in the arts and intellect with each passing decade. The diluted versions of the specialised schools still had some who remained devoted to them, but even these institutions were struggling to stay focused on their original goals as the dissension began to creep into their chambers also.

By two hundred years after arrival, there was little trace of the original culture except in the now tightly cloistered walls of the Living Mystery School and Healing School. These two schools had joined forces, ejected the dissenters, and built several walled communities isolated from the rest of their declining society. As those around them had become more and more like the primitive almost-humans living in the deep forests, preoccupied with eating and sleeping and mating loudly, these few hundred maintained the old Olm way of life to the best of their ability.

The new world Olm, the Olmen as they had named themselves and the planet, had continued to use the robotics for all manual labour. But as less and less of them pursued any kind of academics, they had lost the ability to repair the robotics as they broke down. Growing their own food and maintaining and building their own surroundings was inconceivable to them, so the Olmen began to raid the nearby deep forests, bringing back the primitives by force to provide slave-labour for the Olmen society. Their ancestors could never have imagined the depths to which their descendants could sink. This type of behaviour had been so reviled in their own ancient past that it was rarely even mentioned.

As the Olmen continued their downward slide, the members of the School communities began to formulate a plan for their survival as individuals and as a set of beliefs that was too precious to lose. Since the School communities had never completely lost the skills and technology to repair the robotics, they were well able to both maintain and improve theirs. In this way they were also able to retain their focus on spiritual life, healing, and education rather than on how to feed themselves, clothe themselves, or construct buildings.

While the Olmen had increased in number and needs as a consequence of their frequent and unregulated sexual unions, the Schools had adhered to the old belief system and had maintained a steady population. Each child that was welcomed into one of the tiny Schools communities was considered a blessing, not a burden, and was educated with love and tenderness and regard for life.

The Schools also knew that it was only a matter of time before the Olmen on the outside of the walls began to storm the communities and demand that they turn over their functioning robotics to supplement or supervise the labour of the primitives which were being used as slaves.

These were peaceful people residing behind the walls of each Schools community and the idea of participating in acts of violence, even in the defence of themselves individually or their way of life, was repugnant to them. They were unable to stand and fight, so they decided to leave this planet and seek another home in the stars. If they were unsuccessful in this venture, at least they could assure themselves that they did not get wiped out by the conquering Olmen or, even worse in their eyes, let go of their standards and allow themselves to become absorbed into that unfocused and unspiritual world of the outside Olmen.

They had a potential destination in mind—*Ah-ta-lan*—the home world of those who were later to become the creators of Atlantis on this same planet in another, much later time period.

These beings, somewhat similar in body shape although fairer of skin, eyes, and hair, had paid a visit to the new Olm world during the first century after the evacuation. What had appalled the At-ta-lan people was the growing barbarity of the general population as the elder teachers died and there was no wise replacement to guide these settlers.

But what had impressed them the most was that, during their meetings with representatives of the Mystery School and Healing School, they recognised a common sense of spiritual purpose. This segment of the Olm society was deemed worthy to reconnect with at a later time.

The Schools communities had decided that they could not simply wait and hope to be contacted again by the Ah-ta-lan and they must initiate the contact themselves. They were taking a risk by leaving without waiting for an invitation. But they had a strong belief that their few thousand refugees from the Schools would be welcomed by the Ah-ta-lan people.

They selected the two communities that were located closest to each other and, over a period of many months, the community members from other Schools joined them, a handful at a time. The distances were far for some who travelled in preparation for the space voyage and some of the community members were lost along the way to accidents or attacks by either the large beasts or the primitives. The loss of each member was felt like a psychic ripple through the communities, no matter how far the distance from the actual event.

But there was no time for the Sending Forth ceremony, the joyous Olm death ritual that acted out the return to the Oneness, to be conducted in full and the lost ones were simply buried along the way.

Each of the members of the Schools communities were well versed in the technique of using the Sound That Has No Sound for a variety of purposes from healing to spiritual enhancement, but they had been instructed since birth to never use this human-energy tool to inflict damage of any kind upon another living thing, even in the protection of their own lives. This ancient tradition of energy transmission had been kept alive by the Olm inside the Schools community, but was forever lost to the Olmen, and that was to prove to be their eventual downfall.

They chose two of the ancient landing craft from the evacuation of Olm over 200 years earlier which had lain in nearby fields for all of that time—unneeded and unwanted. The hulls and internal workings of the ships were of a material that never decayed so, although they were overgrown with vines and plants, they were fully intact. But the mechanical workings of the ship required much repair and the dampness of the planet's atmosphere had caused mould to grow on all of the interior surfaces. It took several months to replace each component, clean out each chamber, and then re-equip the ship for the long voyage ahead.

As those preparations were under way, the members of the outlying communities were slowly streaming towards the two selected Schools. Although the separate landmasses that you now see on your planet were joined into one large mass at that time, the distance between communities was still quite formidable since the members were travelling on foot. There were no vehicles on this world and animals were not used for transportation.

Eventually the members were assembled in full, the ships were prepared, and, under darkness of night, the refugees from the Schools communities glided silently upward and out into space towards a location that had been programmed into their guidance system by the scientists. The robotics would pilot and navigate, just as in that long past evacuation from the Olm home world. But this time, the Olm were alone on their voyage without the watchfulness of the Dreamkeepers to accompany them.

A little over a year later, they arrived and were welcomed by the Ah-ta-lan. Their recorded message of impending arrival had been broadcast as they slept during the entire voyage. The Schools community maintained themselves as a distinct unit for several generations afterwards, but eventually their descendants were completely absorbed into the loving and spiritual world of the Ah-ta-lan and they became as one.

Back on the Olmen world, the general decline accelerated. The population continued to grow and with each yearly increase came an increase in competitiveness and aggression as ever-growing segments of the population experienced neediness. No longer was there a guarantee that all would be fed or clothed or sheltered, and those social forces pushed some of the needy into lawlessness to such an extent that, several generations later, there were entire families who had never known any other way of life.

The enslaved primitives had been taught to walk upright and were now able to communicate with hand gestures. But there was a species-wide fear and hatred of the Olmen for removing them from their natural setting in the forest and for separating them from their tribal units.

The ancient ancestors' love of learning and the arts was almost extinct, and the remaining ships and scientific instruments lay covered with mould and forest growth. This apathy was to be the downfall of the Olmen since they had no way of knowing, of being prepared, for the disaster that was headed their way from the skies around them. A belt of meteors advanced steadily on the Olmen world as they lived below in unsuspecting ignorance.

Had they maintained their instruments and been aware of the impending danger, and had they remembered how to use The Sound That Has No Sound in a protective manner, their unified community could have joined their vibrational essences and used this powerful force to redirect the meteors.

The sun had just set on the farthest segment of the huge landmass when the first of the blows to the planet began. Within hours, all human and animal life on this shattered planet was gone as chunks of the surface were torn away and sent spinning into space, lethal gases were vented from beneath the surface, and the ceaseless shuddering and pummelling created a rending and jolting that are beyond your human concepts of earthquakes.

The atmosphere eventually cleared after several years. The sun eventually shone again on the surface of the planet as it assumed a new magnetic direction of spin. But the landmass continued to shudder for many centuries as the planet settled herself and gradually released the memory of the assault. There was no sign of any previous living being to indicate that the Olmen or the primitives had once walked these lands.

The Earth began to slowly, gently renew itself until it was like a prepared field, ready to be sprinkled with the seeds of living plant, animal, and human-creature forms again by the creator-god races from the far reaches of space.

Chapter Ten

The Clearing

We will be explaining in several parts about the Clearing of large portions of human population that is currently under way. We have been telling you for several years that the Earth Changes and social changes that prefaced the larger shift of consciousness are here now. They are not some future event that you can anticipate with dread or procrastinate about facing. All of the foundation of your future life on this planet is happening at this very moment. But why are you asleep to it?

We are concerned that we are not reaching enough people to have the hoped-for effect of changing the consciously-created future rather than simply letting events unfold in a seemingly random manner. You do have the power to change some of what we are about to tell you. That is a great percentage of our purpose in coming here at this time—to allow you to seize control of your own destiny as adult souls who function out of the power of love, for yourselves and for the planet, and not out of the power of fear or greed.

Many of you have been heeding your own inner stirrings and waking up to the changes in planetary weather for several years—but even for those who have been in denial about the shifting nature of the Earth's health, there is no longer any way to dispute what is unfolding now.

The weather and geological events on the Earth have been influenced by everything from the experimental tampering with the Earth's atmosphere via HAARP, to the systematic testing by the government powers of the world with electromagnetic pulsing through the heart and core of the planet, to the warming of the atmosphere due to your rampant reliance on polluting vehicles and your excessive use of power resources.

Your governments have been the direct cause of some of the planet's earthquake reactions, volcanic eruptions, and disastrous weather events. When they continue to do underground nuclear and magnetic pulse testing directly into the body of the Mother Earth, she wrenches and writhes in pain and her movements cause much loss of human life and long-lasting suffering for those who do not have the means to rebuild their lives and homes. [21]

There are other types of testing that are under way of devices that you would consider science fiction. But these things are all too real. We have tried to send images into Deborah's mind to communicate this in a manner that she would understand, but since she has no real grounding in science or physics, she either does not receive or comprehend what we are sending or she is reluctant to examine this very dark energy source.

This last type of energy testing that we are referring to is highly secretive and known to very few within your world governments, but it could be the literal undoing of your planet by dissolving it into a shower of sparkling energy that is gone in an instant.

This must be stopped if disaster is to be averted and your atmosphere is to be saved. The scientists in charge of these projects are 'playing' with substances and technologies that are far beyond their limited abilities and understanding in your current evolutionary stage.

In the past, we have told you that the three primary reasons for the thinning out of the human population—what we will from this point onward refer to as the Clearing—are (1) weather, (2) disease, and (3) acts of aggression. In some cases these reasons will overlap, but for the most part, each of them has a definite stage of arrival. This is what we will be discussing now.

Stage One: Weather

This phenomenon that you call weather has far reaching effects beyond those that you are currently seeing and we will outline some of them for you.

Loss of Life and Bodily Damage

Think back to a mere few years ago. Can you ever remember a time when your evening news or morning newspapers carried the reports of dozens and sometimes hundreds of people who had been killed or severely injured in some random weather event? Those were once or twice a decade events, weren't they? They are now an almost daily event. Some of you may say that this is simply because the news is more efficiently reported now than it was in the past. We say to you, if you need to hold onto that kind of belief to maintain a sense of security, then that is your choice. But the truth is quite evident to those with any kind of recognition.

We are not only discussing the bodily death or injury to humans when we discuss this weather phenomenon. Entire segments of animal and plant populations are being unbalanced by these events and some of them will never fully recover from it. Please take the time to give thoughts and prayers to the non-human occupants of this planet who are stressed or injured.

Loss of Home or Business or Way of Life

For some of you, the pain of losing your homes and businesses is as anguishing as losing another human being. We realise that it is part of your current human nature to be overly focused on possessions and the ownership of 'things' but it is truly time for you to gain a clearer and more mature perspective and realise that if you need them, you can still have these 'things' in your mind and in your memories, if not it physical reality. This is not a criticism of you as humans—it is simply a suggestion to help you remember that these 'things' which you seem to place such value on are temporary aspects of your real life, your soul life. Your memories and imagination are far more real than the objects that you cling to so tightly.

However, we do understand and sympathise with those who are not only losing their homes—their physical means of protection from the elements—but also their businesses and means of supporting themselves and their families. We have no words to soften that kind of blow and would not presume to understand the depth of your type of feelings since we have never been incarnated into a physical human body. We can only gauge how you might feel from the types of reactions that Deborah's body has to loss or worry.

Mental Trauma and Depression

We have dragged a memory out from Deborah's childhood of a house that burned to the ground leaving the entire family with only what clothing they were wearing that day as they escaped the fire. Although she was a small child, she noted the reactions of the adults around her as they went through phases of anger and sadness for the lost house and possessions and worried about rebuilding their lives. The cellular memory in Deborah's body retains the anxiety of feeling dispossessed, uncertain, and uneasy about living in unfamiliar surroundings. She remembers the anger and depression of the adults in the family and does not realise that the tantrums and sleeplessness that she had at the time were also symptoms of depression.

All of these emotions—sadness, anger, depression, anxiety, hopelessness—may be things that you are forced to deal with after weather events that damage or destroy your homes. We can only hope that, as these events continue with such regularity, your governments will recognise the need to have teams of qualified counsellors to deal with this mental distress. Being able to put loss behind you and continue onward will be, to some extent, dependent on both the inner strength that you each have and on the amount of 'strong shoulders' that are there for you in times of stress.

There will be some who are unable to cope with the grief or anxiety. There will be some whose lives are torn apart by weather disasters on more than one occasion and they finally feel that they cannot continue to summon the will to keep going.

If this is someone you know, please bless them in their choices if they decide to leave this earthly life behind. This is not an act of cowardice and we ask you to send them your loving support as they go back to the Light.

The upcoming years will be filled with so many non-stop disasters of one kind or another that you will begin to notice a great many people leaving the planet this way. They are making way for a great event in your near future and are working 'behind the scenes' from a soul level to aid in the transformation of the planet and her occupants. We ask you to respect their personal choices and send them on with love and not with resentment for being left behind.

Interruption of Services

What will you and those around you do to survive when the electrical and gas or oil power that you are so dependent on is unavailable? What will you do without clean and drinkable water? And how long will you be able to cope without a means to cleanse your bodies?

Part of what may calm your mind is to simply be in a mental and physical state of preparation by having adequate food and water set aside for these ever-recurring losses of services. And you would be well advised to have an alternative method of keeping yourselves warm during the cold months.

Contaminated or Destroyed Food Sources

This will be another means of exiting the planet in the future—by death from eating and drinking contaminated food or liquid. It is essential that you have a source of stored food and ample water that is safe to ingest.

The other consequence of the weather will be seen weeks or months later in the lack of certain foods in your markets or in the increased cost of the remaining crops. As the severe weather of all types sweeps across your planet, many crops that are essential parts of your diet will be destroyed. And in some cases, farmers may just recover from one weather disaster and be replanting or ready to harvest a subsequent crop when another weather system destroys the follow-up crop.

It is time for you to make preparation to store several months of food in case of long-term loss of crops. And if you are able, perhaps this is also the time to learn to grow the essentials of what you could survive on in your own backyards.

There were times in your not-too-distant past when humans had to rely on planting gardens in their own yards, whether large or small, for the bulk of their food source since the commercial agriculture had been interrupted by warfare. It may not be convenient or easy for you, but think about the alternatives.

Disease and Medical Issues

Each time a major weather upheaval occurs, there is an increase in the number of incidents of water and airborne diseases. How can you keep your health safeguarded during these times? [22]

We would first advise you to limit your contact with any bodies of water that are not normally in the locations that you are seeing them in. If your rivers have overrun their banks, or water has suddenly gathered in a place that is normally covered with dry land, avoid having this water make contact with your skin and keep it out of your body openings. Not only will currently known diseases suddenly spring to life, but new variations of these will also appear as a result of contact with the contaminants in your soil and air. The spreading of toxic waste throughout your landscapes in buried chambers will now be coming back to haunt you as these substances combine with the weather forces and water to produce deadly illness.

For this same reason, we would urge you to not consume any plants or grains that have been harvested from fields that were under water and covered in this mixture of toxic waste, industrial pollution, chemical pesticides, and water. This is going to seriously limit the kinds of food that you may be able to consume after these types of weather incidents. We are also concerned about the fact that you may unknowingly eat contaminated food months after these events and become seriously ill. These will be incidents based partly on greed and partly on ignorance.

If a field has been replanted following a period of being flooded with water that contains toxic chemical residue, this toxicity will enter the growing plant and subsequently enter the human body that consumes it. You may have no knowledge of the conditions under which your food is grown and may be completely unaware that you are ingesting these substances.

The danger here is two-fold. Not only are you likely to immediately suffer from illness following the consumption of food harvested from contaminated fields, but the toxicity in this food will also build up in the cells of your bodies. This toxic build-up in your major organs can lead to a weakened immune system and, in the case of a build-up in the tissues of the brain, can lead to impaired reasoning abilities and short-circuited motor response. These are extremely serious issues and we cannot emphasise enough how important it is to avoid such contamination.

We would suggest the following ideas. (1) Grow your own food so that you are aware of the conditions under which the plants came to fruition. (2) Shop only from suppliers who will guarantee that the crops have been grown under the strictest of organic conditions. (3) Store food items that are classified as long-term storage *now* so that you are not dealing with toxicity or shortages in the future.

Alternative Housing Options

In the last several months, your news has been full of pictures of people who have lost their homes due to high winds, flooding, earthquakes, rampaging fires, and other natural disasters. We would like you to begin to examine how you would live if there were no available shelter especially since many of you who live in the larger metropolitan areas have not considered these things.

As the weather and wind grows progressively more fierce and the waters of the world's oceans rise, where will you go to stay sheltered? Do you truly imagine that your government relief agencies will be able to provide enough food, medical care, and housing for large groups of displaced people in more than one location at a time without bankrupting themselves or being forced to turn people away? *The weather changes are upon you NOW* and are not some distant in-the-future event.

We have one last thing to propose. We have advocated the creation of smaller, intentional communities that are based on shared spiritual and social belief systems. If more of you are able to move away from your current concepts of single-person or single-family existence and embrace the concept of community living, you will find that you have the built-in safety net that you need. These types of communities are frequently in more rural locations and would be able to rebuild from the available resources surrounding them including mud-brick or adobe, stone, or wood. And with many hands taking care of the construction of one family dwelling at a time, the rebuilding would be accomplished in a much shorter period. Most of the existing and forming communities are well aware of the weather and geological challenges that they may face and have accordingly stored food, water, medical supplies, and building supplies. It is a way of thinking that you would do well to emulate. [23]

Stage Two: Diseases

This is the subject that frightens humans even more than the possibility of weather and geological changes or acts of aggression. But this is also the one that you may need to pay the most attention to. You cannot pretend that you are unaware of the possibility of death or extreme illness through disease, both natural and man made, as you look at your daily news. We have addressed the issue of diseases that arise from the weather changes in the section above, so we need not restate those facts.

In other sections of this book, we have discussed the fact that previously unknown illnesses would be occurring due to the venting of the Earth in volcanic activity and through an ever-increasing number of vents and opening chasms on the floor of your oceans. The ancient organisms and natural chemical substances from deep within the Earth are reappearing in your lifetime to combine with the chemical residues in your water, air, and soil. This concoction of ingredients is making a deadly mixture with the distinct capability of causing intense illness or death for large populations.

Your governments throughout the world have been extremely irresponsible in the storing of both nuclear and chemical materials for the past fifty years. These containers, either senselessly tossed in the ocean waters to corrode and leak, or buried in the soil in metal and concrete containers that are splitting and crumbling from age and allowing their deadly contents to spill into your atmosphere, are ticking time bombs that are about to make a great many of you ill.

As the Earth shifts and reshapes herself, these containers are stressed and shredded and the poisonous substances are released. Even the ocean, the lifeblood of the Mother Earth, is unable to contain these toxic substances as the containers break or disintegrate or—as has happened recently—have been dredged up from the depths of the seas by the strong weather fronts and changing ocean currents.[24, 25, 26, 27]

You must know where these toxic dumps are and insist that they are correctly handled by your governments. We realise that these requests may fall on deaf ears for a while, but if enough of you are determined and vocal in your demands, your governments will be forced to at least begin to acknowledge the errors that they have made with this storage and hopefully they will begin to implement containment of these substances.

This is a lasting shadow legacy of your human aggressive behaviour towards others of your species, and whether you were or were not personally involved in the creation or storage of these deadly substances, both your immediate future and the future of the next generation are demanding that action to resolve this is taken NOW.

The last area that we shall address is the many variations of laboratory-created diseases. These intentionally created diseases may well turn out to be the undoing of your species.

For the last seventy years, scientists in the employ of your world governments have been concocting the most deadly creations imaginable for use upon fellow humans who may have been deemed 'the enemy.'[28,29,30,31]

You would be truly aghast if you knew just how many ways there were to die an agonising death—and all of these ways were created by your fellow human beings. In addition to manufacturing them for their own governments, they have shared these concoctions with governments who may have been allied to them in the past, but who are now considered a threat. You have inadvertently given them the means to destroy your own population!

In many cases, there either *are no treatments* for these created diseases, or the antidotes are strictly controlled by the government and are intended for their use only. The civilian population is considered expendable.

For this reason, in the years to come when you see waves of population being wiped out by the accidental or intentional release of these biological nightmares, do not allow yourselves to become so numb to their more frequent occurrence that you fail to act.

Most of the time, the news media will tell you that there is an upsurge in the number of cases of flu or another respiratory virus. We urge you to stay alert to these particular announcements since airborne transmission is the easiest way to pass these through the human AND animal population.

Once these epidemics begin, they will mutate in the animal world and jump back across the species to reinfect the human population with another variation of the original disease.

We will briefly speak of AIDS. This too is a disease that was created in a government-controlled laboratory and was meant to be used in the future as a type of biological warfare against 'problem populations' that needed to be silenced. The human lab animals that were considered to be expendable were the homosexual community and the tribal black communities of Africa. These were the testing zones where the disease was released and allowed to spread.

The original version of AIDS actually had a vaccine to reverse the course of the illness, but the foolish human scientists in charge of the project did not take into account the rapid mutation factor in the two chosen populations and the disease was soon not only out of control, but it was creating variations of itself each few months. You may note that the two groups that were chosen for testing are groups that are reviled by some intolerant human groups as being less than worthy. [32]

We are aware that if you are reading this book, you are unlikely to be someone who follows that type of angry and limited thought process. But the words that are in Deborah's head as we send these words through her fingers are 'ignorance' and 'bigotry.' The explanation that we now give is not comforting. Many of the laboratories that created these diseases were run by relocated scientists, working as consultants to the U.S. Government, who had formerly pledged their allegiance to the Nazi cause during your war of the 1930s and 1940s. You may understand the mindset now of those scientists and why those particular groups were chosen to be the 'lab rats' for experimentation and potential death.

In every example of laboratory created plague, the potential for both accidental and intentional contamination of large amounts of the population grows with each passing year.

Does this knowledge make you angry? It should! *Only you have the right to control your life and health* and it is completely irresponsible for your governments to assume such an insensitive attitude towards your future. Speak out and demand to know what has been created, where it is, and what provisions have been made for handling this material. Find out why weapons of bioterrorism are now considered by the superpower nations of your world to be a useful method of controlling whatever 'enemy' they may deem worthy of such assault. Weather and natural disasters are one thing, but being removed from earthly life by your fellow humans as a result of their desire for control and power is entirely another issue. Make appropriate inquiries and demands now, before it is too late.

Some of you have asked that we be more specific regarding locations of these sites and timeframes for potential accidents. If we went site by site, country by country, it would take months for us to list them all. However we will tell you of some of the biggest areas of danger.

You ask what we 'see' when we look at your Earth in this context. It is a yellowish green colour that pulsates in an unpleasant way. The vibrations and pulsation of whole and healthy organisms and substances is altogether different from this wavy and irregular energy pattern. But the irregularity that we 'see' is an indication of Earth's instability.

Yes, we have knowledge of the efforts of some segments of Earth's population to cleanse the planet of these deadly substances, but you must be both vigilant in these efforts and more informed of the locations and nature of the other sites that are yet unknown or little known to you. Toxic by-products and nuclear material are deadly to your human bodies, but the laboratory created diseases are your biggest threat—so this is the area that we will primarily address. [33]

In Europe, we will begin with Britain. We must first look at the biochemical and medical laboratories that are away from the large masses of London and are deep in the inner central heart of the country. In places that were formerly known for their production of heavy consumer materials, these laboratories have quietly been established and are creating a nightmare of possible ways to die that are very far removed from a peaceful and gentle death. There is a large cluster of these in the area around Birmingham and Sheffield, there is a smaller cluster in the rolling hills and counties west of London, and there is a research facility that is operated in East Anglia with the assistance of a nearby university.

We see no such labs in at this time in Ireland, one small one near Cardiff in Wales, and one small one near the university in Glasgow, Scotland.

It would have made Deborah quite unhappy to know these things when she was living in England, and since we knew that she would be leaving in a short time, we chose not to share that at the time.

We see the potential for a leak of material originally of an agricultural nature that would be classified by the health service as some kind of rare disease that they would downplay in the media. This would originate in the Midlands and would spread quickly south in the years 1998–2002. [34]

In France we see a set of these labs in the countryside due south of Paris and east towards the border with Germany. And in Germany, the bio-labs are sprinkled all over the country. There are either one or none in the countries of Spain and Portugal, all of the Netherlands and Italy. The one lab that we are seeing in Italy is south and west of Rome in a particularly troubling location since it is on a highly active fault line. The Eastern European countries are dabbling in this work for both the Western Europeans and the Russians, so this also has the potential to be a true danger if these materials are ever used as negotiating tools and the negotiations fall apart. The danger that we see in this area occurs in the 1999-2006 timeframe as a result of a power struggle in an emerging government.

We see none of this in Greece, but the countries of Africa and the Middle East are positively bubbling with the creation of this kind of toxic biohazardous material. This is especially prevalent in Israel, Iran and Iraq, and in the Central African countries.

In Africa, this material is being tested on entire segments of population in 'controlled experiments' that will get out of hand. When you see in your news that a sudden plague has killed off most of an entire tribal area, please know that some of this is due to this kind of senseless testing. The scientists in this part of the world are under the mistaken belief that they can control the path of spread.

This is an especially dangerous area and, for several overlapping reasons, we see a potential timeline that shows this entire continent *running red with blood.* The kinds of plagues that would originate from the use of this biological material as a warfare agent in years to come would quickly spread around the world and result in a large scale loss of life for not only Africa, India, and the Middle East, but also for coastal populations of America and Australia, the financial centres of Japan and China, and any of the larger European cities that are serviced by international air flights.

Central Russia will be unable to fully contain the many varieties of biological warfare that they have developed and we see future contamination and death involving citizens of small towns and rural areas where these secret laboratories are located in crumbling buildings.

The material that we see being incorrectly stored in deteriorating conditions in upper Russia are mainly nuclear and biowarfare agents remaining from the pre-Vietnam war era up through the 1980s. These are seeping into the groundwater of coastal areas and are combining with the decaying nuclear material that has been dumped into the oceans at the top of the world. The citizens of these seemingly pristine areas are actually facing a terrible time of birth defects and slow, lingering death if they do not address this quickly.

Also, although we are not seeing a pulsing as such, from a pair of laboratories in Stockholm we are seeing the potential for the involvement in a larger scale disaster in another part of the world. The theoretical work that they are engaged in at these laboratories would, if it became known to less scrupulously controlled labs of this type, increase the virulence of the disease material that has already been created or is in the last stages of development.

India is developing far too many types of biological agents in the mistaken belief that it will put them on equal footing with the 'big players' of the world. We see serious laboratory safety issues here, but they also have nuclear capability and the primary danger in this part of the world is from political instability.

It is interesting to us that there are almost no laboratories of this kind in South America except for one small one in Brazil. In Central America, there are a handful of labs that manufacture components for the larger material combinations near Mexico City, but they are not processing the finished biohazardous material, only segments of it. We see no potential problems with a specific timeline in this location at this time.

We also see only two of these labs, and they are operating at a very small scale, in all of the vast country of Canada. These are in the countryside near the American North Dakota border and near the large city of Toronto. The danger with the Toronto facility is that a large geological event would allow leakage into the Great Lakes system and a widespread fanning out of the material.

The country of New Zealand is highly unstable geologically and the citizens of this country have blessed themselves and their future by choosing *not* to experiment with or store nuclear material or biohazardous material to any extent that we can see in any energy pulsation. If there are small-scale experiments being done in a university setting or small lab setting, they are not even registering as energy pulses.

Australia has allowed itself to be used as a dumping ground for some of the material being stored by the government of the United States. In central desert locations, toxic, nuclear, and biohazardous material has been stored in subterranean chambers. Yet this agreement may come back to haunt them since the continent of Australia is experiencing an increase in geological instability. This material is not capable of staying in a contained status if the Earth begins to heave and rend and pressure is placed on these storage units. Fortunately, the majority of this material is stored hundreds of miles from the nearest large centres of population.

But the deadliest of the created disease material and stored toxins could spread like wildfire as they are carried on the wind and they settle and interact with the moist and tropical conditions of the coastal areas which contain the majority of Australia's population. We see spurts of this danger as the Earth tosses and rolls more frequently from 2005–2012.

China contains many small-scale stockpiles of this type as they strive to compete in the production of these deadly substances. The dangers that we see in this area are from an ever-increasing series of earthquakes from this point onward. Although the laboratories have what they consider to be adequate earthquake dampening in effect, the preventative measures are rather primitive in some locations and the labs could spill their deadly contents into very concentrated populations resulting in massive death within a very short timeframe. This is another area that we see *bathed in red,* and we will elaborate no further. [35]

Your polar masses even contain some of this material which is being tested and evaluated under the extreme weather conditions there. Your scientists are operating under the mistaken belief that the cold will keep the diseases from spreading. What they have failed to take into account is that the disease life forms will create alternate paths if they are thwarted by a lack of optimum temperatures. As yet, we are not seeing a strong indication of a timeline warning here though.

We have saved the United States for last since it is the country that is most actively engaged in this particularly deadly research. These laboratories are scattered throughout the country and are not always confined to isolated or low-population areas. We shall point out some of the most active states and areas. However, smaller labs exist in almost every state.

In the western states, there are labs from Washington State through Oregon and into California. But some of the biggest producers are in California with several being clustered in an area just south of San Francisco and another cluster is clumped above Los Angeles.

You readers who live in that country are aware that this is a highly unstable area geologically, and most of these labs are on or near major fault lines. This is a very risky gamble to be taking with the lives of millions of people who live in immediate proximity to these facilities.

We see quite a few of these labs in the states of New Mexico and Colorado and most of them are actually under the surface of the earth and invisible for the most part. We are not stating that these labs are safe, but their underground locations make containment easier in the event of a leak, either accidentally or geologically caused.

From coast to coast across the USA, we see a lab here and there and there is another large-scale underground facility in Kansas. But when we look at the east coast of the country, we are seeing another large cluster of these facilities, and they are clumped in the countryside around Washington, DC and in a line from New England through New York and down to Washington. This again, like California, is an area of highly concentrated population.

In our messages over the past several years, we have tried to inform you that both the eastern and western coasts of the United States would be seeing a great loss of life from geological disaster, storm and weather events, and other related causes.

The sweeping of respiratory, brain-swelling, ebola type, and other variants of diseases across these population centres would succeed in thinning out the populations quite effectively and would give your governments cause to take military action into their hands, presumably for your own good.

We are not informing you of these things to make you live in fear, but we have always stated that preparation—

mentally, spiritually, and physically—allows you to be in a safe space in your heart, no matter what the physical outcome to your temporary 'clothes' called a body.

What can you do to prepare for these events? In many cases, there is nothing that can be done other than be informed. In some cases, you can reduce the personal effect of the event by knowing the danger ahead of time and placing yourself well away from it. Or you can insist on knowing what kinds of facilities are dwelling in your neighbourhoods with you.

Access to the kinds of antidotes that the governments have stockpiled for their own usage will not guarantee your survival. In many cases, the cure is more painful than the quick resolution of death and the lingering after-effects may make you wish that you had died.

Equipping yourself with air filtration units and breathing masks may give you some element of peace of mind, but even these will not guarantee that the tiny disease particles do not infiltrate your body through a mere touch by someone who has no knowledge that they are carrying a disease.

Deborah had great reservations about receiving this material. She is aching right now and mentally fatigued from allowing this to come through. But we state and restate that we feel that you have the right to be prepared, to be aware of what is coming so that it lessens the shock to the body and mind when it does arrive.

Those of you who are living away from crowded city areas will be better able to survive, but even the countryside will be affected and no place is truly safe from this time forward.

Stage Three: Acts of Aggression

We will now discuss the third type of Clearing—acts of aggression. It is our belief that you have it in your power to turn this entire situation around—if only you had *both the desire and the action to do so.*

You are already seeing an increase in these acts of aggression, both individually and by countries against their own population or against those that they have named as enemies. This will continue to escalate with each passing year.

Individual acts of aggression are sometimes the most shocking to you since they now include more incidents of children acting out or killing other children. These are things that you, as a society, had never expected to encounter. But your children are a product of their time, and they too feel the increasing vibrational agitation of the planet and are sometimes unable to cope with it. The reduction of family and societal nurturing of children is also leaving these young people in a position of making life-altering decisions when they are insufficiently formed in personality to do so effectively.

Be prepared also to see an increase in individuals acting out against small groups. You have created a society of adults that expects to be appreciated and rewarded and understood at all times and for little or no effort. These people have few coping skills when these expectations are not met or when they are feeling personally rejected—by jobs, by family, by relationships. These people, who have never been taught how to face disappointment or loss, may suddenly lash out and kill or damage those around them. The victims of this aggression may well be unknown or unrelated to the aggressor.

You are seeing an increase in this type of crime in every country of the world and it is not likely to decrease in numbers of incidents until you, as societies, rethink your approach to instilling a sense of security and responsibility in your young. It may be several generations before you are able to turn this around, and *only if you begin to do so immediately.*

Another type of aggression that we will discuss is organised and sanctioned aggression—either by armies against other countries, against their own citizens, or by the ever-increasing number of terrorist groups who aim at a specific target but frequently kill or injure innocent bystanders.

You are now so accustomed to picking up a daily paper or turning on your daily broadcast news and hearing of dozens or even hundreds of people who have died in a single day in one country or another that you are becoming numb to the shock of it and it now barely registers in your consciousness as an event. You have, without being aware of it, been systematically programmed to accept this as the norm. It is a programming that began in the late 1920s when media coverage began to increase in importance in your daily lives. [36]

We bring this to your attention to allow you to be more thoughtful, be more vigilant in your acceptance of news reporting as truth. There are agendas behind what is reported and the emphasis that is placed on certain events and you would be well advised to act now to become educated consumers where news reporting is concerned. Analyse what you are hearing or reading and begin to wonder both why it is reported this way, and then ask yourself what is not being reported. [37]

We find it interesting that many of you view acts of terrorism as a frightening possibility in your future—yet you are equally as likely to encounter difficulties from organised military groups within your own countries who will justify their actions by stating that they are acting for the public good. Terrorism is a reality of your times and it will unfortunately increase incrementally over the next few years. But the loss of your personal freedom is even more imminent and worrying.

As the weather events continue to escalate and geological or social upheavals begin to change your Earth, the armies of *all* of your major countries will be sent to help 'manage' the population. The very act of turning over control of your lives to these organisations implies that you are giving them approval for what they do next. And have no doubt, when armies are feeling powerfully in control because they are utilised in this way repeatedly, the personal and individual freedoms that you now take for granted *may* be swept aside for what the population controllers will call 'the good of the people.'

What if you have no desire to be evacuated to a central location where you are documented and numbered. What if you have made adequate provisions on your own land or in your own community and you are told by these 'officials' that they have orders to move you out, whether you choose to go or not. What if martial law is declared as a means of controlling your future destiny and refugee camps slowly become internment camps for 'troublemakers' who speak out on any number of subjects or concerns.

We are not saying that this type of reality is a certainty by any means. Please note that. But it is one reality that your world governments are *well prepared to implement* and you are living in dangerous ignorance if you refuse to at least examine these possibilities. If you had access to the secret planning manuals of each branch of your government, you would find that central locations had been established for relocation of the government operating centres following social upheaval, weather and geological events, or warfare. On the surface, this would appear to simply be a case of good planning for possible future events.

Yet there is a darker agenda in the minds of many government and military agencies as they ponder a future where personal choice is eliminated and each of you is at their mercy regarding where and how you will live, eat, and act. We find it likely that the ruling world governments will find a method for enacting laws to place you under constant observation and monitoring and that the rights you now take for granted may vanish. And how will you feel about seeing your personal freedoms vanish? These are issues that you will face within a few short years.[38]

We are *not advocating* that you retreat to rural areas and surround yourselves in encampments bordered by ammunitions and barbed wire. But we would like to make you aware that these possibilities do exist and must be thought out *in advance of the events* to come. Maintain your rights to choose whether or not to stay on your own land, in your own home, or with your own group or community.

Finally, there will, in the very near future, be a strong likelihood of multiple-country wars to deal with. We choose not to overly focus on this area since *this potential future can be changed* through imaging the world that you *do* want to live in. Send thoughts of love and healing and, most of all, wisdom to the leaders of your world who could bring these events into reality.

CHAPTER ELEVEN

Cleansed and Remade

We have received dozens of letters in the last few years regarding the Earth Changes and many of them have had questions regarding the location of 'safe places' that will survive the weather and geological upheavals that have now begun to change the appearance of your planet. We have always tried to be honest with you and make you aware that *there are no locations that will not feel this impact.*

There is no so-called 'safe place' and knowing that should assist you to live your lives more fully each day in the here and now.

In the upcoming decades, there are some locations that will cease to be altogether and some that will be radically altered. For those of you who wish to have this information so that you may begin to make plans to relocate to a site that is less likely to be eliminated from your maps, we will take this one continent at a time and will give general information regarding what we see as the *most likely possibility* for the appearance of the remade Earth. These predictions could change in the upcoming decade depending on the severity of other factors. These factors include solar magnetic storms and incoming objects such as asteroids that could seriously damage both your planet's surface and the planetary atmosphere.

We would hope that this information allows you to be mentally prepared for what is ahead and not be in a state of panic. We have observed that some people get quite overwhelmed when they find out that the location where they live may soon be either changed dramatically or simply no longer be there. People in this frame of mind are unable to think in a clear and logical fashion about the alternative possibilities.

If you have decided that the place where you are living is exactly where you wish to be spending your years in this incarnation, then this information will not apply to you in any substantial way for advance planning. It may simply serve to reconfirm to you what you may have already known in an intuitive manner.

For those of you who have made your choices with joy and not fear, we bless you for this loving and purposeful energy that you broadcast into the atmosphere around you that helps to alleviate the general and rising fear that surrounds this subject.

We will go continent by continent in this discussion and will give you a broad overview of what we see as we look at the timeline for your Earth that is the most likely one of many to come true. Please note that many of the timelines for this period are almost identical in outcome and have only slight shades and variations of differences.

North America

The piece of the United States that is named Alaska will find that much of its outer edges are lost to rising sea levels by the middle of the 21st century. In the middle of this landmass, a large chasm will open and eventually become an inland ocean. This chasm will be caused by the tearing of the surface in a repeated series of strong earthquakes between now and 2050. Any towns or cities that are in this area that will open up near the current site of Fairbanks will simply sink into the ground and eventually be covered over with the water from the inland ocean.

The large landmass that is called Canada will be known as one of the safest and least impacted locations on your entire planet after the Earth Changes have settled and the planet is gently humming once again in a harmonious fashion. Yes, this place too will feel the thrust of the winds of change that sweep like a broom across the planet. These high winds will wail and howl in mostly winter storms in this part of the world and will, after the first part of the next century, be accompanied by an increasing series of small to medium sized earthquakes.

Yet even these earthquakes will be mainly 'soft' in this land that thrums with Mother Goddess energy and the citizens of this place will feel truly blessed.

We see that some of the water masses that border the United States will be thrust downward during the shifting of the poles, but there is an abundant amount of underground water in this country that will reappear in many previously unseen locations. The impact of increased solar radiation and the potential realignment of the poles will cause the temperatures to eventually be more temperate than what is currently known there, but it will be a gentle transition for these citizens compared to most of the rest of the world.

The United States of America will be strongly impacted by the Earth Changes as most of both coastlines, east and west, succumb to the ever-rising oceans over the next decades.

We see that part of the west coast of this country will actually begin to sink into the sea long before the actual realignment. This has already begun although the occupants of this area are thus far all too unaware of this fact.

The great volcanoes in the states of Washington and Oregon, along with as-yet-unknown or forgotten ones in California, will roar into wakefulness to signal the movement of the landmasses into a forever changed state of appearance. Those who live near these places would be well advised to understand this fact. If they are relying on an early warning system of preliminary movements or increases in vibration that would signal to them that it is time to evacuate, *there will be no such advance warning.* These slumbering giants will simply rise up and roar in unison and take everything that is in their paths with no prior warning.

On the east coast, great pieces of coastal property will disappear and even the largest of cities that face the ocean will soon be forced to move their occupants away from the water. As the landmasses begin to slowly realign and a potential pole shift unfolds, there will be *no place within 50-100 miles of either coast* that will not be washed over with the rising ocean. If you live in one of these places, then either plan to relocate or embrace the water when it comes and walk into the light of the Oneness with gladness and a complete sense of trust.

Should the pole-movement that we have described come to pass, this, combined with an activation of a fault line that parallels the Mississippi River, will cause a dumping of the water masses that border the country of Canada and a new and rather large inland sea will be created all along the line of the former Mississippi River. The Mississippi River itself will cease to be and this will be the point where the plates separate forever creating two permanent bodies of land. This river will then be absorbed into the inland sea and the many states that had bordered this river will either be reduced in size or eliminated altogether.

Most of Louisiana, Mississippi, Alabama and Florida will simply cease to exist and over half of Georgia and Texas will go into the ocean as well.

We also see a large chasm opening in the mid-upper part of Texas as the movement of water under this landmass causes it to cave in and suck in all the land and towns around it in the process.

The ridge of land called the Continental Divide in the west and the Appalachian Ridge in the east will each become more and more seismically active with each year. The area will have many small mini-quakes and an occasional larger one. But these areas will gradually settle into a calmer phase after the realignment of the poles.

Central and South America

Much loss of landmass, much death is likely to happen to these locations. Central America will be severely reduced in size due to rising water and earthquake activity so that what had been one extended landmass will become a series of both elevated tropical islands and harsh mountainous islands that will barely sustain human life.

In the landmass of South America, we see a series of especially harsh earthquakes and volcanic eruptions which will cause great loss of life in both the initial seismic events and afterwards as no relief aid is forthcoming. Each country will be coping with their own sets of disasters and there will be no organised effort to reach out to other countries during this period.

However, the greatest loss of life in the country of Brazil will be due to a plague that will sweep through the populations and cause a slow and painful death. This plague will also have a devastating impact on the countries of Colombia and Venezuela and the few that do survive may wish that they had not survived as the bodies go unburied and the food and supplies run out.

We currently see that Argentina will survive with the least amount of damage to its citizens and will be another 'mini oasis' of calm similar to Canada when their overall damage is assessed.

The Pacific Islands

For every Pacific Island that simply ceases to be as it washes under the rising ocean, a new landmass will arise to take its place as the renewed volcanic activity of this region creates many tiny new islands over a period of years. None of them will be ready for occupancy for many decades however, so these cannot be considered replacement areas for populations that are seeking a new home.

We see very small portions of the larger masses such as New Guinea, Indonesia, and the Philippines surviving, but their populations will be thrust backwards to a more primitive state of existence as all modern modes of life are washed away or blown away by volcanic movement and large-scale hurricanes.

Australia and New Zealand

We have been with so many of these people in these two places and are pleased that we could let them know what was in their future. We will recap this now for those of you who have not spoken with us directly.

The country of New Zealand will see most of the northern island be lost to a series of earthquakes and volcanoes that will make the air thick with debris and the landmass uninhabitable for awhile for all humans and most animals. The south island will also feel a great series of movements and will resettle into a different appearance. However, in this place there will actually be an increase in the size of the landmass as the pushing forces beneath the crust of the planet shove the small country up and outward to reveal a greater coastline.

For a time the actual coastline and the cities along it will be under water as the seas rise and slosh over the landmass. But the settling will come and the south island will have grown in landmass as it is shoved up out of the sea. Although this area will be highly unstable for a time due to the constant earthquakes, the inland and mountainous areas of the south island will survive with the least amount of damage.

In Australia, the tiny piece of land called Tasmania will also increase in size after an initial reduction due to water overlapping the coastline. If you can picture a string of dots moving across a map between Tasmania and the mid-portion of the south island of New Zealand, you will see that although it is not to become a complete land bridge, this string of dotted mini-islands will stretch between the two places after the pole movement has reshaped the Earth.

Australia's body mass is to change in a similar way to the United States in that great portions of the coastline will be forever lost to the rising seas. Many major cities that are built along these coastlines, especially those on the western coast and the central eastern coast, will be completely underwater.

Unless the Australian government makes plans to move these large population centres inland at the first signs of water encroachment, most of the occupants of these cities will have 'wet feet' as we used to laughingly say in our live discussions.

An interesting thing will happen to the physical body of Australia after the pole shift. The western and southwestern coastline will begin to press downward into the ocean and the crust below. Then the upper northeast corner of the country will be thrust higher. The land that had been claimed by the ocean for a time due to rising oceans will eventually reappear and be at a higher elevation. The inland deserts will begin to bloom as a softer climate allows the rainfall that will transform the appearance and conditions of the place into a more hospitable location for the survivors to reside in.

The western coast of Australia and most of the southwestern coast will stay underwater and will not immediately re-emerge in the years following the shift.

Japan, China, and the Far East

For most of Japan, there is no long-term survival of the final stages of Earth Changes. Small dots of land will remain, yet it is unlikely that anyone could survive the turmoil that this location will be subjected to. These islands will be lost to a series of earthquakes, volcanoes, ferocious storms, and the eventual sinking of the landmasses. Unless there is a plan for a total evacuation to the mainland of Korea, China, or Russia in place, we feel that there is little likelihood of the Japanese people surviving past the end of the next century.

In the countries of China and Korea, we see a severe reduction in population from the weather and geological factors. Yet an even greater reason for a loss of life is due to a man-made plague that sweeps over both countries and is carried on the storm winds. This plague will also affect a great portion of Russia also. Laboratory created diseases that are stored in both of these countries will be unleashed when the geological instability cracks open the containers that they are stored in and scatters this biological plague into the gusting winds. This will not be the kind of lingering death that the citizens of South America will endure. This plague will be swift and deadly and will strike down almost every person that it touches. There will be a great silence in China and Korea and parts of Russia—a very great silence.

There is one exception to this and it is only in the highlands, not in the lowlands of each of these places. In the place known as Tibet and in the country known as Burma, life will be changed by the altered landscape and sweeping storms, but these people will, for the most part, escape the fate of the rest of China. The great silence of death will not extend as drastically into this high and thin air and these people will thrive and continue.

What a jewel the separated landmass of Thailand and Cambodia will be! The movement of the Earth will cause a large channel of water to separate these countries from the rest of the continent and that will be the saving of them. The deep green forests and highlands will be the least touched of all places on this side of the world. Yet they too will be affected by the waves of plagues in nearby countries and Thailand will be hard hit again and again by earthquake activity and rising oceans.

Russia

Sadness, sadness, lingering death is all we can see here with the exception of a few locations sprinkled in the deep mountains of Mongolia. They seem to have so many ways to die in these places—death from plague that is man-made in origin, poisoning by nuclear contamination, death from consuming contaminated food and water, violence and more violence with no thought of helpfulness towards one another. These things are added to the upheavals of the Earth herself. Here too we hear a great silence, but not before the long, long periods of wailing that echo through these lands.

India and Pakistan

Red with blood—red with blood. A few hundred thousand in each segment of this place are all that is left after the rising waters that inundate the coastal centres of population, the plagues of the mid and late 21st century, the chaotic weather, and the mass slaughter of one another. We will speak no further of this.

The Middle East

We find this interesting that in this often hostile place that has so little tolerance for certain belief systems and which is currently known to the rest of the world as a militant and angry location, there is to be a flowering of peace following the realignment of the Earth's landmasses. Yet for your near future, there is a large and looming cloud over this place and it swirls with aggression for many years to come.

There is the sound of wailing rather than laughter for long periods of time. We see an inwardness and a return to suspicion of all things not like them.

Yes, this place too will be sharply impacted by the weather and seismic events and many will be lost as they are crushed to death or swept away. The numbers in these countries will be reduced to less than one in ten which is the same percentage that is left in the United States and continental Europe.

But what is unique in this location is the spirit of helpfulness and community that we see arising from the rubble as the survivors thank the Oneness and share what they have with one another in gratitude. Their resilience will be strengthened by the fact that their lives have frequently been difficult, so they are better prepared to cope with hardship and want. They too will see an eventual blooming of their deserts, just as the inland section of Australia will be transformed, and their lives will be made easier by the fact that they will be able to grow food and rebuild with greater ease after the changes.

The angry energy that currently simmers in many parts of this area is simply washed clean by the larger Earth Changes and never returns. That is the most hopeful thing that we have seen thus far as we have examined your timelines.

Africa

Red with blood—red with blood. From plagues to wars to sweeping winds, there is little left of the population of this place. Desolation and silence are all that we see for many, many decades as the landmass heals itself from the psychic violence and the animals return and flourish long before the humans do.

We see small centres of population returning, but that is more than 300 years into the future and they are not the humans of your present-day world. This place has an odd 'echo' that will be felt for many generations to come as people try to return to this landmass and find that they are unable to cope with the off-kilter energy and they must leave quickly. There is a clinging, lingering sense of horror that is even stronger than that in India-Pakistan and it is a uniquely desolate energy.

Europe

We gaze at this place from high above and see island nations where once there were solidly joined continents. Greece becomes even more of an island country, Italy is broken into pieces, the high and mountainous countries such as Austria and Switzerland become even colder in climate and are shattered by earthquakes, half of Germany and France and all of Holland are lost to the sea, Portugal and Spain are a series of high islands and remote villages that will survive.

England, Ireland, Wales, and Scotland exist only in small dots of land that were the highest altitudes in the pre-changes Britain.

Yet Norway, Sweden, and Finland, although impacted by the harsh weather and battered by seismic activity, survive quite well and are, like the northeast portion of Australia, higher in altitude than previously. They too have been thrust upward by the movement of the Earth's crust and will settle into a peaceful and harmonious state with relative ease.

We have saved Turkey for last. We see great upheaval in this place in both seismic activity and general waves of death and disease. It too has an odd resonance that will make this location undesirable for many decades after the changes. There is some dark energy here that we choose not to examine. The more light-hearted and light-souled of their people will find they are welcomed in the neighbouring and thriving Middle Eastern countries.

Other Places

Greenland will survive with a temporarily reduced coastline, but it too will grow in size and actually get warmer with each passing decade until it is a highly desirable place to live.

Each of the current poles will be 'spun off' for the most part as the warming water washes them away and reduces them to a mass of slush when the magnetic poles slide into a new location.

Antarctica will remain as a landmass once the ice has melted off and will become a warm and fertile homeland for many who flee from other places around the world. Once the ice has melted though, this will temporarily be a smaller landmass until it too is pushed upwards by seismic thrusting and grows in size and altitude in the first few centuries after the Earth Changes cease.

A large mass of land will arise in the middle of the Atlantic Ocean. Most of this is the continent formerly known as Atlantis. This huge landmass was split in two by the seismic forces that sank the continent of Atlantis and it is now in two narrow pieces in your North Atlantic Ocean reaching almost to Greenland, and in your South Atlantic Ocean reaching all the way to Antarctica. It will be many decades before the saltiness of the saturated soils has neutralised enough to support life and agriculture in either of these pieces of the former Atlantis.

As we look at your most likely timeline, the new North pole will be right in the middle of the north island Atlantis landmass directly across from what is now Nova Scotia, and the South Pole will be in the Indian Ocean off the southwest corner of the soon to be submerged coastal Australia.

Please understand this, it will be many years before the dust and debris completely clear from your skies following the final pole movement and resultant eruption of all volcanoes worldwide in a simultaneous clearing of energy. For that reason, you must be prepared to live without freshly grown food for that time period or be limited to only what root vegetables will grow in extremely low light conditions.

There are many challenges for those of you who wish to live through these events and assist in the remaking of your world. Those of you who have learned to live with darkness in a calm and meditative state will be better prepared to cope with this lack of light. We have hope for you as a species and are pleased to note that, for the most part, there is a renewed love of life and respect for the Earth in the survivors. You may not remember signing on for this adventure, but it is certainly not going to be a dull future!

Additional Note: 7 December 2003—The above segments were received in 1998 and although all of the timeframes and site-specific predictions are the same, I see a more gradual movement of the poles that extends over many decades. I stand by the information regarding rising water and drowning coastlines, the geological instability of various continents, and the unfortunate methods of death from disease, contamination, or warfare that I have outlined for each continent or country noted.

The only real revision that I would make in this segment is that I feel the pole movement may be slower and more gentle. But I believe that the slowing and softening is due to a combination of factors including the power of intention by all the masses of people globally who have prayed and meditated about catastrophic Earth Changes.

I also feel that the Earth's magnetic instability and flexing-fluxing in response to the solar magnetic discharges may be preventing the type of full-on cessation of planetary rotation and resultant reversal—what we had all come to expect as the classic pole shift in a stop-start fashion.

Since the writing of this book, it is now a scientifically documented fact that the poles are moving slowly to new locations. The slowness of this activity allows the human populations of this planet to be better prepared for what is upcoming in the decades ahead.

—Deborah

Chapter Twelve

IMAGINATION AND RENEWAL

The long prophesied changes for your world are here *now* and there is no escaping that fact. Events in your present and very near future will keep you off balance and feeling uncertain unless you give yourself the tools to cope with these changes as they arise. The Earth needs to renew and cleanse herself and it is important for you to understand that this is a naturally reoccurring and cyclical event and is not aimed at the destruction of you personally.

Some of you may be trading in your human-incarnation 'clothes' for a body of light in the coming years, and that too should be nothing for you to fear. It is merely a return to your true form and your true state of being.

As the Earth births herself into a new state of being, it eases her pain if you share in this process by consciously sending her the energy of love and healing. And it also aids in the transformation if you are able to release your fear of death and allow her to remake herself with a more balanced population.

Finally, if you are able to calm your agitated minds and psychic states by re-visioning the world that you *do* choose to live in during your time on Earth, it will send out waves of soothing and serene energy into the psychic and spiritual aura of the world as a whole and transformation will truly begin.

We have told you throughout this book that you have the power to change both your life and your future destiny, and this power lies within you, waiting to be tapped. It is the imagination, the creation of an image of the life that you want, that will activate these changes.

Deborah: The Dreamkeeper has offered the following meditation to help you achieve these things. It may be helpful to read this into a tape recorder so that your own voice can softly guide you through the steps.

Recreating Your Life and Your World

We would like you to find a comfortable place to either sit for an extended period of time or, if you prefer, lie flat. We find that sitting is preferential since the act of lying down sometimes induces a sleep state rather than a meditative state, but it is your choice. Please loosen your clothing if necessary so that there is no constriction that will cause you to be distracted as time passes.

If you can find a quiet room in your home or a peaceful location in nature, these are ideal conditions. However, if you live in a noisy environment, you may want to either mask the sound by putting on soothing background music, or you may choose to insert earplugs that block out the majority of the sound around you. Sitting on a well-padded cushion or comfortable piece of furniture will also eliminate the strain on your spine that may cause you to come out of your meditative state prematurely.

Close your eyes and begin to take slow, deep, and regular breaths. As you take these deep breaths over the next minute or two, feel all of the tensions of your day sliding off of you and disappearing forever. Once you have completed this relaxation breathing, you are ready to begin.

With your eyes closed and all of your limbs relaxed, take a slow, deep breath and picture a cleansing of your mind—take another deep breath and picture a cleansing of your body—and take one more deep breath and picture a cleansing of your spirit. You are now prepared.

Maintain a deep and regular breathing pattern as we relate these things to you. You are now surrounded by two warm and safe kinds of energy that are originating from two different locations. From the Mother Earth, picture a deep and golden energy swirling slowly and thickly up in a spiral around your body. This energy wraps you in a feeling of warmth and safety and your body is responding by sending shoots of energy, like roots on a new plant, deep into the body of the Earth. You are now completely safe and grounded to your source of life.

Continue to breathe slowly and deeply as you see in your mind a second kind of energy—a sparkling shower of twinkling gold and silver that is raining down on you from the Universal Oneness of God that is above, below, and all around you at all times. This cool and tingling energy rains softly on every part of you, washing you clean of all worries and concerns.

You are safe—you are grounded and anchored securely into the planet that you reside on—you are surrounded with soft and loving energy from the Oneness. Your entire body and the aura space around your physical form are filled with this glowing light and you allow the sensations to fully sink in until you are peaceful.

Now you will create a movie for yourselves and you will pick the setting. Is it a cool and wood-fragrant forest? Is it the seashore with its pulsing rhythm? Is it the top of a mountain with a panoramic view stretching below? Is it a comfortable chair in front of a crackling fire while the snow falls silently and softly outside? Whatever place feels most comfortable to you, pick a location and see yourself transported there. You are about to create your future and you need no distractions—so know that you are in this place in precious solitude.

Continue to breathe in a slow and relaxed way as you take note of the beauty that is all around you. In your own life, you would like to have this kind of beauty available to you at all times. You are worthy of this—you deserve this—now, let's create this.

As you feel yourself more and more relaxed with each passing moment, you notice that a spot of light has appeared before you. Slowly—slowly—the spot is growing closer and closer until you see that it has become the shape of a movie or television screen.

Perhaps for some of you it is the shape of a blank canvas on an easel. Pick the shape that is most familiar and comfortable for you because you are about to direct the unfolding events in your future.

Picture yourself gently dematerialising in a shower of sparkling light and then re-forming on the screen of your choice. You are now inside of the movie of your future that you are creating.

Look down and see your body. Is it in a state of good health? Is it the shape that you desire? Do you feel good about what you see? If any of these areas are of concern to you, picture your body now in perfect health and fitness and feel that sensation. Send thoughts of love and blessings to your body as it is now and as it is in its future state and allow those loving thoughts to register as warmth throughout your entire being.

Look now at the conditions in which you live. Is there abundance? Do you have a safe place to live, warm clothes and good food, and the financial resources to allow you to have peace of mind? If these things are lacking in your life or need improvement, create a picture now of the way that you would like to be living. See yourself free of financial worries and living in an ideal and harmonious setting. Hold onto that picture in your mind for a few minutes as you enjoy the sensations of security and safety.

See yourself always attracting these kinds of conditions and mentally say thank you for the abundance in all areas of your life. Then envision yourself saying aloud that, "*I am grateful for my blessings and feel safe in the knowledge that they will always be there.*"

Repeat this phrase three times and allow the truth of it to fully sink into every cell of your body. Does it feel comfortable and natural? If there are any shadowy doubts trying to work their way into your movie, repeat this phrase of gratitude and affirmation three more times—and then three more times—until you are certain down to the depths of your heart that it is how you are meant to live.

So far you have been alone in this movie, but now it is time to move on and include those around you in the movie of your re-created life.

Are the people that are in your life those that make you feel good about your life choices? Are they fun to be with? Do they encourage you when you have new interests and enthusiasms? Are they there for you in times of need or periods of discouragement? Do they honour your spiritual and psychic insight?

Picture now that you are surrounded by people with all of these desirable qualities and *know in your heart* that from this point forward, *you will draw these people into your life.* Take this part of the movie slowly—play it over and over again as you see yourself interacting with happy and energetic people who bring out the best in you. Feel those sensations of love, acceptance, and encouragement—and let those feelings wrap around you like loving arms.

Then, to deal with those who are already in your life who may not be supportive or who are negative in thought and action towards you, picture them tightly wrapped with a clear film that has the words LOVE and POSITIVE THOUGHTS written all over it.

Surround them with this material and know, *and believe,* that their words or actions will simply slide off of you in the future with no negative effects. You have sent them nothing but good things and have shielded yourself from future harm.

Now see the work that you do or the activities that fill your daily life. Are these activities or careers making you feel happy and fulfilled?

If they are, simply wrap that picture in a golden aura of happiness and move on. If your days are not filled with joy and purpose, then we want you to see this change for the better.

What do you dream of doing with your life? What career would you like to have? Or would you rather have the financial ability to retire and do good works by volunteering with those in need? Do you long to spend your days writing or painting or gardening?

Whatever is your dream, now see yourself doing those things. Walk slowly through this portion of your movie and feel the sensations of doing those things every day. Picture your surroundings and the working or playing conditions. What items would you be holding in your hands?

Take it slowly and let it sink in until you are certain that you have 'lived in' this scene enough to know that it is your future.

See yourself moving now into a comfortable chair. In your movie you are watching the news on a television, or listening to the news on the radio, or you have just opened the morning paper and are reading the unfolding events of the world. Is this the kind of world that you want to live in? Are these realities comfortable for you?

Picture yourself now getting up and moving across the room to sit at a writing desk. In your hand is a lovely pen and in front of you on the desk is stretched a long scroll of parchment paper. The scroll is blank and waiting for you to create your wish list for the world. See yourself dipping the pen slowly and deliberately into the ink well at the back of the desk—and begin to write.

What do you wish for? Are your wishes of a personal nature? Do you wish to correct the out-of-balance areas of your life? Do you wish to strengthen and increase the goodness that is already there?

Be thorough and write as many wishes and dreams for your personal life as you desire and write these things with confidence.

What about your life as you grow old? How would you like to be living? Who is surrounding you at this stage of your life? How will you approach your coming reunion with the Oneness when you leave your Earthly life behind?

See yourself surrounded with love and purpose and happy companions. Feel the energy of that vision. Now see a glowing door opening on the other side of the room. Through that door you hear the soft voices of those you have known and loved who have gone on before you. They are calling out to you reassuringly from that glowing light.

You may now see your future-self walking slowly yet firmly towards the glow, looking back one last time and knowing that you have done all that you came to do in this lifetime, and then see your future-self stepping confidently into the light. There is no doubt—there is no fear—and you feel completely safe as you step forward. You have prepared yourself for a gentle transition, when that time comes.

Return now to the present time. Is your next set of wishes for the planet and for all of humankind? Envision peace and prosperity. Truly see an end to all war and oppression and want and see all beings living in harmony on this planet.

Are you thinking big enough—ahead to a time when all who you know have passed on and the world is still here? Envision the world that you wish to survive into the next generation and many more generations ahead—and then write that on your scroll.

With every line that you write, know that these things will come true as more and more people awaken to their ability to reshape the future. Write and write, line after line after line, until you can no longer picture any changes that you would like to make or wishes and dreams that you would like to implement.

Then see yourself walking to the front door of the building that you are in and see yourself holding the scroll out into a ray of sunlight. Watch as a breeze scoops it from your open palm and softly wafts it higher and higher—on out into the Universe to be acknowledged and answered.

Now, walk slowly back inside and sit peacefully for a few moments. Then open the newspaper that is lying beside you. Is this a more peaceful and loving world that you are reading about now? You may repeat this section of the meditation as many times as you need to until you are convinced that you have done your best to imagine and thus to re-image a better world into being.

We have one last vision for you to create. Come back from the life in the screen. Picture yourself sitting quietly in the actual space that you are now meditating in. You are still wrapped in comfort and serenity and a sense of purpose.

Now, deep within your chest, see a glow begin that spreads out like a tiny sun. Let it grow until it fills the space that you are in. Then picture hundreds, then thousands, then millions of similar suns glowing brightly all over the Earth. Know that as you are seeing this, you are not alone in your recreation of the world. Know that you are connected through love and intent to all of these others—and feel the shared glow of your work. Sit quietly and bask in that sensation for a minute longer.

Take a moment to express gratitude for your life and the many blessings in it. Then slowly—slowly—see yourself releasing the energy of the Earth back into the heart of the planet. Then release the energy of the universe back outwards in a sparkling burst. And when you feel comfortable about coming back into the present, gently open your eyes and come back to the room where you are meditating.

You are blessed by the power of this set of intentions for all and for yourself and you are a blessing to the planet in your willingness to make a positive impact with your life and your spiritual work. *Know and believe in the power of this statement.*

CHAPTER THIRTEEN
Questions And Answers

Deborah: During the past several years, I have received wonderful feedback from the readers of the web site—sometimes in comments, sometimes in criticism, but mostly in questions for the Dreamkeeper. In some cases, those who participated felt comfortable having their name and location published along with their question, and in some cases you will note that only initials are given and no location is noted.

Many of the questions that came up during the live-audience sessions have already been covered at the beginning of the book in the chapter ORIGINS in which the Dreamkeeper explains who and what she is all about. It has been very gratifying to see how much thought and curiosity is reflected in the questions below. For all of those who participated, I again thank you for the time and effort involved in contacting me.

Ruth Fisher: I too, have had a gift since I was a child. For many years it lay dormant, as my life took turns that made it impossible. However, since July of this year I have been having visions, both in altered state and just the voice in my head. In the altered state, I have what I refer to as a spirit guide. I know who it is at present, someone who has gone before me and I am comfortable with. I have been told by him that another will be taking his place that will be of far more assistance. I guess my question for the Dreamkeeper is this. Is this real? I have seen so many things and they are now coming fast and furious. When in altered state, my guide keeps telling me not to doubt. To get the word out. Alert people and keep assuring the message of coming together on a spiritual level that contains working together and loving one another.

I have friends that are serious doubters, and when discussing this with them, all they want is proof. As for me, I feel kind of alone here, but I am inclined to believe what I am seeing. No, I do believe it! I also believe that I have a message that I am presently trying to put in book form. Any help your Dreamkeeper can give me would be greatly appreciated.

Dreamkeeper: We are feeling the truth of your words and the emotional dilemma that you are currently experiencing. This is a difficult time of transition, and Deborah did not always fare well with it when we first re-entered her life and asked her to allow us to use her body. We will assure you that it will get easier with time. Your mission has been simply stated to you, but it is indeed one of importance and it requires strength and courage to live in this manner when you may be subjected to criticism by family and friends.

You must believe in the truth of the message that you are receiving from your guide. The spiritual work necessary to allow us to recreate the world in an image that is peace-filled and whole and interconnected is a great and important mission. Please believe in the integrity of the work even when you have times of darkness and doubt. You may find it helpful to stay in contact with Deborah in this regard since she has been through this emotional and social turmoil in her own life and can relate to what you are living through.

Yes, write what you are hearing and allow the world to share the message! Know that we encourage you and are pleased at your dedication to helping humankind.

RF: I presently live in Massachusetts but am quite uncomfortable here. No mountains! I desperately need mountains. I was recently told by my guide that by late next summer I would be living in Northwest New Mexico.

Dreamkeeper: We are aware that many of you are being drawn to this part of the country and we will explain. The sacred energy of the Earth is very easily accessible in this place, yet there are problems that must be addressed. What you call the four corners states, Colorado, Utah, Arizona, and New Mexico, have a combination of geological and natural sacred energy that has been revered by the native people for many generations.

There was a deliberate and well-planned choice that was made when the government of your country began to do testing of instruments of war, both nuclear and biological, in this place. These sites were chosen not only for their remoteness but also for the resonant qualities that 'supplement' this dangerous work.

Those of you who are being drawn to this place may be doing so because you are aware on an unconscious level that this place needs the extra positive and loving energy of those who are willing to do the psychic combat needed to reclaim this location for the welfare of humankind. Be aware that this is a deep soul commitment that you have made before you incarnated into this lifetime. It is not an easy path, but we encourage those of you who are dedicated to this path to counteract the negativity that is currently being placed there.

Susan Sanders, Port Orchard, Washington, USA: I have lost 3 people who were very close to me this year. You have said that many will be choosing to leave and I know that is true. How can those of us who are left deal with the grief and loss of our loved ones?

Dreamkeeper: You are asking about the loss of companionship and physical presence of many of those that you love during a short period of time. This is not an easy issue for you since the loss is not only of that person that you knew in this lifetime, but of the soul-essence that you have known in other lifetimes and other shapes. We are sensing that all three of these people have travelled with you through time and have reoccurred as important landmarks in your life over and over in the past and future.

Perhaps that will help you to understand that you have not lost them. They are still with you in those lifetimes in the past *and* in the future that are occurring simultaneously with this current one. If you had the ability to move through the ribbons of time, you would realise that they are never, ever lost to you. They are simply in another form or lifetime, and you will meet them again.

This is an important point though. The soul essence of each human is never fully invested in the three-dimensional form you call a body. The soul essence is simply 'lending' a piece of itself to the human form for the duration of earthly life, but it is always in residence in that vast cosmic expanse called the Oneness. It is as if a holographic projection of soul is allowed to come into the human body, but it is up to the individual human, during the path of spiritual growth in their own lifetime, to realise that they are simply a reflection, an image, of the real totality that is the soul and that until they are reunited with the family of all souls and with the Oneness, they are never truly complete.

Your loved ones have simply gone home for a while—to their true selves in their highest state. However, they have not abandoned you to this Earth. They are with you in moments of prayer and meditation and sleep when you can slip out of the shackles of human consciousness that is so limiting. Relax into those moments and do not feel frantic if it does not come easily at first. But trust in what we say, you will be able to hear them and feel them holding you and counselling you when you release your third-dimensional barriers as much as possible.

It is likely that they have a great purpose that they, in their life on Earth, could not have fulfilled for this planet in transition. You must try to cheer them on as they move forward into their greater role.

We know that these words will not ease the ache in your body and heart when you think of them and miss them. But we promise you, it will get easier with each passing day.

If you are able to access them and get reassurance while you are in your unconscious state, it will greatly aid in your own healing process. We hope that these words have helped you.

J.P., United Arab Emirates: Do you know of any white man's soul mate who was found in a black person, or vice versa? Do souls have colour discrimination?

Dreamkeeper: What an interestingly human question! In the realm of the Oneness, and in your more natural state of soul life, all souls are sparks of the Oneness, bright and twinkling sparks. Your soul *has no colour*, and therefore has no concept of attraction or non-attraction due to such reasons.

Yes, if two human beings were in a state of true soul recognition and had no concern about the artificial human concept of colour barriers, two beings from different races could most certainly find one another again after being separated by time and space.

The memory of past lives and shared events is a strong pull when you meet someone that you recognise in this way. It is up to you, as a mature human, to realise that all souls are beautiful and shining pieces of light and that it is a human concept to judge people by the colour of the skin-clothing that they are *temporarily* wearing. We hope this helps you.

Theresa, Cairns, Australia: Do you know the aboriginal people and would they recognise you?

Dreamkeeper: We are well known and remembered in the legends of many native people around your planet. When your tribal populations had settled, we would make random visits with the spiritual elders of these races and interact regarding their role on the planet as keepers of wisdom and guardians of the welfare of the Earth herself.

Deborah was unaware that we were part of the legends of these people throughout the world since this is part of the native sacred wisdom tradition and she had no access to this. When we were living in the country called Australia, she began to receive letters from native people in different tribal units around the world that told her of the legend of the being with the starry face and hands whose return would mark the beginnings of the cleansing of the planet.

To answer your original question, yes, the aboriginal elders would know who the Dreamkeeper was and would not be afraid if we reappeared in their presence.

Shari J., Dallas, Texas: How can I be sure that you are what you claim to be and aren't some evil creature who means us all harm? My preacher told me I wasn't supposed to read your web site anymore after I told him about it because you were not a human or an angel and that's all that God allowed to be on the Earth, so he says you must be some creature out of hell.

Dreamkeeper: Does that feel true to you? Do we seem to be telling you anything dangerous or dark? Do you feel any sense of fear when you read our words?

We would ask you to do this. Go within and ask. In a time of peaceful meditation, ask *your* inner self if this feels right for you to read our words. If the words of the man that you call preacher are that important to you, then perhaps you are not ready to make independent decisions as a free-thinking human. We pass no judgement on this. It simply may be where you are in your developmental stage and you may only feel safe if *someone else tells you* what is real and what is not real.

Our words are of love for one another and love of the great Oneness that is God—so why does this man called preacher find that to be incorrect in his eyes? We will say nothing to criticise this person except to state with firmness that he is not correct in his belief that God only allowed certain beings known as angels or humans to reside on this planet. There are many that have come and gone from here with the blessings of the Oneness as you matured and developed and it is a particularly human characteristic to think that you are the only ones who are 'allowed' here.

If you feel that you are doing something bad by reading our words, then it would be better not to place that burden on your heart and simply do not read them after this.

Loru, Paris, France: I have been reading your work for several years and notice that you do not mention the problems in Africa very often. Why is that? I am studying at the university here in Paris, but my home is in Rwanda. My brother was killed in what was called a 'civil action' and my father left home long ago. Only my mother is left there and she will not leave my grandparents alone in that place. She tells me to study hard and try not think of what I read in the news. She also tells me to never think of coming back there since I would have no future. What do you see for Africa?

Dreamkeeper: We sense that there are actually three questions that you are asking here, not just the two that we see on the page.

You ask why we do not mention Africa very often. If you have read the pages we write, as you have said, then you will notice that we rarely bring up issues in specific countries. We receive so many letters from people asking if their particular town or city or state or country or region will survive the Earth Changes.

But we do not think that is your only concern. We think you want to know why we do not name current places and problems in Africa.

Each month when we give Deborah new information for the internet location, we give, for the most part, items that will be of interest to all humans no matter where they are in the world. Our concerns are not site-specific.

NOTE from Deborah: Due to time constraints, I stopped updating the Dreamkeeper website with monthly updates several years ago.

We do not mean to sound disinterested—it is not that. But we would be writing for days if we mentioned every area of worry to humankind in our notes and all of these things would have to be updated almost daily. We are not trying to provide the services of a newspaper. We feel that it is better if we give encouragement and meditations and news about upcoming changes in your world to you *all* and not just to specific segments.

It also seems that in your question about what do we see for Africa, you are asking what do we see for your future there in that place. You may be wanting to know whether you should go back there or listen to your mother and stay away from an area of chaos.

The second part of the question is something that only you can answer. If you think that you can help to heal your country by taking your educated perspective back there and trying to work for a positive future for your country, then that may be right for you. But if you are going back to a country that is not safe, and if you could do more good for the world at large by staying elsewhere, then that may be another idea for you to consider.

Before we finish this book, we will be taking a section-by-section look at the world and what we see for the future of various parts of the planet. It will not be an easy thing for you to read when we get to the vision of the future Africa. We see a great deal of death from sweeping illnesses and violent warfare in the next ten years. We hope that you are able to continue your education and make a decision for your life that will give you a peaceful heart. [39, 40]

Christian M., Little Rock, Arkansas: What does the Dreamkeeper have to say about the rapture? Is this how we will all leave the planet so we don't have to worry about our bodies during the Earth Changes?

That's what they keep telling us at church and although my wife believes that, I'm not so sure. She keeps yelling at me about losing my faith and saying I won't get 'saved' if I don't believe in the rapture and I won't end up in heaven with her and the children. I just found out that she has called the pastor and a group of people are coming over to our house tonight to try and talk sense into me. Can you help? Can you tell me something that I can read to her so I can convince her that I know what I'm talking about?

Dreamkeeper: We have picked your question because it is one of many that we have received on this subject, but you also mention that you are getting pressure to conform from the woman that you share your life with.

In other areas of this book, we have addressed the problems that arise when humans begin to awaken to the fact that sometimes when they are told that *they must* believe or are pressured into accepting a belief system so they fit in and do not 'rock the boat,' it suddenly no longer feels authentic to them and they are perplexed by that.

Yes, it is a difficult thing to be living in a house with two strongly different opinions on such subjects, but we hear about this kind of problem in almost daily mail from our readers.

How do *you* feel about this? It sounds as if you are wondering about the authenticity of what you have simply accepted all of your life and never questioned. Questioning is good and it shows an awakening consciousness!

We are going to cause anger in some readers with this statement, but we feel that truth is more important than happy little fairy tales to keep the humans calm. The concept of rapture that your religious leaders keep drumming into you is partially correct but has great flaws. There is a path away from pain and suffering at the moment of death, but it is not this rapture that you have referred to.

The being who was Jesus will not suddenly descend out of the skies and lead you all to heaven! Is he to descend simultaneously in billions of places at once? How do they explain *that* to you? Do you really believe that all of the dead for these many millennia will suddenly rise up from their slumber and waft upwards into heaven with the man Jesus? Have they really been forced to simply wait in the darkness for all of these years? Would a merciful God do that to its believers?

Do you truly think that great masses of angels will suddenly appear in only the Christian skies and lead you to safety so that no one who believes in the man Jesus will perish in the Earth Changes? Are those who have other belief systems not equally worthy of the love of God and equally worthy to be saved?

We find it both sadly human that you as a species have this childlike need to believe that you will be saved from any pain at the hour of your death, and also worrying that you have such faith in a fairy story that is being given to you for the purpose of keeping you calm in the face of impending change on a planet-wide scale.

No, the dead have not been lying in wait in their graves for all these centuries waiting for the Judgement Day. *This is a total fabrication from the minds of HUMANS!* The Oneness never made such claims and we ask that you be more discerning in your judgement in these issues.

There are many, many books written by scholars that will point out the flaws in the writing of the books of the Bible and will show why they were written that way as teaching tools. They are not meant to be taken as literal fact and are quite inaccurate if you are concerned with reality. But even the words of scholars are not enough. The authenticity that you seek lies within you and every human that is currently on this world. Whose truth are you to believe—your truth or that which you are *told* or convinced to believe is truth?

What your Bible does have that is accurate, and which we highly praise, is that sense of gratitude and love and wonder for the magnificence of all creation by the Oneness. We think that these writers did their best, at the time that they were living in, to convey their concept of the 'bigness' of God to an uneducated group of people through a series of 'magical stories.' Can you understand how marvellously exciting it would be to see angels swooping down on clouds and trumpets sounding to welcome you to a clean and glorious city filled with beautiful food, clothes, and houses if you were living in a dry and dusty desert and were scratching to make a living? These writings were meant to appeal to the simple minds of the times, but they were not meant to be carried forward for two thousand years as the literal word of God.

We find that the thing humans fear most about death is not the idea of leaving their human life behind, but it is the idea that death might be painful. *That is a normal concern for the current developmental state of your minds.*

Please understand this, the moment of death is not meant to be a long and protracted affair, and although the concept of 'rapture' as you call it is not quite correct, *there is a light that is there for you to walk into* and feel no further pain or fear. That does not, however, mean that armies of angels will be descending and taking you all away as soon as the wars, geological upheavals, or massive social changes begin.

If you and your wife have sharply different opinions about this issue, just reading this to her will not solve anything. It will most likely make her cling to her beliefs even more than before and if she has called in outside help to convince you that they are right and you are wrong, you will be unlikely to find them willing to listen with open minds to your point of view.

We have no solutions to offer to you regarding this situation in your household. However, we do encourage you to be true to what you believe is *your personal truth.* We wish you good luck and many blessings in your personal search.

Hanna J., Copenhagen, Denmark: When I was a little girl, my grandmother took me into the forest just before she died to introduce me to her friends, the fairies. I *do remember seeing them,* but I was only 5 years old and my mother told me that it was just my imagination. I inherited my grandmother's house when my own mother died and after extensive renovation, I use it now as a holiday home. It had been almost completely unused for most of my life since my mother never liked the atmosphere of the place and never took us there as a family after my grandmother died.

I have grandchildren of my own now that are almost 1 and 3 years old and I would like to have them meet the fairies and feel that magic that I felt. My daughter thinks I am eccentric, but she finds it harmless and doesn't object. But I can't seem to see them anymore. Did I only imagine them or are they real creatures?

Dreamkeeper: You have not imagined this and yes, there are creatures that are fairies. Does that make you feel better? There are many kinds of small creatures that are seen all over the world and are written about in stories for a reason. There is a resonant memory of them long after you are adults and have lost the ability to see them. How interesting that your grandmother could see them even into adulthood!

Some of these small beings are as tiny as insects and have wings. Frequently they glow when they move because they are moving in a different time and space ratio than that of humans and they give off a spark of light as they move from place to place.

Not all of these creatures are winged. Some of these non-winged ones are called Elves, or Leprechauns, or Trolls or simply Little People. They are part of the mythology of all cultures worldwide because they do exist!

Children in every country can tell you that they have seen or interacted with these special little beings and they are speaking truth. Deborah used to leave treats outside in a specific place in her special tree in the apple orchard because she interacted with these little creatures as a child.

The little beings called Morona in New Zealand are a race that was left over from an early colonising attempt on this planet. The Morona are genuinely human-like in appearance and are like miniature versions of you. Their home world was a planet of snow and ice and you will find writings about these lovely pale creatures with red or yellow hair in countries where there is a cold and mountainous climate such as the Southern Alps of New Zealand, the Alps of Europe, parts of Siberia, and the far northern countries such as Sweden and Norway or in the cool and green places like Ireland, Scotland, Tasmania, Canada, the states of Washington and Alaska in the USA, Tasmania in Australia, and the cool and high countries of lower South America. These little beings do not thrive in heat or bright weather.

The creatures that you call nature spirits or devas do not have the same almost human appearance of the others and are usually glimpsed as tiny beings that emit a softly coloured light. All plants and minerals have a life force of their own, but the devas and nature spirits coexist with the actual life energy of these species.

The human-like appearance of the fairies and fee and others is a bit deceiving though. They are actually more light-energy and, in some cases, more insect-like in appearance. Yet they have the ability to project their visual representation to you in a way that makes you feel at ease and safe. They know that this is especially important for children and they are both powerfully magical and quite considerate in that regard.

We have spoken before of the layers of societal conditioning that alter the 'filters' of your eyes as you grow older and change what you are able to see. This is the reason that Deborah can no longer see us in physical form and it is the reason why you are no longer able to see the fairies. That is why we remarked that it was unusual for your grandmother to have retained that ability as an adult.

Yes, it is sad if you are not able to regain that vision, and no, you did not imagine it. But we can suggest that when you think the grandchildren are old enough to be able to communicate to you what they see, take them to the forest and introduce them to the fairies as if you could still see them. Then listen to what the children tell you they see and hear and enjoy the interaction in that manner.

Kim Tanaka, Tokyo, Japan: Why are there so many different kinds of people appearance-wise in the world? You have mentioned creator races from other planets, but why did they make so many different looking versions?

Dreamkeeper: The different races of creator-beings arrived and departed from your planet over a long period of time. It was decided prior to their arrival that each of them would focus on a specific area of the planet.

Different races of beings arose because different races of creators each had their own vision of what the final product should look like. You must remember that you were also created for a variety of reasons ranging from the need to create a worker population to do heavy labour for more advanced societies, to medical and genetic testing, to those races that simply wished to see something beautiful grow and flourish through trial and error as they had done in their own remote past.

Your physical features are a mixture of what each particular creator race found pleasing to look at and your own bodies' adaptation to the locations and climates you were living in. There was never any one ideal human image or skin colour for all locations around the planet.

Linda B., Palo Alto, California, USA: I don't feel safe in California any more. Am I imagining this? My children (3rd and 5th grade) keep having nightmares of huge earthquakes then water washing over them and our house and dogs are swept out to sea. We do not live that close to the ocean, so I'm not sure where this is coming from. But I too find that I am constantly edgy as if I'm waiting for something terrible to happen.

I am a single mother and have a good career, safe neighbourhood, lots of friends and social activities, all of what we call the good things in life.

I started searching the internet for prophecy-related information and I found your website by accident and sat here nodding my head for two nights reading it saying yes, yes, yes, as I read.

I am a computer programmer and have had a job offered to me in Raleigh-Durham, North Carolina that I turned down. But now these people have called again and offered me the job with an even better salary. I feel like this is some kind of a sign that I'm meant to leave here. Am I just reading things into it that I want to see? My parents in Sacramento are furious that I would think of taking the children so far away from them. I'm in a dilemma and would appreciate any ideas you could offer.

I never even write letters to the editor, but I'm writing to some non-human and I don't know why!

Dreamkeeper: You are not alone in your visions of the fate of the state that you call California. It is for this reason that many of your citizens are streaming away into the nearby mountain states where they feel safer. [41]

We have said before in previous sessions that some people receive direct visions, some hear voices, some have prophetic dreams (such as the ones your children are having) and some people simply get an urge to do something *right now* and that is their means of receiving psychic warnings.

You must do what feels correct for you and your children in spite of the difficulties that you may face with your parents. You are responsible for the lives of the three of you and you *are allowed* to live in a manner that is authentic to you. Your parents made their choices as adults and now it is time for you to make your own choices. If you feel that this job in another place is 'singing' to you, then perhaps you should answer that call. Your parents will come to understand the rightness of your decision when they see that you are happy in your new location and that their grandchildren are no longer troubled by bad dreams.

Thank you for feeling that it was acceptable to write to a non-human and ask for advice.

Ron Mauer, Virginia, USA: Can you predict the most probable year when the 200mph to 400mph winds will sweep the Earth clean?

Dreamkeeper: We have explained before that precise dates are not available. However, we can look at the most likely time period based on what we are seeing of your future timeline from the present. The yearly build up of challenging weather conditions will escalate from this point on and there will actually be a series of 'mini shifts' over a period of several decades before the final shift that will realign the positions of your landmasses and your magnetic poles.

This is an event that has happened repeatedly throughout the history of your planet, yet you are feeling it in a collective and societally personal way because there are a much greater number of humans on this planet than in the past, and your means of communication, such as this computer contact, allow you to know what geological and weather trends, and the resulting emotional responses, are happening on a global scale.

At this time—and we must emphasise again that this can change according the actions of humankind and off planetary forces—we are seeing the greatest of the deadly winds arriving between 2010 and 2013 of your Earth years. The winds will originate from a point in space and descend onto your world. There will be a great loss of life as a result of this 'broom' that sweeps the surface of your planet and lasts for many days.

Keiran, Brisbane, Australia: Are we going to keep on finding out new stuff about ancient ancestors on Earth?

Dreamkeeper: This is a subject that the woman who is Deborah loves to learn new information about. We have heard many people say over the last few years that most of the important archaeology must have been done in the past and there probably isn't much left to find since your cities are so all-encompassing in places where previous civilisations were known to dwell.

But does that mean that all the mysteries have been solved? Do you not think that these places that you already know from your studies of history might not reveal new secrets? And what of places and objects that have been hiding in plain sight?

In spite of the chaos and wars and disease on your planet in the coming decades, you will continue to make discoveries and be fascinated once again by your ancestors and their link to your own way of life. [42, 43, 44, 45, 46]

Harriet, London, England: I have recently attended several lectures about the changes on this planet that are coming up after the year 2000. And one of the speakers kept saying we are all going to be tagged like they tag wild animals that are caught for study and then released into the wild. It sounds too unlikely to contemplate. Do you think it will ever come to that?

Dreamkeeper: Unfortunately, we do see this coming quite soon. We have been telling people in our group lectures for several years that the world governments will begin to implement this as soon as they can find some way of convincing you that it is for the public good. Right now your animals can be tracked with tiny computer chips that are embedded under their skin. We think that the public will soon be told that they need to implant their children, even infants, with these devices to keep them safe from predators who would kidnap or harm them. On the surface that might sound logical. But once the implant is in place, the person will be able to be tracked for the rest of their lives through technology that knows where they are at every moment of the day. [47]

We have explained that there are many laboratory created diseases that will enter your world in the next few years. The miniaturisation of this technology will continue to the point that it is so small that it can be injected through a needle into your skin while you are supposedly getting a vaccine for one of these man-made diseases. [48, 49]

Jason Anderson, Ohio: Why am I seeing more and more of what the newspapers and online chat groups call contrails every month? There are days when the skies are filled with this criss-crossing pattern. It doesn't feel right. And my girlfriend always get wheezy within a day after seeing those things in the skies.

Dreamkeeper: This again is another method of both damaging the human immune system and spreading the laboratory created illnesses that we have told you about in earlier parts of this book. We know that there are government officials trying to convince you that there is nothing to worry about, but any activity that increases the amount of illness in a community immediately following the fly-over should be considered suspicious.

We say this to you with firmness. This has nothing to do with eradicating insects and it is all aimed at reducing the quality and quantity of your life. It is another control mechanism to keep you ill and unable to think or act clearly in a time of crisis such as the one which will soon be arriving in your world. [50, 51]

Marcia B., Ontario, Canada: What are your thoughts about the genetic testing that is being done on everything from food to humans? Are we going to see artificially created babies or half robot people in a few years?

Dreamkeeper: The technology is already in place for these events and the first laboratory created infants are already a reality. It is merely a matter of time before the research with robotics leads to the fusion of human and machine. These are dangerous paths to tread because these very acts have been the undoing of many civilisations on other worlds.

You would be well advised to not numb yourselves to this news and speak out to your lawmakers if they begin, and they will, campaigning to shift your thinking about these subjects so that you will eventually accept them as normal and necessary.

You are living in a critical time period and the future appearance of Earth in many areas, including the occupants of this planet, is being decided now, not then.[52, 53]

Veronica A.S.: Are there any such things as Indigo Children or Crystal Children, or is that all made up nonsense?

Dreamkeeper: These are terms that have been created by human writers to try and explain why so many gifted and psychic children are being born at this point in your history. Many of them arrive with full knowledge of the events that are ahead and it is not your imagination when you notice how alert, aware, and communicative these children are at a very early age. Most of them will possess strong psychic ability in a variety of forms and if you as a parent are unprepared for this fact, it can prove to be a bit unnerving.

These children will often return with past life memories quite intact and you will find that they will be able to tell you quite easily about other places, other countries, and other time periods. This is especially disconcerting to a parent who knows that the child is too young to have ever read books or seen movies about these places. These children will also have strong future-vision skills as well as the past-life memory.

Our main concern is that not all of these children are entering into families that are aware of these things and who will nurture these abilities rather than attempt to suppress them. There are simply not enough open-minded and prepared parents worldwide to be receiving the huge influx of these very special children. So many of them are being born into 'unawakened' families.

We would ask that if you have one of these children in your own home, please know that they are quite advanced souls who have come back to be islands of calm and reason in the turbulent decades ahead. But they will not achieve this potential without the appropriate nurturing and intellectual stimulation. If you are tempted to simply look upon them as hyperactive and leave it at that, please take the time to re-examine this position in case you are squelching the vivacious and intelligent gift that has been presented to you in the form of this child.

We ask also that you be alert to those children around you, perhaps those of other members of your family or the children of friends, who exhibit these same psychic abilities and high levels of reasoning and intelligence. If the parents are unable or unwilling to go out of their way to encourage the child, perhaps you could do a service to the planet by being a loving mentor to this child.

Giselle, South Africa: Is there any point in continuing to plan for the future if there may not BE any future for many of us? There are many of us here who teach at the university and we have noticed that there is not a great sense of hope for the future amongst ourselves and our students.

Dreamkeeper: There is *always* a future! It just may not be what you feel is safe and familiar to you at the present time. Unless one specific timeline unfolds that involves a massive and global catastrophe, it is likely that there will continue to be humans on this planet for many more centuries until you have all worked through this stage of development and are ready to move on to something even more wonderful. We can assure you that whether you go or stay during the upcoming years, it is an exciting adventure that lies ahead. Be not afraid of this upcoming time. You are safe at all times in the love of the Oneness.

CHAPTER FOURTEEN

Going Home

September 26, 2001

Posted online after the World Trade Center bombing in New York City

When last we spoke to you at length, we told you to expect a great change in planetary energy, an infusion of feminine energy onto the planet that would activate the insecurities and anger of those whose energy was out of balance. We also warned you to expect acts of aggression against groups of people in events such as small-scale wars (and acts of terrorism qualify as this) and in increased aggression and anger that is aimed at women. We are not pleased to see that these events have unfolded.

At all times, when we come to you and speak of events that might soon come to pass, it is given with the hope that those events or patterns that you consider to be negative may be lessened or softened. We are feeling the distress and rising anger on your planet—all of us who observe your world are feeling this like a series of waves that are vibrating from your Earth.

You may remember that we have spoken of the waves of people who will be leaving the planet in the chapter called The Clearing. These are not unexpected events, but the violent nature of the soul migration is what seems to be the most shocking to you as humans. Let us give you some clarification regarding that.

When the human physical body is separated from the soul, no matter how violent the event is that takes the physical life of the human in question, there is NO pain or suffering. At the very moment of separation, all sensations are removed and we can assure you that the departing soul does not feel the event in any physical manner. This applies equally to the types of incidents you saw in the recent terrorist attacks and to what you term 'everyday crimes' or even car accidents.

Now we will clarify further. *There is soul distress in some cases.* When a soul is snatched out of the body with such suddenness, many times the soul in question is left confused as to where they are and how they got there. Many of you who are reading this will note that you have felt a disturbance in the atmosphere in the last two weeks that was unlike anything you had experienced prior to this. What you were feeling was the sheer number of confused souls that had perished in one period and who were wandering for a time through the veils of your atmosphere. You will note that this response was felt most strongly during the first few days after the event.

For many of you who are highly psychic, you could literally feel the stream of souls moving, moving, moving, and some of you may have had sightings of some of these departed ones.

In the case of large numbers of humans who perish in events such as cyclones and floods or earthquakes and volcanic eruptions, there is not as much disturbance to the soul energy of those who are departing. What disturbance you who are left behind feel is positively muted compared to that which was felt worldwide two weeks ago.

Before we explain further, it may be helpful to understand that prior to your arrival on this planet, your soul makes certain choices regarding future events in your life. That is why many of you know when you are going to die and are not surprised when those events unfold in just the manner that you have foreseen. That tickling at the back of your memory is just that—a recollection of what you agreed to prior to the incarnation on the planet.

But we will also tell you that the Universe does NOT plan every single action of time down to the finest detail. That would negate the concept of free will that we embedded in you as a species. It is one of the least understood and most talked about concepts of humankind—that you DO have free will regarding your life and outcome and that *timelines can be changed!* We have restated this fact many times.

Yet, for all the advance preparation that a soul receives prior to incarnation, that same soul cannot always assimilate the event when it goes counter to the departure method that the soul had previously agreed to. That is why the soul is in such distress. Someone else, another human or humans, made the decision about how these souls in New York and Washington were to die. And that decision was counter to the planning that those souls had done prior to incarnation. Can you now understand their confusion? Their unconscious state had always known how they would leave, yet this was not what eventuated. For this reason, many of these souls were wandering in a dazed and confused state for several days and *this confused soul energy was what you were feeling.* Add to that the sheer pain and anguish that was being felt by the families, friends, and unbelieving witnesses to these events and you have created a potent cocktail of psychic vibration that carried not only around your world but out into the Universe itself to be felt by us and others.

Know now that these souls have been gently led away into the waiting presence of loved ones 'on the other side.' There they will rest for longer than the usual period to absorb and then clear themselves of what they have encountered in this particular incarnation.

Trust that they are well watched over as they accomplish this step. Just as many of you have felt the overwhelming need to sleep for the last few weeks, they too will sleep for a long time to allow their souls to heal. You have heard the phrase, "As above, so below" used many times and for many reasons, have you not? This applies to the restorative power of sleep as well. It is literally universal in its effectiveness in the healing process for both humans and non-incarnational souls.

We wish you love and hope that the healing process on the planet proceeds without further violence and hatred intruding into your lives.

Endnotes and Articles

[1] SOLAR MAGNETIC STORMS:
http://www.sec.noaa.gov/index.html
Very comprehensive information.

[2] SOLAR SUPERSTORM
http://science.nasa.gov/headlines/y2003/23oct_superstorm.htm

[3] SOLAR MAGNETIC STORMS
http://edition.cnn.com/2003/TECH/space/10/28/solar.flare/
Sun Erupts in Biggest Storm in Years. Earth in path of solar-ejected cloud.
By Kate Tobin, CNN, October 29, 2003

[4] THE EFFECTS OF SOUND ON THE HUMAN BODY
http://www.quiet.org/quiet-list/msg00156.html

Extract from an article entitled: 'Healing Sound', by Michael Rault, in the Oct/Nov 1989 issue of Odyssey. Address: The Wellstead, 1 Wellington Avenue, Wynberg. 7800. Republic of South Africa. Tel: 27 21 797-8982

Music can intensify feelings, summon images and memories, fill you with awe, or simply charm you. Sound vibrations can both heal and destroy, and can have far reaching effects even on our cellular structure.

We are subject to a continual barrage of noise from traffic, aircraft, vacuum cleaners, televisions, fridges, typewriters, lawnmowers, air-conditioners, barking dogs, power tools.... Even should you wear earplugs when you sleep, noise will still get through to you as sound vibrations are received by your whole body, not just your ears. The human body absorbs the impact of sound waves as they pass through the skin through to the deeper tissues. The individual molecules comprising the many millions of molecules in human tissue are excited by different frequencies.

When struck by the sound wave nearest to their own inherent frequency they will oscillate more strongly and will resonate to it. The direct consequence of molecular impact is the creating of alternating compression and dilation zones - in effect an intensive form of massage at cellular level. However, we can get 'massaged' by very undesirable sounds as well as those that are therapeutic.

[5] THE EFFECTS OF FLOURESCENT LIGHTING ON THE HUMAN BODY

http://society.guardian.co.uk/publicvoices/prisons/story/0,12261,799260,00.html

Fluorescent lighting was not meant to come into such general use: it was a temporary, emergency feature that was only ever intended to keep factories working 24 hours a day during the second world war.

In 1999 at the International Light Conference at Reading university I heard a speaker called Anne Silk talking about the lack of darkness causing serious medical and emotional problems since it interfered with the body's ability to manufacture vital brain chemicals. To illustrate her talk she showed a picture of a prison cell at night, lit up by the perimeter security lighting. I listened to world scientists confirming my beliefs about mal-illumination being linked to depression, impotence, sleeping disorders and skin cancers. At the very least, according to some of them, certain types of fluorescent tubes leak radiation and some may lead to a depletion of brain chemicals such as serotonin and melatonin. This can lead to the kind of depression that in extreme situations precipitates suicide.

The partial answer seemed to be in a new breed of lighting tubes that were more like daylight in that they covered the whole colour spectrum rather than just a section. Doctors with whom I am studying have also told me that the letters SAD (seasonal affective disorder) may be substituted for the letters PMS (premenstrual syndrome) - that in effect they share similar symptoms and a similar cause.

This is not a new idea to the Germans, the Russians or the Americans. Based on the research of Dr Fritz Hollwich and others, cool white fluorescents are legally banned in German hospitals. Americans developed a type of full spectrum lighting to facilitate human survival underground in the event of a nuclear holocaust. They grew roses and lettuces underground. The average English office or hospital cannot even nurture a houseplant under their lighting, that's why they are all silk or plastic! And if a live plant can't thrive what price a human?

Russians have been using full spectrum lighting with excellent results in factories where colds and viral infections had resulted in unacceptable levels of absenteeism. But research is available in Britain too. As far back as in 1982, the Lancet published an article about research being undertaken at the London School of Hygiene and Tropical Medicine and the University of Sydney's melanoma clinic. Dr Helen Shaw found that the people who had the lowest risk of developing skin cancer were those whose main outdoor activity was sunbathing. Twice the risk of developing melanomas was found in office workers who had to work indoors all day under fluorescent lights. She also demonstrated that office lighting caused mutations in cultures of animal cells.

[6] EFFECTS OF COMPUTER AND MOBILE PHONE USE
http://bit.ly/Ghoqa

[7] SOLAR RADIATION AND HUMAN HEALTH
http://www.who.int/inf-fs/en/fact227.html
EXTRACT from: A report by the World Health Organization
SOLAR RADIATION AND HUMAN HEALTH

Too Much Sun is Dangerous

Sunlight, an essential prerequisite for life, may be extremely dangerous to human health. Excessive exposure to the sun is known to be associated with increased risks of various skin cancers, cataracts and other eye diseases, as well as accelerated skin ageing. It may also adversely affect people's ability to resist infectious diseases, and compromise the effectiveness of vaccination programmes.

Sunlight is electromagnetic energy, which is propagated by electromagnetic waves. Healthwise, the most important parts of the sunlight electromagnetic spectrum are: ultraviolet radiation (UV), invisible to the eye; visible light that allows us to see; and infrared radiation, which is our main source of heat but is also invisible. Excessive exposures to them poses particular risks to health.

Skin*:* Excessive UV exposure results in a number of chronic skin changes. These include various *skin cancers* of which *melanoma* is the most life-threatening; an increased number of moles (*benign abnormalities of melanocytes)* and a range of other alterations arising from UV damage to keratinocytes and blood vessels. UV damage to fibrous tissue is often described as "photoageing". Photoageing makes people look older because their skin loses its tightness and so sags or wrinkles.

- United Nations Environment Programme (UNEP) has estimated that more than 2 million nonmelanoma skin cancers and 200,000 malignant melanomas occur globally each year.
- In the event of a 10% decrease in stratospheric ozone, an additional 300,000 nonmelanoma and 4,500 melanoma skin cancers could be expected worldwide.
- Caucasians have a higher risk of skin cancer because of the relative lack of skin pigmentation.
- The worldwide incidence of malignant melanoma continues to increase, and is strongly related to frequency of recreational exposure to the sun and to history of sunburn.
- There is evidence that risk of melanoma is also related to intermittent exposure to UV, especially in childhood, and

to exposure to sunlamps. However, the latter results are still preliminary.

Eye: UV exposure of the eye depends on many factors: ground reflection, the degree of brightness in the sky leading to activation of the squint reflex, the amount of atmospheric refection, and the use of eyewear.

- The acute effects of UV on the eye include the development of photokeratitis and photoconjunctivitis, which are like sunburn of the delicate skin-like tissue on the surface of the eyeball (cornea) and eyelids. While painful, they are reversible, easily prevented by protective eyewear and have not been associated with any long-term damage.
- Chronic effects include the possible development of pterygium (a white or cream coloured opaque growth attached to the cornea), squamous cell cancer of the conjunctiva (scaly or plate-like malignancy) and cataracts.
- Some 20 million people worldwide are currently blind as a result of cataracts. Of these, WHO estimates that as many as 20% may be due to UV exposure. Experts believe that each 1% sustained decrease in stratospheric ozone would result in an increase of 0.5% in the number of cataracts caused by solar UV.
- Direct viewing of the sun and other extremely bright objects can also seriously damage the very sensitive part of the retina called the *yellow spot*, *fovea* or *macula leutea*. When cells of the fovea are destroyed, people can no longer view fine detail. This is a serious visual impairment making it impossible to read, sew, watch TV, recognise faces, drive a vehicle or do any task which requires recognition of fine details.

Immune system: UV also appears to alter immune response by changing the activity and distribution of the cells responsible for triggering these responses. A number of studies indicate that UV exposures at environmental levels suppress immune responses in both rodents and humans. In rodents, this immune suppression results in enhanced susceptibility to certain infectious diseases with skin involvement, and some systemic infections. Mechanisms associated with UV-induced *immunosuppression and host defence* that protect against infectious agents are similar in rodents and humans. It is therefore reasonable to assume that UV exposure may enhance the risk of infection and decrease the effectiveness of vaccines in humans. Additional research is necessary to substantiate this.

Thermal Effects: Heating of tissues in the human body is the principal effect of infrared radiation. Excessive infrared radiation can result in heat strokes and other similar reactions particularly in elderly, infirm or very young individuals. At moderate levels of exposure, the warmth experienced from being in the sun is relaxing and restorative.

Protective Measures: Methods for personal protection from solar UV exposure include adequate clothing, hats and the proper use of sunscreens to protect UV-exposed skin. For eye protection, UV absorbing sunglasses are needed.

Changes in behavior could minimize solar UV exposure. These include staying out of the sun, either indoors or in shaded areas, during the four-hour period around solar noon when UV levels are at their highest. During summer, when daylight saving time is in effect, solar noon in most of Europe is at 14.00 hours (2 p.m.); in the UK and countries with a similar longitude, it is at 13.00 hours (1 p.m.).

Broad-spectrum sunscreens should be used when other means of protection are not feasible, and then to reduce exposure rather than lengthen the period of exposure. While topical applications of sunscreen are preferred for absorbing UVB, some preparations do not absorb the longer wavelength UVA effectively. Moreover, some preparations have been found to contain ingredients that are mutagenic in sunlight. People using sunscreens should use those with a high sun protection factor (SPF) and be aware that they are to protect from the sun and not for tanning purposes.

The reflective properties of the ground have an influence on UV exposure. Most natural surfaces such as grass, soil and water reflect less than 10% of incident UV. However, fresh snow reflects nearly 80% while sand reflects 10-25%, significantly increasing UV exposure for skiers and bathers.

For further information, journalists can contact: WHO Press Spokesperson and Coordinator, Spokesperson's Office, WHO HQ, Geneva, Switzerland / Tel +41 22 791 4458/2599 / Fax +41 22 791 4858 / e-Mail: inf@who.int

[8] THE NUTRITIONAL BENEFITS OF ORGANIC FOOD
Nutritional Benefits of Organic Foods

Growing crops in healthy soils results in food products that offer healthy nutrients. There is mounting evidence that organically grown fruits, vegetables and grains may offer more of some nutrients, including vitamin C, iron, magnesium and phosphorus, and less exposure to nitrates and pesticide residues than their counterparts grown using synthetic pesticides and fertilizers.

- Reviewing 41 published studies comparing the nutritional value of organically grown and conventionally grown fruits, vegetables, and grains, certified nutrition specialist Virginia Worthington has concluded there are significantly more of several nutrients in organic crops. These include: 27% more vitamin C, 21.1% more iron, 29.3% more magnesium, and 13.6% more phosphorus. In addition, organic products had 15.1% less nitrates than their conventional counterparts. She also noted that five servings of organic vegetables (lettuce, spinach, carrots, potatoes and cabbage) provided the recommended daily intake of vitamin C for men and women, while their conventional counterparts did not.

  Source: "Nutritional Quality of Organic Versus Conventional Fruits, Vegetables, and Grains," by Virginia Worthington, published in *The Journal of Alternative and Complementary Medicine*, Vol. 7, No. 2, 2001 www.foodisyourbestmedicine.com/organic.pdf.
- Organic crops appear to be higher in vitamin C, essential minerals and phytonutrients, according to the 87-page report

prepared for The Soil Association of the United Kingdom and released during 2001.

Source: "Organic Farming, Food Quality and Human Health: A review of the evidence," written and researched by Shane Heaton, The Soil Association, United Kingdom, 2001.

- A study commissioned by the Organic Retailers and Growers Association of Australia (ORGAA) found that conventionally grown fruit and vegetables purchased in supermarkets and other commercial retail outlets had ten times less mineral content than fruit and vegetables grown organically.

  Source: Organic Retailers and Growers Association of Australia, 2000, as cited in *Pesticides and You*, Vol. 20, No. 1, Spring 2000, News from Beyond Pesticides/National Coalition Against the Misuse of Pesticides.

- A comparative study conducted by researchers at the Research Institute of Organic Agriculture (FiBL) in Switzerland found that organically grown apples were of higher quality than conventionally grown apples with respect to parameters that relate to health and taste (taste score, sugar-acidity-firmness index, nutritional fiber content and other factors used for quality assessment).

  Source: "Are organically grown apples tastier and healthier? A comparative field study using conventional and alternative methods to measure fruit quality," F.P. Weibel, R. Bickel, S. Leuthold, and T. Alföldi), Acta Hort. 517: 417-427 (2000).

- A study has shown that organic soups sold commercially in the United Kingdom contain almost six times as much salicylic acid as non-organic soups. Salicylic acid, which is responsible for the anti-inflammatory action of aspirin, has been shown to help prevent hardening of the arteries and bowel cancer. The average level of salicylic acid in 11 brands of organic vegetable soup was 117 nanograms per gram, compared with 20 nanograms per gram in 24 types of non-organic soup.

  Source: *New Scientist* magazine, March 16, 2002, page 10; *European Journal of Nutrition*, Vol, 40, page 289.

- Research by visiting chemistry professor Theo Clark and undergraduate students at Truman State University in Missouri found organically grown oranges contained up to 30 percent more vitamin C than those grown conventionally. Reporting the findings, Clark said he had expected the conventional oranges, which were much larger than the organic oranges, to have twice as much vitamin C as the organic versions. Instead, their scientific testing revealed the higher level in the organic oranges.

  Source: *Science Daily Magazine*, June 2, 2002
- Reporting on its study examining pesticide residues in foods bought around the country, *Consumer Reports*, January 1998, noted: "Our side-by-side tests of organic, green-labeled, and conventional unlabeled produce found that organic foods had consistently minimal or nonexistent pesticide residue."

  Source: "Greener Greens? The Truth about Organic Foods," *Consumer Reports*, January 1998, page 13.
- Analyzing U.S. Department of Agriculture's Pesticide Data Program data comparing the relative amounts and toxicity of pesticide residues in different foods, a Consumer Union report found that fresh peaches, frozen and fresh winter squash, apples, grapes, spinach, pears, and green beans had some of the highest Toxicity Index ratings. As a result, the Consumers Union recommended purchasing organically grown apples, peaches, pears, grapes, winter squash, spinach and green beans.

  Source: "Do you know what you're eating? An analysis of U.S. Government Data on Pesticide Residues in Foods," February 1999, Consumers Union of United States Inc., Edward Groth III, project director.
- Organic fruits and vegetables have only a third as many pesticide residues as their conventionally grown counterparts, according to a study by Consumers Union (CU) and the Organic Materials Review Institute. Study findings are based on pesticide residue data collected by the U.S. Department of Agriculture, from tests conducted on foods

> sold in California by the California Department of Pesticide Regulation, and from tests by Consumers Union. Data covered more than 94,000 food samples from more than 20 crops, with 1,291 of the samples organically grown. USDA data showed 73 percent of conventionally grown foods sampled had residue from at least one pesticide, while only 23 percent of organically grown samples of the same crops had any residues. When residues of persistent, long-banned organochlorine insecticides such as DDT were excluded from the analysis, organic samples with residues dropped from 23 to 13 percent. More than 90 percent of USDA's samples of conventionally grown apples, peaches, pears, strawberries and celery had residues. The California data found residues in 31 percent of the conventional food, and 6.5 percent of the organic products. Tests by the Consumers Union, meanwhile, found residues on 79 percent of conventionally grown samples and 27 percent on the organic products.
>
> Source: *Food Additives and Contaminants*, May 8, 2002. Also, see www.omri.org.

Reprinted with permission from the Organic Trade Association. The Organic Trade Association is the leading business association representing the organic industry in the United States, Canada, and Mexico. Its more than 1200 members include growers, processors, shippers, retailers, certification organizations and others involved in the business of producing and selling certified organic products. www.ota.com

[9] ANTIBIOTICS ON THE FARM: September 2000
http://news.mpr.org/features/200009/25_newsroom_antibiotics-m/steil.shtml

Antibiotics on the Farm By Mark Steil, reporting for Minnesota Public Radio, September, 2000 Extract from MPR's Fighting the Superbug series (permission applied to reproduce)

The use of antibiotics in farm animals is coming under increasing criticism by those who believe the patients who farmers are really treating are themselves and their fellow humans.

Research has found that using the drugs causes some dangerous animal-borne bacteria to become resistant to even the most powerful antibiotics, creating untreatable "super bugs" which can infect humans. Farmers say antibiotics are a long-standing tool they need to raise livestock and poultry efficiently.

Hundreds of animals hip-and-shoulder their way to steel food troughs. The trough holds an oatmeal-like slurry containing typical farm-grown staples like soybean meal and corn. But most people might be surprised to learn the daily feed ration also contains low levels of antibiotics. The regular dose helps hogs grow faster, in fact that's what the pork industry calls the feed-based use of antibiotics: Growth promoters.

[10] WHO URGES END TO USE OF ANTIBIOTICS FOR ANIMAL GROWTH: Washington Post, August 13, 2003, MARC KAUFMAN
http://www.mindfully.org/Farm/2003/WHO-Animal-Antibiotic13aug03.htm

The World Health Organization will recommend today that nations phase out the widespread and controversial use of antibiotic growth promoters in animal feed, saying the move will help preserve the effectiveness of antibiotics for medicine and can be done without significant expense or health consequences to farm animals.

Based on a study of Denmark's experience following a 1998 voluntary ban on antibiotic growth promoters, WHO concluded that under similar conditions the use of low-dosage antibiotics "for the sole purpose of growth promotion can be discontinued." WHO's findings and recommendation do not require nations to act. But they will add to the growing movement to stop routine use of antibiotics on farms, and to the kind of public pressure that led the McDonald's fast-food chain to recently tell suppliers to cut back on antibiotic growth promoters. WHO officials say that about half of the antibiotics used by livestock growers worldwide are low-dose growth promoters, the type that public health experts say are most likely to promote the growth of bacteria that are resistant to antibiotics.

"We have believed for some time that giving animals low dosages of antibiotics throughout their lives to make them grow faster is a bad idea," said Peter Braam, project leader for the WHO report. "Now we have solid scientific information from Denmark that producers can terminate this practice without negative effects for the animals and growers, and with good effects for the human population."

According to the Animal Health Institute, 13 percent to 17 percent of antibiotics used on U.S. farms was for growth promotion. But the Union of Concerned Scientists, an advocacy group, said it had found that about 50 percent of the antibiotic use was in the form of low-dosage growth promoters.

[11] MELTING ICE WILL SWAMP CAPITALS
http://www.commondreams.org/headlines03/1207-04.htm
Melting ice 'will swamp capitals'
By Geoffrey Lean Environment Editor, The Independent,
07 December 2003

Measures to fight global warming will have to be at least four times stronger than the Kyoto Protocol if they are to avoid the melting of the polar ice caps, inundating central London and many of the world's biggest cities, concludes a new official report. The report, by a German government body, says that even if it is fully implemented, the protocol will only have a "marginal attenuating effect" on the climate change. But last week even this was thrown into doubt amid contradictory signals from the Russian government as to whether it will allow the treaty to come into effect.

Global warming already kills 150,000 people a year worldwide and the rate of climate change is soon likely to exceed anything the planet has seen "in the last million years" says the report, produced by the German Advisory Council on Global Change for a meeting of the world's environment ministers to consider the future of the treaty in Milan this week. It concludes that the protocol must urgently be brought into force, but only as a first step, insisting that "catastrophic" climate change "can now only be prevented if climate protection targets are set at substantially higher levels than those agreed internationally until now".

The report, written by eight leading German professors, says that "dangerous climatic changes" will become "highly probable" if the world's average temperature is allowed to increase to more than 2 degrees centigrade above what it was before the start of the Industrial Revolution.

Beyond that level the West Antarctic ice sheet and the Greenland ice cap would begin gradually to melt away, eventually raising sea levels world wide by up to 30 feet, submerging vast areas of land and key cities worldwide. London, New York, Miami, Bombay, Calcutta, Sydney, Shanghai, Lagos and Tokyo would be among those largely submerged by such a rise.

Above this mark too, other "devastating" and "irreversible" changes would be likely to take place. These include a cessation of the Indian monsoon and the ending of the Gulf Stream, which would dramatically worsen the climate in Britain and western Europe, even as the world warms. Another risk is the so-called "runaway greenhouse" where rising temperatures lead to the release of huge reservoirs methane stored in permafrost and the oceans, adding to global warming and starting a self-reinforcing cycle that would eventually make the earth uninhabitable.

To avoid such catastrophe, the report says that industrialised countries will have to cut emissions of greenhouse gases like carbon dioxide by at least 20 per cent by 2020, and by up to 60 per cent by 2050. The Kyoto Protocol would at best cut them by 5 per cent by 2012, and probably less, even if it were brought into force and fully implemented.

In the meantime the world looks as if it will greatly exceed the targets. Writing in The Independent on Sunday today, Michael Meacher, the former environment minister, calculates that global emissions of greenhouse gases could increase by 75 per cent by 2020, "putting the world well on the way to doomsday".

[12] THE EFFECTS OF SHIFTING MAGNETICS ON ANIMALS

http://www.pbs.org/wgbh/nova/magnetic/animals.html
Impact On Animals by Peter Tyson

Would a dramatic change in the earth's magnetic field affect the animals that rely on it for migration?

Late on a January night in 1993 I found myself on a beach on the Pacific coast of Costa Rica, kneeling in the sand beside a leatherback sea turtle. Like a giant mango with wings, the huge black turtle had hauled herself up the beach in great stentorian gasps of air and was laying her eggs in a pit she had laboriously scooped out with her hind flippers.

Knowing basic facts about her ecology and physiology, I was in awe. How her kind, the largest living reptiles, had been around for 120 million years. How she lived solely on jellyfish, a thing more water balloon than animal. How she could collapse her lungs and dive to depths that would cause you or me to implode. How she had traveled thousands of miles around the Pacific Ocean, only to return there to the very beach she was born on years before.

That navigational and homing ability astonished me more than any other. How did she navigate around a trackless wilderness larger than the world's total land area and find her way back to that same short ribbon of sand? One hypothesis was just starting to be floated in those days: that to aid their long-distance migrations leatherbacks and other sea turtles appear to use the Earth's magnetic field (see Figure 1).

When I learned recently that our planet's magnetic shield is rapidly weakening and may be ready to reverse its polarity, causing compasses to point south, I immediately wondered what that would mean for leatherbacks and the many other species that use the magnetic field to orient themselves and find their way around. Could they withstand a significant dwindling of the field's strength or even a reversal? Or might extinctions, perhaps mass extinctions, be in the offing?

Animal Magnetism

One of the first concrete signs that animals can tap into the magnetic field was observed, as in many a great discovery in science, by chance. It was the fall of 1957, and Hans Fromme, a researcher at the Frankfurt Zoological Institute in Germany, noticed that several European robins he kept in a cage were becoming restless and were fluttering up into the southwestern part of the cage. Nothing unusual there: it was known that migrating birds in cages become edgy at that time of year, and European robins in Germany migrate southwestwards to Spain to overwinter.

What made it striking was that the birds were in a shuttered room. They could see neither visual landmarks, nor their fellow, non-captive robins, nor the sun or stars, which were known to serve them as navigational aids. Clearly they were acting on something invisible, and Fromme deduced it must be the Earth's magnetic field.

Numerous experiments undertaken by him and others since then have shown that many living things avail themselves of the magnetic field. Organisms as diverse as hamsters, salamanders, sparrows, rainbow trout, spiny lobsters, and bacteria all do it. "I would go so far as to say that it's nearly ubiquitous," says John Phillips, a behavioral biologist at Virginia Polytechnic Institute and State University who has discovered this ability in everything from fruit flies to frogs. (There's no scientific evidence that humans have this "sixth sense," though curiously, our brains do contain magnetite, the mineral thought to aid other animals' brains in detecting the field.)

How do we know organisms have this ability? A standard method to test for it is to throw a magnetic curve ball, as it were, at experimental subjects. In an effort, for example, to determine if the blind mole rat, a subterranean rodent that builds a home of branching tunnels with no exits to the surface, can sense the magnetic field, Tali Kimchi and Joseph Terkel of Tel Aviv University built an eight-armed maze within a device in which they could alter the magnetic field. They then tested two groups of rats—one in the Earth's magnetic field and the other in a field shifted by 180°—to see whether they had directional druthers for siting their sleeping nests and food chambers. The first group showed a significant preference to build their beds and pantries in the southern part of the maze, while the second group opted for the northern sector.

So they can sense it, but can they use it like we do a compass, to orient themselves? In another experiment, Kimchi and Terkel trained 24 blind mole rats to reach a goal box at the end of a complex labyrinth. Then, when all had mastered the task, they had half the rats do it again under the natural field and half under a reversed field. Lo and behold, the latter rats' performance fell far short of that achieved by their magnetically unmanipulated fellows.

Undersea Superhighways

Other animals take things a step further than the blind mole rat, using the magnetic field like we do the Global Positioning System, to determine their location on the surface of the Earth and using that to negotiate unseen pathways during migration.

Kenneth and Catherine Lohmann of the University of North Carolina at Chapel Hill and their team have shown through many experiments that during their 8,000-mile migration around the Atlantic Ocean, young loggerhead sea turtles can detect not only the field's intensity but its inclination, the angle at which magnetic field lines intersect the Earth. The turtles use these two pieces of information, which vary at every point on the planet's surface, as navigational markers that help them advance along their migratory route (see Figure 2).

Sometimes this navigational ability can serve its practitioners only too well. A mystery long bedeviling marine biologists is why otherwise healthy whales beach themselves, often in large groups. In the early 1980s, a British biologist named Margaret Klinowska first noticed a correlation between where whale strandings tended to occur along the coasts of England and where magnetic lineations written into the seafloor intersect those coasts. (These lineations, or anomalies, are different from those produced by the main magnetic field.) Joe Kirschvink of the California Institute of Technology and his colleagues later showed a similar association on the east coast of the U.S. Whales, it seems, follow these magnetic lineations during migration (see Figure 3). "If that's your game plan, and you get off track, and you follow a sharp magnetic anomaly that curves and runs into the coast, bang, you end up on the beach," says Kirschvink. Because whales are very social, if the leader makes this mistake, so does its entire pod, hence the mass strandings.

Rising To The Occasion

If whales can run into trouble when the field is reasonably strong, what might happen to them and other creatures that rely on it if the field becomes feeble or even flips? Hans Fromme had found in Frankfurt that when he placed his European robins into a steel chamber and reduced the strength of the ambient magnetic field by a third, the birds' flutterings were no longer directional. This suggested that the birds needed the magnetic field to be a certain intensity to be of use. But Fromme's colleague F. W. Merkel later showed that the birds were able to acclimatize to the new magnetic field within a number of days.

Indeed, the researchers I spoke with all thought that organisms would be able to adjust to an acute weakening or even complete reversal of the magnetic field. "My gut reaction is it's not going to have an impact," says Frank Paladino, the Indiana-Purdue University leatherback researcher whose project I was visiting that night in 1993.

History seems to back this up. There is no firm evidence that the many magnetic field reversals that have taken place throughout our planet's history (see When Compasses Point South) have coincided with or triggered extinctions. Reversals take hundreds if not thousands of years to complete, and because for any one type of animal that represents hundreds or thousands of generations, species have time to accommodate to the change. Moreover, Kirschvink notes that even if the main dipole field were to collapse—an event that can last for up to 10,000 years during a reversal—residual fields 5 or 10 percent as strong as the main field would remain on the surface, and animals would be able to use those quite well for migration.

So as I watched that leatherback in Costa Rica use her oar-like front flippers to expertly disguise her newly laid nest with sand and then begin dragging her massive bulk back to the surf, I needn't have worried, it seems, that she and others like her might lose their way and thus rupture the cycle leatherbacks have maintained since the Age of Dinosaurs. That's a relief considering how many threats she and other wild animals already face today.

[13]SOLAR STORMS AND THEIR HUMAN IMPACT

http://sunearth.gsfc.nasa.gov/sechtml/storms.html

Solar Storms and Their Human Impacts

A Roman garrison was mistakenly ordered to march to the coastal town of Ostia because Tiberius Caesar in 34 AD thought that the red glow seen on the northern horizon at night was Ostia in flames. (The Aurora, p.12) In China, the "Yellow Emperor" in 2000 B.C was conceived during an auroral display. Up until very recently, this was about all you could find to indicate that there were genuine 'other-worldly' influences upon us instigated by the rather passive sightings of sunspots or aurora. Even today, the average person is unaware of either sunspots or aurora since neither are easily observable.

In just one generation, our reliance upon uninterrupted power supplies to run our computer-rich, internet-laced, civilization; our colonization of near-earth space with hundreds of billions of dollars of satellite; and manned human activity, have placed all of these enterprises at risk for damage by solar storms. Like settlers to Kansas discovering tornadoes for the first time, we now have to reach a grudging accommodation with aurora and their invisible confederates that ply the ether above our heads. Unlike these settlers, however, we have to be frequently reminded that there is a problem at all. Fortunately, many examples of what this solar mayhem can do are easy to come by.

Hello? Is anyone there?

Beginning with the invention of telegraphy in 1841 and the telephone in the 1870's, vast systems of telephone and telegraph lines were strung-up across many of the continents. It didn't take very long before these new modes of communication began to turn up, not just an occasional long-distance call from Aunt Mabel, but some entirely unintended messages from Mr. Sun. During solar storms, "earth currents" induced by the changing terrestrial magnetic field, were so powerful that telegraphers didn't need a battery to send their messages down the line; Some were even treated to near-electrocution!

You can also find many references to earth current problems in the American Journal of Science and Arts, (e.g. vol. 29, May 1860)

William Ellis of the Royal Greenwich Observatory provided the first solar storm forecast in 1879 informing the telegraphic community that sunspots are correlated with periods of strong auroral activity. He noted that in the most recent years, there was little magnetic activity, and that telegraphic technology had taken a turn towards even more sensitive apparatus, and thousand-mile cables. He worried that with the next solar maximum only a few short years away, the new technology would be even more susceptible to magnetic 'storm' damage.

Nobody cared. By 1881, as if on queue, and after a lull in numbers of 'mysterious' surges, a new generation of reports began to accumulate as the solar cycle reached its maximum. Once again telegraph lines in Boston and London operated without batteries as auroral currents began to surge.

For other references to magnetic storm disturbances, consult the Journal of the Society of Telegraph Engineers and Electricians, vol. 1-10.

As solar storm particles arrive at the Earth and enter the magnetosphere, they temporarily set-up an invisible, circulating flow of charged particles around polar regions of the earth: The Ring Current. This current causes magnetic field fluctuations near the ground which in turn induce currents to flow in wires. This accounts for the shenanigans we have just encountered in long telegraph lines. But it doesn't matter if these wires are under the ocean because electromagnetic energy can pass through water with little hindrance. In the Atlantic Cable between Scotland and Newfoundland, voltages up to 2,600 volts were recorded during the March 1940 magnetic storm. A February 9-10, 1958 storm caused severe interruptions of telephone service on Western Union's North Atlantic telegraph cables, and disrupted phone calls carried by the Bell System's coaxial cable link between Newfoundland and Scotland.

"Hey...Who turned out the lights!"

Spectacular auroral displays can be breath-taking, but too much of a good thing can spell serious trouble. The pathways for this trouble can be as common as the power lines that criss-cross your own neighborhood. The March 24, 1940 storm caused a temporary disruption of electrical service in New England, New York, Pennsylvania, Minnesota, Quebec and Ontario. A storm on February 9-10, 1958 caused a power transformer failure at the British Columbia Hydro and Power Authority. On August 2, 1972, the Bureau of Reclamation power station in Watertown, South Dakota was subjected to large swings in power line voltages up to 25,000 volts. Similar voltage swings were reported by Wisconsin Power and Light, Madison Gas and Electric, and Wisconsin Public Service Corporation. A 230,000-volt transformer at the British Columbia Hydro and Power Authority exploded, and Manitoba Hydro in Canada recorded power drops from 164 to 44 megawatts in a matter of a few minutes, in the power it was supplying to Minnesota. Have a nice day!

Power Outages: American Geophysical Union, March 1997 report on transformers and solar storm effects. *For more information about power surges, read* 'Our Turbulent Sun' by Kendrick Frazer, (Prentice-Hall, 1980).

Perhaps the most dramatic, recent impact occurred in March 1989 during the peak of the last sunspot cycle, when the sun produced one of the most powerful storms ever recorded. On March 13, 1989 Alaskan and Scandinavian observers were treated to a spectacular auroral display. In fact, this display was seen as far south as the Mediterranean and Japan. Although many millions of people marveled at this beautiful spectacle, many millions more were not so happy about it. Hydro-Quebec on Saint James Bay did the best it could to stabilize the power surges its lines received but ultimately failed the challenge. For 9 hours, large portions of Quebec were plunged into darkness.

March 1989 Blackout in Quebec IPS Radio and Space Service report. According to John Kappenman, who is in charge of Transmission Power Engineering at Minnesota Power and Electric, the frequency of transformer failures is higher in geographic regions where magnetic storms are also more common such as the Northeastern US region which had 60% more transformer failures. Moreover, the number of failures follow a solar activity pattern of roughly 11 years. A conservative estimate of the damage done by geomagnetic storms to transformers by Minnesota Power and Electric was $100 million. Oak Ridge National Laboratories estimated that the collateral impact to the economy of another March 1989 storm of only slightly greater severity would produce a Northeast United States blackout, and cause $6 billion in damage. The North American Electric Reliability Council placed the March 1989 and October 1991 storm events in a category equivalent to Hurricane Hugo or the San Francisco earthquake in their impact upon the national economy.

Power Outages: AGU Report on transformers and solar storm effects Minnesota Power and Electric report by John Kappenman on transformer outages.

Just as good for generating large induced currents as telegraph and power lines are long, uninterrupted segments of oil and natural gas pipelines. Currents flowing in pipelines are known to enhance the rate of corrosion over time, and this can have catastrophic effects. On June 4, 1989 a powerful gas pipeline explosion demolished part of the Trans-Siberian Railroad engulfing two passenger trains in flames. Rescue workers at the Ural Mountain site worked frantically to rescue passengers. Of the 1200, all but 500 could be saved. Many of the victims were children bound for holiday camps by the Black Sea. Apparently gas from a leak in the pipe line was ignited by the two passing trains. The gas settled into the valley that the trains were passing through at the time. Rumors of sabotage were wide spread among the local population, but no one suspected the aurora and the invisible corrosive currents it spawned over time. The Alaskan oil pipeline is a newer technology and is specifically designed to minimize these geomagnetic currents, but the Siberian pipeline was an older technology without these safeguards in place.

Summaries of newspaper reports in this catastrophe can be found at IMAGE/POETRY's Space News page.

You would think that all this catastrophe would surely be picked up by major newspapers, but you would be quite wrong. The Chicago Tribune, The Washington Post and the London Times were curiously silent about the March 1989 blackout. Only the Toronto Star on March 13, 1989 reported that "Huge Storms on Sun linked to blackout that crippled Quebec" The problem is that many of these calamitous events are at the nuisance level, and they are seemingly unrelated. No grand conspiracy is afoot, and only small, geographically remote segments of humanity seem to be affected. But now times have definitely changed as we enter the Satellite Era with hundreds of millions of subscribers relying on the flawless and reliable working of satellite technology.

They call them 'Satellite Anomalies'

There is a long list of satellites that have been confirmed to have been directly affected by solar storms and the enhanced particle fluxes the satellites intercept. It is also this category of impacts that seems to contain the greatest controversies among satellite designers, insurance companies, and scientists working behind the scenes.

GOES-4 (November 26, 1982) visible and infrared spin-scan radiometer was disabled for 45 minutes after the arrival of high-energy protons from a solar flare. Marecs-B, a marine navigational satellite, was disabled by the strong electrical currents flowing during a week of intense auroral activity in February 1982. GOES-7 weather satellite lost half of its solar cells during a large proton release by the sun during the powerful March 13, 1989 storm which cut the operating life span of this satellite in half. ANIK E-1 and E-2 (January 20-21, 1994) two Canadian communications satellites were disabled due to the elevated activity of high-energy electrons in the magnetosphere. A similar disturbance in August 1993 was implicated in causing temporary pointing errors in five Intelsat satellites. The Intelsat-K satellite began to wobble a few hours before the January 20, 1994 event which affected the Anik E1 and E2 satellites. Intelsat-K also experienced a short outage of service during this time.

On January 11, 1997 at 6:15 AM EST, AT&T experienced a massive power failure in its Telstar 401 satellite. A few hours before Telstar 401 began to show signs of malfunctioning, the GOES-8 weather satellite experienced its own difficulties. Meanwhile the plasma from a solar storm had just arrived hours before.

January 1997 CME —The technical details of the January 1997 coronal mass ejection

October 7, 1995 Intelsat 511 Satellite outage caused by the sun; IPS Radio and Space Services report by Richard Thompson. *Information about the ANIK satellite failures can be found in articles appearing in* Aviation Week and Space Technology, Jan 31, 1994, and in Satellite Communications, March 1994.

It is important to realize that simultaneous events need not be correlated. The SOHO satellite recently showed two comets plunging into the sun, and hours later, the sun disgorged a massive cloud of plasma. These are "simultaneous" events but not connected by cause and effect. Also, if there are thousands of working satellites in space, why is it that a specific storm only seems to affect a few of them, if any at all? Despite the dramatic consequences for Telstar 401, no military satellites were apparently affected by this particular storm, and Hughes Space and Communications which manufactured over 40% of the commercial satellites now in orbit, had also not received any reports of any anomalies related to the storm among other satellites of similar type. If solar storms are so potent, why don't they take- out many satellites at a time? Solar storms are at least as complex as tornadoes, and we know that tornadoes can flatten one house while leaving its neighbors untouched, but that doesn't persuade us to deny the existence of tornado damage. We can see tornadoes coming with our own eyes. Not so for solar storms: The ultimate Stealth Bombers of the solar system. CNN's article on the SOHO Comets

During the last year it has become popular to blame any odd event on El Nino from a 'bad hair day' to droughts in Texas. Literally billions of dollars of commercial satellite insurance money rides on whether a satellite failure was an 'Act of God' (uninsurable) or a subtle satellite design flaw (insurable). A scientist's guarded opinion cannot be submitted as evidence to support one side or the other of an insurance claim. There must be a rigorous and precise statement in the court of law that 'Event A caused Satellite B to fail, but did not affect at the same time Satellites C, D, E ....Z'. Usually, this kind of guarantee cannot be provided scientifically because the satellite is unrecoverable, and only apparent correlations in time and space can be offered as evidence that a specific solar event affected a satellite in a specific way, leaving its neighbors unaffected. This often allows commercial satellite companies to claim that no natural 'Act of God' event was indisputably involved. Sometimes, after all, satellites DO simply malfunction in orbit after many years of operation.

"Insurers Beleaguered by Rash of Failures in '98", Space News, August 31, 1998.

"Insurers Battle with Satellite Manufacturers over Quality Control", Space News, April 28, 1997.

It was widely reported in the media such as Aviation Week and Space Technology, that a solar storm had damage the Telstar 401 satellite, but some scientists were not so ready to implicate the solar storm as the proximate cause of the damage to the satellite. Robert Hoffman, a NASA scientist and PI for the POLAR satellite, was quoted in Aviation Week and Space Technology as saying that, although the satellite was located in an affected area of the magnetosphere, *"We have no idea what caused the failure"*. Physicist Geoff Reeves at Los Alamos National Laboratory also supported this cautious position. *"We know that these conditions can cause problems for satellites, but unless we can go up with the space shuttle, bring the thing back, and look at it in the lab, we'll never know exactly how it failed." "Faulty Materials Blamed in Failure of Telstar 401"*, Space News, May 26, 1997.

Where's the beef?

Scientists do, however, know a thing or two about how radiation affects satellites, at least in the case of research satellites which represent a very non-threatening population. When research satellites fail, scientists do not get paid satellite insurance dividends, nor are there national security issues involved. Instead, some scientists may quietly lose their careers, and taxpayer money is silently lost in the accounting book work.

The most destructive ingredient of solar storm activity for satellites seems to be in the high-energy electrons rather than the other types particles. These electrons do their damage by producing 'deep dielectric charging' in unprotected parts of the satellite. Data taken by the SAMPEX satellite of the energetic electrons near geosynchronous orbit, against the times when the Anik satellites were affected, shows that the failures happened near the peaks of this activity. Data provided by Rice University and NOAA and NGDC scientists show that satellite surface charging 'anomalies' detected by the GOES-4 and GOES-5 spacecraft in geosynchronous orbit, correlate very well against a period when electrons were injected into this orbit due to the passage of a disturbance from the geotail region into the inner magnetic field regions around the earth. Some satellite designs, or satellite orbital locations, seem to have a higher risk for solar storm affects than others.

One recent, and spectacular, satellite outage occurred on May 17, 1998 when the PanAmSat's Galaxy IV satellite, insured for $165 million, lost control, and shut down service for millions of pagers in North America. Hughes investigators believe this was due to a rare buildup of crystals in a switch designed to control the flow of electricity to satellite processors. Hughes vice president Jeff Grant is quoted as saying that Hughes officials do not feel that the processors on the other 30 satellites of similar model type (HS-601s) are likely to fail but that, *"We feel we could have another processor failure on a spacecraft in orbit. I don't think we would be immensely surprised." Jeff Grant's quote is from*—Space News, July 13, 1998.

The electrostatic discharge scenario is mentioned in—Space News, July 13, 1998.

The crystal build-up scenario is discussed in—Space News, August 17, 1998.

Was there a solar storm or other geomagnetic storms in progress at that time? Between April 27 and May 6 NASA satellites detected 7 CMEs and two very powerful solar flares which temporarily produced a new radiation belt orbiting the Earth. Several magnetic storms were recorded on earth on May 2 and May 4 causing New England power companies to reduce their power-sharing capacity with Canada as a precaution. On May 2, the Equator-S satellite failed, but the connection between the solar storms and the satellite failure is currently in dispute. The May 6 storm affected the POLAR satellite which had to be shut down for several hours to recover. According to plots made of the high-energy electron fluxes near the Earth by Geoff Reeves (Los Alamos Laboratories), the period from May 15-19 recorded the maximum electron fluxes during this storm period. So, did Galaxy 4 fail because of the high-energy electron environment or because of faulty switch design? This is the core of the controversy over commercial satellite failures. *Iridium satellite losses are mentioned in*—Space News, May 18, 1998.

Of particular concern are the so-called 'phantom switches' where data bits are switched from '1' to '0' or vice versa because of a discharge in the electrical device caused by a high-energy particle strike. A nearly perfect correlation can be found between specific bit-switches and energetic electron enhancements detected by the GOES-7 and METEOSAT-3 satellites. The switches seemed to happen most often during periods when the electron impacts remained high for several days at a time. It isn't a single intense storm that seems to do the dirty work, but a sustained period of high electron 'storm' activity near the spacecraft. Even commercially available hand calculators on-board the MIR have been used to track bit switches.

Solar activity doesn't have to take a direct swipe at a satellite to do it harm by throwing high-energy particles at it. There is an old Irish saying 'May the road rise up to meet you". For satellites during heightened solar activity, the earth's atmosphere can puff up like a balloon and offer increased atmospheric friction. The premature demise of such satellites as the Solar Maximum Mission (SMM April 1990) and Skylab (July 1979) is the result. During the March 1989 storm, U.S. Space Command had to post the new orbital elements for over 1000 objects whose orbits had been affected by the momentarily increased air resistance hundreds of miles above the earth's surface.

That was then...this is now!

Between 1997 and 2007 it is estimated that as many as 1000 new satellites will be launched with 75% for commercial use. Most will be located in nearly a dozen satellite networks located in low earth orbit (LEO) between 200 and 800 km. Among the heavily used satellites already in place are the Motorola Iridium network of 66 satellites in LEO, the Intelsat network of 25 satellites in geosynchronous earth orbit (GEO) near 34,000 km, and the Global Positioning System with its 24 satellites at 11,000 miles costing $10 billion. Individual Investor magazine (June 1998) announced on its cover 'The Sky's the Limit: In the 21st century satellites will connect the globe'. The International Telecommunications Union in Geneva has predicted that between 1996 to 2005, the demand for voice and data transmission services will increase from $700 billion to $1.2 trillion, and that the fraction carried by satellite services will reach a staggering $80 billion. To meet this demand, many commercial companies are launching aggressive networks of LEO satellites (See table). But there is more than satellite technology riding on the line for the next solar maximum.

Planned Commercial Satellite Networks for 1999-2005, Computer technology History

Also read "Merrill Lynch Bullish on Space Industry Worldwide" published in the 'International Space Industries Report', May 7, 1998.

Most people have an instinctive fear of radiation and its potential biological effects. No matter where you live, you receive a free dose each day of environmental radiation which adds up to 360 millirems (4- 5 chest X-rays) per year, and you have no control over this. Cancer risks are generally related to radiation exposure, and one obtains between 12 and 100 cancers per 100,000 people for every 1000 millirems of additional dosage per year. This has been translated into 'acceptable' risks and dosage levels for different categories of individuals and occupations. Some careers are worse than others for producing large lifetime dosages such as, nuclear plant operators and astronauts.

During the Apollo program, there were several near-misses between the astronauts walking on the surface of the Moon and a deadly solar storm event. The Apollo 12 astronauts walked on the Moon only a few short weeks after a major solar proton flare would have bathed the astronauts in a 100 rem blast of radiation. Another major flare that occurred half way between the Apollo 16 and Apollo 17 moonwalks would have had a much more deadly outcome had it arrived while astronauts were outside their spacecraft playing golf. Within a few minutes, the astronauts would have been killed on the spot with an incredible 7000 rem blast of radiation.

The MIR space station has been inhabited for over a decade, and according to Astronaut Shanon Lucid, the daily dosage of radiation is about equal to 8 chest X-rays per day. During one solar storm towards the end of 1989, MIR cosmonauts accumulated in a few hours, a full- years dosage limit of radiation. Meanwhile, the Space Station will be assembled in an orbit which will take it through the South Atlantic Anomaly. Moreover, Space Station assembly will involve several thousand hours of space walks by astronauts. The main construction work will occur between the years 2000 and 2002 during the sunspot maximum period of Cycle 23. We can expect construction activity to be tied to solar conditions in a way that will frustrate the scheduling of many complex activities and the launches of Space Station components.

Shannon Lucid's MIR adventures are reported in Scientific American, May 1998.

So, what do we do?

The next solar cycle is already upon us, and if the blackouts, communication outages and satellite problems of the last few cycles are any indication, we could be in for some interesting news headlines, or interesting denials of cause and effect.

Increasingly more people are becoming sensitized to the need for paying attention to solar storm effects upon satellite operability. For instance, in Satellite News (June 1, 1998 p.3) an essay notes that,

"...The sun is nearing the peak of its 11-year activity cycle, signaling an increase in solar flares. This may lead to waves of radiation and high energy protons bombarding the planets throughout the coming months and years, rendering billions of dollars of satellite constellations vulnerable to extreme conditions."

So, why not make all satellites 'radiation hardened' or equip them with lots of radiation shielding? In one word 'Cost'. Shielding is dead weight, but it costs just as much as million-dollar technology to put into space. So, satellites are designed with the minimum shielding that the engineers think, they can get away with to keep the satellite functioning without breaking the bank. There is nothing wrong with this strategy, provided you are willing to take the gamble that you can anticipate accurately what the typical environment will be like during the satellite's lifetime. If you guess wrong, the shielding is inadequate and your satellite is lost. As pointed out by William B. Scott in Aviation Week and Space Technology magazine, *"Austere defense budgets also have increased reliance on more affordable, but perhaps less robust, commercial off-the-shelf hardware...expensive radiation-hardened processors are less likely to be put on some military satellites or communication systems now, than was once the case according to USAF officers...newer chips are much more vulnerable than devices of 10-15 years ago."*

"Operations Place High Value on Space Weather Forecasting" in Aviation Week and Space technology, September 1, 1997.

"Stormy Weather in Space" in IEEE Spectrum, June 1995.

"Solar Flares Show Vulnerability of High-Tech Communications" in Florida Today Space Online

From the first day of the Space Age, engineers recognized that the geiger counters inside scientific research satellites such as Vanguard and Explorer were madly ticking away the cosmic ray traffic even from inside the skin of the satellite. There are many well-known elements to this problem that are by no means a mystery to satellite designers. In the mid-1960s, NASA became a leader in developing and refining models of the earth's environment through the Trapped Radiation Environment Modeling Program (TREMP). The most recent of these models for the high-energy electrons and protons are called AE-8 and AP-8 models. Because they are strictly statistical averages over time and space, these 30-year- old models do not include solar storm events which can produce a years worth of radiation damage in a few hours. Despite the incompleteness of the AE and AP-8 models, they are in widespread use today. NASA has now begun to invest millions of dollars in research satellites and newer generations of models that will be substantially more accurate. They will for instance, not average many different data together, but will follow the detailed changes in many different data sets across time, space and energy. As 'physics-based' models, they will take advantage of more than 30 years of advances in plasma physics theory to improve upon their predictability. But the new models are not ready yet, and so satellite designers rely on older models to calculate spacecraft shielding.

"US scientists warn of rise in solar flares" in Space News, December 1, 1997.

"NASA urged to pursue study of radiation effects" in Space News, January 6, 1997.

"Space weather monitoring faces funding woes" in Space News, June 30, 1997.

In an age where "cheaper, faster and smaller' drives many satellite designs, satellites have become more susceptible to solar storm damage than their less sophisticated predecessors. Amazingly, as more satellites become disabled by 'mysterious' events, we are having to rediscover the importance of old lessons in satellite design and the costs are passed on to us as the end users.

"Satellite makers Use Cheaper, Faster Approach"—Space News, Feb 18, 1998.

"Protecting US assets in space" in the International Space Industry Report, June 8, 1998.

Meanwhile, the next time you hear about power outages or satellite failures in the next few years, don't blame 'El Nino', instead you might also consider blaming ol' Mr. Sun. After all, he's been up to the same old shenanigans for over a century now. Perhaps this time we will find ourselves a bit more prepared for his mischief!

[14] CULTURAL THEFT AND MISREPRESENTATION
http://www.powwows.com/gathering/734623-post596.html

Over the years many individuals, both Hopi and non-Hopi, have purposely distorted and exploited Hopi spirituality and the Hopi way of life to suit their own ends. The reasons for this misrepresentation vary as much as the people who engage in it. The most common motives, however, are notoriety, profit, or political manipulation. Irrespective of the intent, it all results in an unwanted intrusion by outsiders on the Hopi. Many, and perhaps most, Hopi people believe that religion is a private matter and that there is already too much information available to non-Hopis about Hopi spirituality. A great deal of knowledge that may have been shared with guests as a courtesy or as privileged information, even in moments of undeserved trust, has been published. These published accounts, be they accurate or misleading, have been misused to replicate Hopi ceremonies and spirituality for profit. In many cases, information has been altered in a way that ignores any spiritual context and religious significance.

Hopi religion is so complex that it is impossible for any one Hopi, traditional group or political faction within Hopi, to know it entirely. Hopi culture and religion as a whole is multifaceted, but there are also variations from village to village, and much of the Hopi ceremonial cycle is secret even among the Hopi. Specific clans and societies are responsible for different aspects of the ceremonial cycle, which in its entirety, make a complimentary whole. Beware, then, of any one person professing to be a traditional spokesperson for the Hopi or even a "traditional' Hopi. No one person can possibly speak for all Hopi people. Some who profess to do so do not practice the beliefs of Hopi religion or participate in its priesthoods.

[15] HAARP

http://www.earthpulse.com/src/category.asp?catid=1

One of the most comprehensive sites on this subject and FAR too many articles to list individually.

[16] HAARP FACILITY TO QUADRUPLE POWER: October 2003

http://www.arrl.org/news/stories/2003/10/29/2/

HAARP facility to quadruple power: Technical Specialist Richard Lampe, KL1DA, represented the League at the 2003 High Frequency Active Auroral Research Project (HAARP) RFI meeting September 24 at the HAARP site near Gakona, Alaska. "Joint funding through DARPA will allow HAARP to quadruple in size from its current 960 kW output to 3.6 MW," Lampe says. "When completed in 2006, HAARP will then be the premier ionospheric research facility with beam-steering capabilities that other similar arrays worldwide don't have." Under terms of its experimental license, HAARP must transmit on a non-interference basis, and Lampe—who is ARRL liaison to HAARP—says the staff at the control center immediately shut down the transmitters when harmonics were detected on 75/80 meters during experiments last year. "Alaska hams monitor the bands and aid HAARP engineers by reporting RFI issues as soon as they happen," Lampe said. Other participants at the meeting included representatives from the Aircraft Owners and Pilots Association, the US Air Force, the US Navy and on-site staff and research students.

[17] DO YOU BELIEVE IN GOVERNMENT MIND CONTROL?
http://www.bibliotecapleyades.net/scalar_tech/esp_scalartech16.htm

This report was filed by a television station in Northern California, USA, REPORTER Ross Blackstone, KOVR 13 News (CBS affiliate station), APPEARED ON News at 5:00, News at 6:00, THE 10:00 News (11/17/00)

Imagine everywhere you go, someone is watching you, reading your thoughts, and controlling your mind. Periodically over the past several decades, we've heard of situations when the U.S. government has experimented on human beings. Some cases have involved nuclear weapons, others, LSD and mind control. Is it possible something similar could happen to us right now without our knowledge? In this special assignment, Ross Blackstone introduces us to northern Californians who say it is and they have proof. They believe the government is sending radio waves to directly effect the unique electromagnetic waves in their brains.

[18] MICROWAVES AND BEHAVIOUR
Extract of published article named above.

Victor Frankenstein surgically fathered the famous fictional monster, but the fiend was conceptually mothered if not physically spawned by electricity in the form of lightning from the heavens. Perhaps unwittingly, perhaps intuitively, author Mary Shelley (1831) touched a deep truth in the maternal metaphor: Life did originate from electrical discharges into the primeval fog. Indeed, life continues to preserve in all of its earthly forms from the most primitive cell to the most complex organism an elemental dependence on electrical phenomena. Understandably, the curiosity of the scientist about the electrobiological goings-on of the earth's flora and fauna is shared by the layman. A large popular literature is accumulating and embraces experiments and anecdotes that range from the ostensibly respectable to the seemingly bizarre.

Recently published texts by Tompkins and Bird (1973) and by Burr (1972, 1973) are not only exemplars of the literature but are rich sources of reference materials. One reads, for example, that plants have nervous systems that yield differing electrical signals on "stimulation" by kind or *malevolent thoughts* of human beings (Backster, 1968).

One also reads that many Soviet scientists are giving credence and careful study to ESP and related phenomena, not in defiance of Marxian dictates of materialism but quite in keeping with them. The Soviets are championing earlier theoretical notions of Georges Lakhovsky (1934) to the effect that each plant or animal cell is an oscillatory system capable of transmitting and receiving high-frequency electromagnetic energy over a distance.

Microwaves and Behavior DON R. JUSTESEN, *Laboratories of Experimental Neuropsychology, Veterans Administration Hospital, Kansas City, Missouri*

Requests for reprints should be sent to Don R. Justesen, Laboratories of Experimental Neuropsychology, Veterans Administration Hospital, Kansas City, Missouri 64128. The author is also at the Department of Psychiatry, Kansas University Medical Center, Kansas City, Kansas 66103

[19] SUBLIMINAL PROGRAMMING THROUGH TELEVISION

Copy of U.S. Patent #5,270,800 : Description on application for patent. Subliminal message generator

Abstract

A combined subliminal and supraliminal message generator for use with a television receiver permits complete control of subliminal messages and their manner of presentation. A video synchronization detector enables a video display generator to generate a video message signal corresponding to a received alphanumeric text message in synchronism with a received television signal. A video mixer selects either the received video signal or the video message signal for output. The messages produced by the video message generator are user selectable via a keyboard input. A message memory stores a plurality of alphanumeric text messages specified by user commands for use as subliminal messages. This message memory preferably includes a read only memory storing predetermined sets of alphanumeric text messages directed to differing topics. The sets of predetermined alphanumeric text messages preferably include several positive affirmations directed to the left brain and an equal number of positive affirmations directed to the right brain that are alternately presented subliminally. The left brain messages are presented in a linear text mode, while the right brain messages are presented in a three dimensional perspective mode. The user can control the length and spacing of the subliminal presentations to accommodate differing conscious thresholds. Alternative embodiments include a combined cable television converter and subliminal message generator, a combine television receiver and subliminal message generator and a computer capable of presenting subliminal messages.

[20] LASER WEAPONS IN U.S. SIGHTS: OCT. 21, 2003
*Quote: "Contrary to science fiction, the lasers will not be visible streams of light. Instead, targets will simply explode."
The entire article may be found at
http://www.cbsnews.com/stories/2003/10/20/tech/main578998.shtml

[21] WEATHER AND ECO-TERRORISM BEING USED AS A WEAPON
http://www.cheniere.org/video/sovietweathervideo.html

U.S. Defence Secretary Cohen expresses concern about eco-terrorism using scalar electromagnetic weapons. “Others [terrorists] are engaging even in an eco-type of terrorism whereby they can alter the climate, set off earthquakes, volcanoes remotely through the use of electromagnetic waves... So there are plenty of ingenious minds out there that are at work finding ways in which they can wreak terror upon other nations...It’s real, and that’s the reason why we have to intensify our [counterterrorism] efforts.”

Secretary of Defense William Cohen at an April 1997 counterterrorism conference sponsored by former Senator Sam Nunn. Quoted from DoD News Briefing, Secretary of Defense William S. Cohen, Q&A at the Conference on Terrorism, Weapons of Mass Destruction, and U.S. Strategy, University of Georgia, Athens, Apr. 28, 1997.

[22] HEALTH ISSUES FOLLOWING FLOODING
The entire article may be found at
http://www.geotimes.org/oct01/geophen.html

*Quote: “The major post-disaster disease risk in the Mobile study area is from eastern equine encephalomyelitis (EEE), an often-fatal inflammation of the brain and spinal cord. Carried by mosquitoes, the disease occurs in focal locations along the eastern seaboard, the Gulf Coast and some inland Midwestern locations of the United States. Small outbreaks of human disease have occurred in the United States, and outbreaks among horses can be a common occurrence during the summer and fall. Humans develop symptoms four to 10 days after being bitten by an infected mosquito. These symptoms begin with a sudden onset of fever, general muscle pains and a headache of increasing severity. Many individuals will progress to more severe symptoms such as seizures and coma. About one-third of all people with clinical encephalitis caused by EEE will die from the disease. Of those who recover, many will suffer permanent brain damage, with many of those requiring permanent institutional care.

The EEE virus also can produce severe disease in horses; some birds, such as pheasants, quail, ostriches and emus; and even puppies. The whooping crane, an endangered species, is highly susceptible to EEE. Cases in horses usually precede those in humans, making horse cases a good surveillance tool." Posted October 2001.

[23] Intentional Communities on the Web

As extensive a collection as we are aware of... though for perspective, these Web savvy groups are only a portion of the 600+ communities described in the Communities Directory. We have included here the communities listed at the web sites of Ecovillage Information Service and the Cohousing Network and the Federation of Egalitarian Communities To access this website and list, go to http://directory.ic.org/

[24] World's Oceans Used As Toxic Waste Dump
http://www.latimes.com/
Seattle Times on Wednesday, March 29, 2000, 07:53 p.m. Pacific
by Marla Cone, Los Angeles Times

LOS ANGELES - The U.S. Environmental Protection Agency plans an unprecedented experiment this summer to cover 180 acres of ocean floor south of Los Angeles, a potentially risky effort to deal with the world's largest deposit of the pesticide DDT. The pilot project, in which tons of sand will be dropped into deep ocean water off Palos Verdes Peninsula, is the first tangible step toward resolving a decades-old problem that haunts Southern California's marine environment.

For 25 years, through 1971, chemical manufacturer Montrose Corp. dumped residue into the Los Angeles County sewer system, allowing 110 tons of DDT to spread across 17 square miles of the ocean floor in depths up to 200 feet. The chemical, linked to cancer and reproductive problems, is still contaminating fish consumed by some Southern Californians and killing bald-eagle chicks.

DDT, banned in the United States since 1972, was widely used and touted as safe for killing mosquitoes and other pests until scientists discovered that it accumulated in the fat of fish and consequently, in animals and humans.

[25] Toxic Dumping In The Waters of Tasmania
http://tasmaniantimes.com/
Kelly approves waste dumping in ocean
By Andrew Watson

HOBART—Pasminco Metals-EZ has been given the go-ahead by the federal government to continue dumping the toxic waste product jarosite into the sea until 1997. Federal environment minister Ros Kelly has extended the company's deadline for sea dumping by two years. The decision contravenes the recently ratified London Convention on Ocean Dumping, of which Australia is a signatory. This bans all countries from dumping toxic waste into the sea from December 1995.

Greenpeace described the government's decision as an "international disgrace" which is protecting one of the country's worst polluters. A Greenpeace spokesperson on toxic waste, Dr Paul Brown, said the decision makes a mockery of Kelly's recent claim in parliament that the federal government had a "very high international standing" on waste management.

Since 1973, Pasminco Metals-EZ has been dumping approximately 200,000 tonnes of jarosite per year into Bass Strait. This waste includes 15,400 tonnes of zinc, 38 tonnes of cadmium, 5760 tonnes of lead, 0.36 tonnes of mercury, 2280 tonnes of arsenic and 576 tonnes of copper. Despite company and government claims that the dumping has had "no harmful effect on the environment", elevated levels of cadmium have been detected in seabirds which feed in the vicinity of the dump zone, 60 nautical miles south-east of Hobart. The company's own May 1993 Jarosite Report revealed high concentrations of heavy metals in marine animals at and near the site. In particular, cadmium levels in fish were well above national food standards.

[26] Allies Dumped 70 Boatloads of WWII German Chemical Weapons In The North Sea-Sept.12, 2000
http://www.rense.com/general3/ns.htm

MOSCOW (AFP) - A deep sea dump of Nazi chemical weapons threatens to pollute the North Sea and the Baltic, a team of Russian scientists warned Tuesday. The leader of the team, which has just returned from an expedition to Denmark and Norway, told AFP the Allies had dumped the hazardous chemicals in containers near the Gulf of Skagerrak at the end of World War II.

The scientists measured "levels of arsenic between 50 and 100 times the norm, and a concentration of heavy metals twice the norm," said expedition leader Vadim Paka, of the Russian Academy of Sciences. He said the concentration levels did not pose an immediate threat to the nearby populations, but added that the effects of erosion in the open sea, "when the containers rust and break up, risk causing an ecological catastrophe."

Paka added that the expedition had taken measurements at depths of between 190 and 215 metres (yards) in the Gulf of Skagerrak, which lies between Denmark and Norway, where about 20 vessels loaded with chemical weapons had been dumped.

Almost 70 boats in total had been dumped in different parts of the North Sea and the Baltic, he said. "We have gathered a number of readings which show that toxic agents have infiltrated the water," Paka said before urging the governments of the region to undertake a detailed study of the submerged vessels. "There is no more time to be lost, because no conservation scheme is technically possible without a detailed study," he said, underlining that Russia did not have the money to finance such a project.

[27] British Dumping of WWII Chemical Weapons Threatens Europe
http://www.heraldscotland.com/
London, Sunday Herald, June 17, 2002 By Rob Edwards, Environment Correspondent

More than half a century ago, Britain dumped over 100,000 tonnes of the Nazi's deadly chemical weapons in the sea. Now they are coming back to haunt us. Scientists fear millions of ancient shells and bombs resting on the short stretch of seabed between Denmark and Norway have begun to leak their lethal payload. Danish fishermen have been injured, Norway has launched an investigation and coastal authorities are worried a 'historic time bomb' could be about to explode.

The Sunday Herald has obtained a copy of a report by the Ministry of Defence which details for the first time the extraordinary scale of the postwar operation to get rid of Germany's chemical weapons. Between 1945 and 1947, at least 112,000 tonnes were loaded into 33 German boats, which were then scuttled in Skagerrak, the strait across the North Sea that separates Norway and Denmark (see table). The chemicals, confiscated from Hitler's Third Reich at the end of the second world war, were mustard gas, phosgene, tabun and lewisite, all of which can inflict appalling injuries. They may also have included hydrocyanic acid and Cyclone B, two of the poisons used to murder millions of Jews in Nazi concentration camps.

Before they were packed into the hulls of ships, the weapons were put into wicker baskets by German workers. The hope was that any chemicals that leaked out would be absorbed by the wicker, and prevented from contaminating the sea. That may have been a false hope, however. An expedition to Skagerrak by Russian scientists has discovered evidence that the weapons—sometimes only two hundreds metres deep—are falling apart and spilling their contents into the marine environment.

The investigation by the Russian Academy of Science in St Petersburg found levels of arsenic up to 200 parts per million around one of the dump sites. This was 'extremely high', they said, and was probably due to arsenic leaching from corroding weapons. They also detected high concentrations of lead and other heavy metals. The weapons could poison fishermen who pulled them up from the seabed, were a target for terrorists and posed 'a large danger to the environment', the Russian scientists warned. 'It is a terrible menace for Europeans,' said Albert Bikmullin, from the International Ecological Parliament, a Russian environmental group. 'Poison gas, dissolving slowly in the water, is able to pollute vast areas and get into food chains.' He added: 'Plankton absorbs poison gas very easily, is mutated and gets into fish as a food. Fish, in their turn, get to carnivores and in this way poison gets into a man's meal.'

The Russian government has formally approached NATO, seeking support for a programme to monitor and prevent leakages from the chemical dumps. But NATO, which is considering the request through its Committee on the Challenges of Modern Society, has not yet decided what to do. Meanwhile the Norwegian Pollution Control Authority has just begun its own investigation, which involves sending a remote-controlled mini-sub marine to the seabed to take pictures and samples. 'We have to keep it under control to make sure that it doesn't harm people,' said Hilde Keilen, the authority's senior executive officer.

Danish studies have suggested that over 150 fishermen have accidentally brought up chemical munitions in their nets. In some cases, they have been burnt by leaking mustard gas, which, despite its name, is a thick, viscous liquid. KIMO, an organisation which brings together over 100 local authorities representing five million people around the coasts of northern Europe, is planning a Scottish conference on chemical dumps at sea this November. Due to take place in Ayr, it is entitled Time Bombs From The Past. 'We are increasingly concerned about the historic time bomb which is ticking away at over 80 dump sites in northern seas. We are asking governments to investigate the exact locations of chemical and conventional weapons dump sites, compile inventories and make this information available,' said KIMO's Rick Nickerson.

'These materials are increasingly washing up on our coasts and endangering fishermen at sea. It is important that a clear picture is obtained of the state of these dumps so that appropriate action can be taken if and when a site becomes a problem.'

The cause has been taken up by the Labour MP for Glasgow Baillieston, Jimmy Wray. He has put down an motion in the House of Commons calling on the British government to combat the pollution from the sunken ships, and has been backed by 28 other MPs. 'It is important that this kind of pollution is dealt with soon. These ships have been sitting on the seabed for the past 50 years and are now rotting away. Dangerous chemicals are being leaked into the sea, and we could have an environmental catastrophe on our hands within a few years,' he said.

The British government, however, has no plans to even monitor the chemicals dumped in Skagerrak. 'The consensus of international scientific opinion is that munitions on the seabed present no risk to human health or the marine environment, provided they are left undisturbed,' said the defence minister, Dr Lewis Moonie. He confessed that much of the historical documentation detailing the dumping had been lost. 'After the second world war it was the administrative practice to destroy records of sea disposals of munitions, including chemical weapons, when such records were perceived to be of no further administrative use,' he explained. The admission has infuriated Wray. 'It is terrible that important documents have been destroyed by the Ministry of Defence,' he declared. 'It doesn't bear thinking what other documents have been disposed of.'

[28] Government Created Diseases: The Smallpox Wars
http://www.prospect.org/cs/articles?article=the_smallpox_wars_101901
Extract from The Smallpox Wars by Wendy Orent

"It's been just over a year since the publication of the first press reports revealing that Soviet researchers had weaponized smallpox. But the U.S. government has known this since the early 1990s, from at least three intelligence reports from 1991 and 1992, which revealed that stocks of smallpox existed in several places in Russia. Furthermore, by 1993, rumors of another ominous development began to surface, this time from a KGB report that suggested that smallpox was also in the hands of North Korean bioweapons researchers."

[29] Laboratory Created Diseases
Earth Trends by Martin Khor Monday 15 Jan 2001
http://www.twnside.org.sg/title/et0104.htm

LAB-CREATED KILLER VIRUS SPARKS BIOTECH FEARS

News last week that a new deadly virus was created during a genetic engineering experiment has set off warning bells that the use of the technology should be very carefully monitored and regulated. In the experiment that went wrong, an engineered mousepox virus acquired the capacity to damage the immune system and killed all the mice involved. The scientists warned that it is "not too difficult" to create similar viruses that are deadly to human beings. Are we in danger of new diseases created in poorly-regulated labs?

The potential hazard of applying genetic engineering for medical purposes was dramatically publicised last week when Australian scientists revealed they had accidentally created a killer version of the mousepox virus that killed all the mice in their experiment. If the same method had been used on the smallpox virus (which is similar to mousepox), it may have resulted in a more dangerous form of that virus that can destroy the immune system and thus be extremely lethal to humans.

Hundreds of experiments are taking place around the world in which scientists genetically modify viruses and bacteria. As the Australian case has shown, it is possible for new dangerous viruses to be created, with or without the intention of the scientists, and with potentially catastrophic health consequences.Last week's revelation is likely to spark a major controversy on the need to strictly regulate genetic engineering research, experiments and use in animals and humans. In recent there have been serious concerns, and many public protests, regarding genetic engineering. However, they have mainly focused on its use in agriculture and on the safety of genetically-modified foods. The Australian mousepox case can be expected to cause similar concerns on the use of genetic engineering in medical applications and purposes, or for biological warfare and acts of terrorism.

The scientists who carried out the experiment have themselves publicised the dangers that can arise from it, warning that terrorists could without much difficulty use their method to develop a new lethal strain of smallpox to carry out biological warfare. "We discovered that if we modified this virus in a particular way then suddenly animals were dying that would normally be resistant to the virus," said Bob Seamark, the head researcher, according to an AFP news report. "It was a concern that this same modification could be made to human viruses and this would enhance their virulence or at least strengthen their ability to kill people." Seagate and the Cooperative Research Centre issued a global warning to guard against misuse of their research.

Another scientist, Annabelle Duncan, called for the tightening of the Biological Weapons Convention to make it "very, very hard" for terrorists to use the results of scientific research to create deadly new weapons. Duncan is molecular science chief at the Commonwealth Scientific and Industrial Research Organisation (CSIRO) which helped create the virus, and was formerly deputy leader of a United Nations team that investigated bio-warfare agents in Iraq.

Whilst it is right for the researchers to warn about the misuse of scientific data by "bio-terrorists", equal attention should also be paid to the hazards posed by scientific research and experiments, including those like the Australian case, that may be perfectly legal but nevertheless potentially harmful. What if the new lethal mousepox virus escapes from the laboratory and moves freely about? And, worse, what if genetically-modified viruses that can cause more lethal versions of life-threatening human diseases (such as smallpox) or even new diseases.

The Australian case was first reported in the New Scientist magazine last week, and then was publicised worldwide through the BBC and major news agencies. The New Scientist report began dramatically as follows: "A virus that kills every one of its victims, by wiping out part of their immune system, has been accidentally created by an Australian research team. The virus, a modified mousepox, does not affect humans, but it is closely related to smallpox, raising fears that the technology could be used in biowarfare."

The researchers were trying to make a mouse contraceptive vaccine for pest control, and did not intend to produce a killer virus. Two scientists, Ron Jackson of CSIRO and Ian Ramshaw of Australian National University inserted into a mousepox virus a gene that creates large amounts of a molecule, interleukin 4 (IL-4), that is naturally found in the human body. The molecule was supposed to stimulate antibodies against mouse eggs, and thus make the mice infertile. The mousepox virus was used as a vehicle to transport the egg proteins into mice to trigger an antibody response and the gene for IL-4 was added to boost antibody production.

"The surprise was that it totally suppressed the cell-mediated response—the arm of the immune system that combats viral infection," says the New Scientist report. Mice normally suffer only mild symptoms from mousepox, but with the added gene, it killed all the mice in nine days. "It would be safe to assume that if some idiot did put human IL-4 into human smallpox, they'd increase the lethality quite dramatically," said Jackson. Moreover, the modified virus is unusually resistant to vaccine as the vaccine applied to the mice to protect them against mousepox worked in only half the mice exposed to the killer version. If a human version of the virus is created, vaccination programmes would be of limited use.

In light of the incident, the New Scientist report poses a vital issue: "Is it possible that research into new vaccines against cancer and other diseases could inadvertentl create lethal human viruses? Many of the most promising modern vaccines depend on viruses to transport genes into the body, and contain genes that directly alter the immune response. "But researchers have not been too concerned because the evidence until now suggested that changes in the genetic make-up of viruses invariably makes them less virulent, not more."

Meanwhile the researchers decided to go public with the results of their experiment. "We wanted to warn the general population that this potentially dangerous technology is available," said Jackson. "We wanted to make it clear to the scientific community that they should be careful, that it is not too difficult to create severe organisms." The warning by these scientists poses many questions. What if they had covered up instead? How many other scientists have been involved in genetic engineering research that also resulted in lethal viruses, but who did not publicise the findings, or who did not even know the effects their modified organisms are capable of?

Are there adequate regulations to prevent the production and spread of potentially dangerous modified viruses and bacteria? Do the authorities in each country and in international agencies even keep tabs of the experiments going on? In view of the seriousness of the Australian case, these questions need to be answered, and extreme caution is required, before an accidental (or even an intentional) release of deadly microbes takes place. The emergence, spread and effect of the AIDS virus is an outstanding example of the devastation a new virus or bacterium can inflict on human lives and health, in this case a virus that damages or destroys the body's immune system.

Last week's news that a new virus was created in a laboratory that can kill all its victims by wiping out an important part of their immune system should serve as a warning for regulatory action to be taken before it is too late.

[30] Laboratory Created Disease: Gulf War Syndrome

http://www.all-natural.com/riley.html

Biological Warfare Conducted on U.S. Military Members, and Corporate Bio-Genocide Levied on the Planetary Population

EXTRACT from A Lecture By Captain Joyce Riley in Houston, Texas on January 15, 1996

Extract #1

The basic fact is that biological agents were used on our troops. Chemical agents were used on our troops. Germ warfare was used on our troops—using biologicals that *were made in the United*

States of America. It was made in Houston, Texas and Boca Raton, Florida. It was passed through the Centers for Disease Control (CDC) and through companies such as American Type Culture Collection (ATCC) in Maryland. It was passed to Saddam Hussein—sold to Saddam Hussein, as late as 1989. Just prior to the war. The American government was involved in the provision of biological warfare (components) to Saddam Hussein. They knew exactly what they were doing. Our troops did not know what to expect, nor were they protected. We later found out that we had no adequate biological/chemical detection capability. The lies are going on and on. I released the story on my radio show on May 4, 1995 with Drs. Garth and Nancy Nicholson. We had security in the studio because I had made the mistake of sending out some news releases in advance. I was afraid that we would be stopped from doing the program. We had someone there to argue a temporary restraining order, if necessary. But, we didn't need it. Drs. Garth and Nancy Nicholson named names, places and times. The sad part is that it is real. When I heard them naming names and places, I thought "oh, my word. I'm going to have ten lawyers on my door tomorrow." No one showed up. No one has come to me and said, "you shouldn't be saying this". The reason being that they don't want to fight me in court. They know its true. So, what I am going to show you tonight is absolute evidence of the saddest story in American history.

Extract #2 [Editor Note: Here she is referring to the Reigle Report. We might also remind you that the father of the Chairman of the Joint Chiefs of Staff was in the Nazi SS].

Active Duty Military Intimidated Into Silence

I was approached at one point in time by someone who lead me to Drs. Garth and Nancy Nicholson, who are heroes in my mind. They are both Ph.D. scientists at the M.D.Anderson Cancer Center. Their daughter was in the 101st Airborne that did deep insertions into Iraq. Many of the 101st Airborne have called me and many of them are sick. The 82nd Airborne is sick. Men and women at Fort Hood, Texas are sick. Camp Pendleton. Camp

LeJeune. Fort Riley is really sick right now. These people are not allowed to talk about this in the military. They are not allowed to tell people about the Gulf War Illness. They are not allowed to admit to it. I have even visited Gulf War vets at Brook Army Medical Hospital, and they are not even allowed to talk about it. I took some Gulf War information over there *and the patients had to hide it so the doctors would not see it.* So, the Nicholson's daughter came back from Iraq sick. She gave the disease to the family - to Garth and Nancy, who live in Houston, and also to the family cat. The cat died. Before the cat died, they tested all of their blood. They found that *they were positive for something called Mycoplasma Incognitas,* which is the chief biological agent we find to be responsible for a lot of the illness of the veterans.

Mycoplasma Incognitas

I will explain this to you by saying that *Mycoplasma Incognitas* is between the size of a bacteria and a virus. It travels through a population, and as long as your immune system is all right it will not affect you. But, according to the Nicholson's, who are both Ph.D. cellular biologists, they found that *the scientists who were involved in this horrible plot inserted 40% of the HIV envelope gene into the Mycoplasma.* What this means is that it doesn't give you HIV, *but it gives you the symptoms.* So, they found this and realized that they had a germ warfare agent on their hands. It is the *first* biological agent identified. There have been others.

U.S. Government Refuses to Dispense Known Treatment to Affected People

The Nicholson's went to the laboratory to discover how to treat this. They found that an antibiotic called Doxycycline was the most effective. *The United States military will not allow military members under their control to have Doxycycline or VA hospitals to dispense Doxycycline.* They are simply not allowed to have it. I got a call from a Special Forces commander who had been retired for one year. He said: "I have had it. I came home. I served my country. I got my blood sent to Dr. Nicholson for free testing and got my prescription for Doxycycline. I went to have it filled and not only did that *take away my military ID card*, but *they would not allow me to have the Doxycycline to save my life*." You see, *the disease is contagious, and now the wives and children are getting it.* It is going to affect *you* in the *general population.* That is why it is so important to understand how serious this is. *It is not just the United States. It is a worldwide program.* There were 28 countries that served with the United States in Iraq. All 28 countries now report that their men and women are also sick. But Drs. Garth and Nancy Nicholson revealed that *a Houston company was involved in the manufacture of a biological weapon that was sold to Iraq and was used on American soldiers in the Gulf War.* Since we came out with the names of these companies, there have been lawsuits filed against those corporations.

Symptoms of the Syndrome

These are the symptoms of the syndrome. You may look at this and it may not seem very significant to you, so if you look at *aching joints* and go to your doctor and say "I have aching joints" or you say "I have *chronic fatigue* ", or you say "I don't have the *memory* I used to", they will not say anything. When I am talking about memory loss, I am talking about the kind where you have to wear a beeper so your family can find you. One young man told me, "I can only remember today. I can't remember what happened yesterday." He was 27 years old. We are talking about a problem known as *night sweats.* Any Gulf War veteran who has the Mycoplasma knows about night sweats. You have to change your linens twice a night. The *muscle spasms* get so bad that you can't stand it and people scream in pain. There is also *loss of eyesight, breathing problems,* and *chest pains* because the Mycoplasma settles in the atrium of the heart. All of these are problems that become worse. The problem is that the government is telling the people of the United States "there is no Gulf War Illness". The doctors in this country *think* there is no Gulf War Illness. So, when people come in and complain about the *symptoms,* they are turned aside and told that the problem is psychological in nature.

Deformed Children Caused by U.S. Corporate Genocide

Now, you are not being told about the *babies that are being born deformed.* There is a Gulf War Baby Foundation formed to register babies who have contracted the syndrome. There are so many that are being born deformed. You are not being told about this. Dan Rather doesn't tell you about it, does he? No. And so, you think that if it isn't on the nightly news it must not be true, right? If a tree falls in the forest and Dan Rather doesn't cover it, does it still make a noise? Think about it.

Gulf War babies are severely deformed. In fact, according to *Nation Magazine*, "studies have shown that *67% of babies born to Gulf War veterans are deformed.* What have they done to our future generations? What have they done to their DNA?

There was an article that appeared in *Life Magazine* in November 1995 featuring a man in the 82nd Airborne at Fort Brag, North Carolina. This young man has a child with no arms and no legs. I know of a nurse in San Antonio who knows of 50 children like this. When our soldiers risked their lives in the Gulf, they never imagined that their children would face these consequences or that their country would turn its back on them. You are hearing what perhaps 1% of the country knows today. It will take your help to get this story out. There is no way these parents can afford to take care of these children. (Shows pictures of children).

The Reigle Reports and Congressional Knowledge About the Problem Covered Up

This is something that the government is trying to keep you from knowing about. The Reigle report is evidence that biological and chemical weapons *were* used on our troops. It was presented to the United States Senate, but it has been withheld from you. They don't want you to see it. A news release went out that Senator Reigle from Michigan was a brave man for doing this. He is no longer in the Senate. He had to pay for the report to be done. The Feb 1994 news release said, "Reigle Uncovers U.S. Shipment of Biological Warfare Materials to Iraq Prior to Gulf War". The release went on to say, "there is evidence of transmission to family members. I am deeply troubled that the United States permitted the sale of deadly biological agents to a country with a known biological warfare program." There is no *blood ban* stopping Gulf War veterans from donating blood to the general blood supply that the *general population* uses. Reigle also sent a letter to Secretary of Defense Perry on Feb 9, 1994 and talked about the exposure of Gulf War veterans and the transmission of the disease to spouses and children. He found out that we had been *exporting* these biological substances through ATCC. *This information is known to every Senator that was in office in 1994.* Why aren't they doing something about it. Why weren't you told about it? Reigle also said to Secretary Perry, "without proper treatment and testing, their condition will worsen. They cannot wait. Many are now destitute, with their savings spent on medical care not provided by the government.

According to Senator Reigle, "the Department of Defense refuses to acknowledge any part of the problem. Their blanket denials are not credible. To my mind, *there is no more serious crime than an official military cover-up of facts that could prevent more effective diagnosis and treatment of sick U.S. veterans. It is an astonishing example that the Defense Department is going to deny reality.*" The Veterans Administration is *not treating* Gulf War veterans, but only *monitoring their blood to see how well the biological warfare agents worked.* They are not treating the Gulf War veterans.

(Here she details the bacteriological substance shipped. See attachment from the Reigle Report at the end of this transcript).

Proof of Chemical Weapon Use from the Schwartzkoff NBC Log

(Slide Shown) Here is how we know the biologicals were used. What I am showing you was once a classified document. It is part of the Chemical-Biological log that belonged to General Norman Schwartzkoff in CENTCOM. He was responsible for central command. The NBC log is sort of a roadmap of the war and what transpired. You can see here that it says, "Colonel Dunn has confirmed that the soldiers of the 3rd AD have blisters, characteristic of mustard chemical agent, on upper and lower arms." Remember the official statement? "No Biological or Chemical Weapons Used". The log continues, "ARCENT advised that casualty happened on afternoon of 28 Feb, a reddening of the skin and small blisters." I want you to know that I talked to several of the MEDIVAC flight nurses who accompanied the troops out of the theater of operations, and they told me that *many of the men had no skin on them, that their skin was falling off.* Evidence of a chemical burn. So, this is known information. Some of the autopsies done at Dover, Delaware found that some of the deaths were due to chemical poisoning.

Schwartzkoff's NBC log continues, "Msgt Blue called. Subject: Commanders Guidance for Disposition of captured chemical and biological munitions." They had captured them and they knew they existed. Continuing, "field destruction is OK, but bulk destruction may have international implications." I have a number of these pages that were released under a FOIA request, and there are about 100 pages that were released to the Gulf War Veterans of Georgia. My hat is off to all the Gulf War Veterans that have been trying to take this message to the public for the last four years.

(Slide Shown) Anybody who was in Desert Storm knows what these are. The little "PB" pills which are a pre-treatment pill for a nerve agent. In other words, if you were going to be affected by a nerve agent such as Soman, you would take this pill in advance and it was supposed to help you. However, you should *never* take this unless you actually *are* affected, because it builds up in the body and it creates many problems.

International Media Comes to the U.S. to Investigate

(Slide Shown) This is an article that came out of the *Sunday Times* in London. The BBC has been over here investigating this quite heavily because they have so many people in England that are sick from all of this. The Italian equivalent to "60 Minutes" has been over here filming on the subject, because the Italian soldiers are sick also. It's country after country.

U.S. Companies Sold Iraq New Genocidal Anthrax Toxin

This is why I am scared about what is going on with the biological warfare. *It hasn't stopped*, because Saddam Hussein still has these things. Reading the *Sunday Times* article, we see that "Russia has developed a powerful new poison with no antidote that could be used in biological weapons. It is a variation of the anthrax toxin that causes death within days. *It has been genetically engineered to make it resistant to antibiotics.* The toxin is so powerful that *a tiny amount that would fit on a pinhead would theoretically kill 500,000 people.*" Can you imagine what that would do to the *WATER SUPPLY*? Saddam Hussein had *thousands of pounds of this substance* that was given to him *by United States companies.*

Veteran Medical Files Destroyed or Missing

Guess what happened to our veterans medical files? They are destroyed. There was actually an attorney who was sent to prison for destroying veterans medical files. Many of the medical files of Gulf War veterans are missing. No only are they missing, but now the proof that they received the vaccinations is now missing.

Gulf War Participants Force-Injected With Experimental Vaccines

Let's talk about how we were affected on the biological side. The first way was with the immunizations. We were given 10 or 11 immunizations prior to going to the gulf. We don't know everything we got. Some of us got sick afterwards. The Anthrax vaccinations were given over in the Gulf, in the theater of operations, *and you were forced to submit to it.* If you didn't take it, you were court-martialed. People were put into a room like this, the doors were locked, and they had security guards with side arm who stood by while people were forced to take this injection. Why? Why would they do this to people? The Anthrax "vaccine" had not been approved and was experimental. The injection for Botulism was also dangerous. All of these things in combination created a problem.

The Soviet Doctrine: The Biological Cocktail

But, the *real* problem that we believe to be the main transmission agent was via the SCUD-B and FROG missiles. You see, the SCUD missiles that Hussein used on us had biological and chemical agents in them. When the Patriots shot them down, it rained biological and chemical agents down on the troops. In terms of biological warfare, they used what is called the SOVIET DOCTRINE, in which 18-20 biological agents were mixed together in the tanks of the SCUD missiles. Because the batch contained so many biological agents, *it effectively confuses the diagnosis and the treatment process.* Now, ask yourself this.

Media Projects Responsibility on Iraq for U.S. Crimes

What is the press coming out and saying? If you read the media, which I hope you don't, you will see an article in the *Kansas City Star* on October 14th that said, "Iraq Sanctioned", in which they claimed "Iraq lied to us about having and using biological weapons." You know as well as I do that they have satellites in the sky that enable them to see what you are having for dinner. You know they knew what Hussein had, *because they sold it to them.* Absolutely.

This is what I want you to be watching for, because this is going to be the cover story. They are going to have to *deal* with the Gulf War illness because so many people have it now. In fact, I will tell you now that because we know that over 10,000 have already died, and we believe 500,000 of our Gulf War veterans to be sick, Dr. Nicholson told me that 20% of the people *around* the theater of operations (United Arab Emirates, Bahrain, etc.) are now sick. *It is coming to a place near you,* believe me. The chronic fatigue syndrome. I got a call from a doctor the other day who told me that he has 15 patients with CFS, *and they don't know anyone who went to the Gulf War.* It's transmissible through sex and through kissing, because it is now found in the dental floss test, where you can see evidence of the mycoplasma. It is communicable and it is going to be growing.

A doctor called me the other day, and he said, "I don't know what's going on. I volunteered to take care of these Gulf War veterans because the VA wouldn't take care of them, and now I'm sick with the same problem. Can you help me understand why I'm sick?" I said, "don't you know its a communicable disease?" He had no idea, because the official position of the U.S. Government is that "there is no Gulf War illness."

Peter Kawaja has been talking about the fact that "GF" was used during the war. Nobody ever mentioned "GF" or even heard of it, except Peter Kawaja, and he kept saying "GF was used." Well, the substance called "GF" is *made by the U.S. Department of the Army.* The government made it. I have evidence in the government logs of "GF" having been used during the war, but no one ever addressed "GF" until a *U.S. News and World Report* article came out on September 11, 1995. In this, they have the UN inspector going over to Iraq and inspecting the SCUDS and voicing the "sudden realization" that "Oh, they had all this nasty stuff over there after all that the Iraqis didn't tell us about". Well, I have evidence in a Pentagon report that shows that *we knew about it more than 30 days before the war started.* The U.S. government *knew* it was in the SCUDS, because the U.S. companies sold it to Iraq in the first place. It's interesting that in this story the UN inspector is trying to cover himself by saying what he did. The fact that "GF" is mentioned in Schwartzkoff's NBC log also proves the military knew it was there.

The True Origin of The "New" Emerging Biological Diseases is the Biological Cocktail Thrust on the Planet By U.S. Companies, Disguised in the Media as "Mysterious New Diseases" from "Nowhere" In Order to Cover Up Crimes Against Humanity and Genocide.

An article came out in *Scientific American* in October 1995 that was very fascinating reading. They have to deal with the results of this biological warfare, because too many people are getting sick and too many people are dying. How are they going to deal with it? The title of the article in *Scientific American* was, "Dangers from new viral plagues." Have you been seeing anything in the newspaper about Dengue fever in South America, or about these "strange" viral hemorragic diseases that are "*suddenly attacking us*" from "*nowhere* "? Guess what. *They came out of the Gulf War!* And, they are now calling it "emerging viruses". Hemorragic fever viruses are among the most dangerous biological agents known. The Ebola virus. *You didn't hear about that before the Gulf War, did you?*

The article in the *Scientific American* wants you to believe that all of a sudden we are going to be having all these incredible viruses, *all over the world*, appearing *for no reason at all.* Many biologists are saying that they never heard of any of these things before. How many of you ever heard of the Hantavirus before the Gulf War? Remember the Hantavirus in New Mexico, caused by "mouse droppings"? I guess we didn't have mouse droppings before the Gulf War, right? We didn't hear about Ebola before the Gulf War. We didn't hear so much about Chronic Fatigue before the Gulf War. A lot of these things we never had a problem with before the Gulf War. A lot of them were used during that time and supplied by United States companies.

Now, the media tells you "why" we are "going to have this incredible problem." *Scientific American* tells us, "the primary cause of most cases of hemorragic fever is ecological disruption resulting from human activity." In other words, we cut down too many trees in the rain forest and those bugs are going to get us. That's what they are trying to get you to believe, that it is because of cutting down too many trees in the rain forest. Well, they are calling them *hemorragic fever viruses* now. I've never heard of hemorragic fever viruses. I've been a nurse for 25 years and I have never heard about them. But, now *some of the Gulf War illnesses contain hemorragic fever viruses.* Some Gulf War veterans have called me and have said that they are bleeding from every part of their body. *It is similar to the Ebola virus,* but it takes two years to kill them - slowly. How many of you have seen the movie *Outbreak*? That is your homework.

Were the 1995 Chicago Heat Wave Deaths Really Something Else?

Why am I concerned about this? I was having lunch with Peter Kawaja, and I noticed this article in *USA Today*, and I couldn't believe what I was seeing. Remember when there was that period of incredible heatwaves in Chicago and all these people were dying? Well, look here in this article, where it shows lines of refrigerated trucks brought in to store bodies. Since when did we have so many bodies that we had to put them in trucks? This is the part that concerns me: The bodies were stored in *nine donated refrigerated trucks* that were *to be destroyed after use*. Now, if we went and destroyed every hospital and funeral home after a body was in there, we wouldn't have much left, would we? Why would they want to *destroy* the trucks? Were they *contaminated?* Was there a disease? I don't know. All I know is that *when you read material in the newspaper, check it out very carefully*. Ask questions! Don't assume they are telling you the whole story.

U.S. Ships Enough Biological Agents To Iraq to Kill the Entire Planet

(Slide Shown) Now, this was faxed to me by people in Britain. Remember that we said that this new Anthrax toxin could kill 500,000 people with an amount on the head of a pin? United States companies shipped Saddam Hussein *1,500 gallons* of Anthrax. It had already been loaded into bombs and missile warheads in Baghdad. Out of *39 tons* of biological warfare agents imported by Iraq from the United States, *each ton could have produced ten tons of biological warfare material.* How much *does* he need, anyway?

The Post Gulf-War Emergence of Flesh-Eating Bacteria

Over 50,000 U.S. and British troops have suffered symptoms, ranging from broken down immune systems to *wasting flesh*. How many of you have heard of *flesh-eating bacteria*? Didn't hear about it before the Gulf War, did you? Wonder why? It's part of it. Some of the Gulf War babies are born with flesh-eating bacteria already hard at work.

U.S. Government Increases Budget to Bury Veterans But Denies Them Money for Assistance

(Slide Shown) This is an article from a British newspaper. It says, "the U.S. Defense Department has increased its budget for burial of Gulf War veterans." They haven't announced this too widely in the United States, have they? That's what they are doing. They are denying the problem exists, denying that biological weapons were used, and increasing the capability to bury people. How can we treat people like this?

The Attempt to Bring George Bush to a War Crimes Tribunal Thwarted by U.S. "Justice" Department in 1993

Did you know that George Bush was almost brought up before a Grand Jury? He was subpoenaed in an illegal export case that involved shipment of biological agents to Saddam Hussein. You didn't know about that, did you? He was. In 1993 the "Justice Department" said, "he doesn't have to do it." George Bush was brought up before a *war crimes tribunal*. You didn't know about that either, right? Get the book by Ramsey Clark.

Emergence of Post-Gulf War Biological Problems Coincides With Massive National Injection Programs

So, what are we doing in America? *We are inoculating everybody.* Why? Why is the government so big on inoculating everybody? Every newspaper in the country had a front page color picture of inoculation. They are trying to justify it. Why? In Houston, you can drive down a certain street where they have nurses lined up along the street. You put your arm out the window of the car and they inject you. Why? America, we have to stop holding out our arms to anybody that comes along and says, "We're from the government. We are going to help you. You need this shot". Why do I need this shot? I got too many shots during the Gulf War and I paid dearly for it. I will never do that again. Know your rights.

U.S. Troops Inoculated Before Going to Bosnia Are Coming Down With the Same Symptoms

(Slide Shown) Why does this picture appear in the paper? *They are inoculating all the troops going to Bosnia.* I am just now starting to get reports from the troops in Bosnia that *some of them now have the characteristic rash,* which is a cardinal clinical sign *of the Gulf War Illness.* Its the only sign you can see at this early stage, until they start losing weight, their hair, and start aging. Many people come to me when they discover that they have this rash. It's a sign of *biological and chemical warfare. WE ARE DOING IT TO OUR TROOPS IN BOSNIA.*

U.S. Troops Inoculated Before Going to Somalia Are Coming Down With the Same Symptoms

The U.S. troops that are coming back from Somalia are coming back sick, too, with all the same symptoms and problems as the Persian Gulf veterans.

Bush and Clinton "Justice Departments" Refuse to Prosecute. Bio-weapon Supply Companies Under the Trading With the Enemy Act

Now, I want to show you this. It appeared in *Media Bypass* recently. It was January 1996. In this issue, Sarah McClendon, who was a wire service person in Washington, has kind of seen the light. She is in her 80's now, but she follows every story. I want you to see what she has written, because she was a "government person" beforehand. And now, I will tell you, that she has truly "changed sides."

She writes, "Proof is building up stronger than ever that big U.S. corporations [Editor Note: The U.S. Government is also a corporation] made the weapons that Saddam Hussein used to kill American soldiers in the Persian Gulf War. These corporations also provided the chemical and biological weapons that the Iraqis used to make thousands of surviving soldiers ill. *Both the Bush and Clinton Administration Justice Departments agreed not to prosecute for TRADING WITH THE ENEMY.*"

Excerpt #3

Media Mistakenly Releases Truth About Doxycycline Then Issues Cover-up Stories

(Slide Shown) Ok, this just came out the other day. I was in Connecticut doing a radio show on the Gulf War issue, and I was taking a break for a commercial, when all of a sudden CBS radio comes over the main feed and says, "the Gulf War illness is found to be helped by the antibiotic Doxycycline." I couldn't believe it. We pushed the federal government to admitting this.

[Editor Note: I thought you might find it interesting that CBS has had long time connections to the Central Intelligence Agency]

I called CBS news and they faxed me the news release. I thought, "now they'll be able to get Doxycycline from the military." Guess what happens the next day. Good old Associated Press, the cover-up news agency, comes out with "Report Urges More Attention to Psychological Problems". Here we are, back again, to saying that all the symptoms are psychological. And so they had another cover-up news release that came out just this past week to cover-up the one that came out that told the truth. That's what's happening.

[31] U.S. Develops Lethal New Viruses

29 October 03

http://www.newscientist.com/article/dn4318-us-develops-lethal-new-viruses.html

A scientist funded by the US government has deliberately created an extremely deadly form of mousepox, a relative of the smallpox virus, through genetic engineering. The new virus kills all mice even if they have been given antiviral drugs as well as a vaccine that would normally protect them. The work has not stopped there. The cowpox virus, which infects a range of animals including humans, has been genetically altered in a similar way. The new virus, which is about to be tested on animals, should be lethal only to mice, Mark Buller of the University of St Louis told New Scientist. He says his work is necessary to explore what bioterrorists might do.

But the research brings closer the prospect of pox viruses that cause only mild infections in humans being turned into diseases lethal even to people who have been vaccinated. And vaccines are currently our main defence against smallpox and its relatives, such as the monkeypox that reached the US this year. Some researchers think the latest research is risky and unnecessary.

"I have great concern about doing this in a pox virus that can cross species," said Ian Ramshaw of the Australian National University in Canberra on being told of Buller's work. Ramshaw was a member of the team that accidentally discovered how to make mousepox more deadly (New Scientist, 13 January 2001). But the modified mousepox his team created was not as deadly as Buller's.

No rebound

Since then, Ramshaw told New Scientist, his team has also created more deadly forms of mousepox, and has used the same method to engineer a more deadly rabbitpox virus. But this research revealed that the modified pox viruses are not contagious, he says. That is good news in the sense that these viruses could not cause ecological havoc by wiping out mouse or rabbit populations around the world if they escaped from a lab. However, this discovery also means some bioterrorists might be more tempted to use the same trick to modify a pox virus that infects humans. Such a disease, like anthrax, would infect only those directly exposed to it. It would not spread around the world and rebound on the attackers. But there is no guarantee that other pox viruses modified in a similar way would also be non-contagious. Ramshaw's team made its initial discovery while developing contraceptive vaccines for sterilising mice and rabbits without killing them. The researchers modified the mousepox virus by adding a gene for a natural immunosuppressant called IL-4, expecting this would boost antibody production. Instead, the modified mousepox virus was far more lethal, killing 60 per cent of vaccinated mice. The addition of IL-4 seems to switch off a key part of the immune system called the cell-mediated response.

Maximised production

Now Buller has engineered a mousepox strain that kills 100 per cent of vaccinated mice, even when they were also treated with the antiviral drug cidofovir. A monoclonal antibody that mops up IL-4 did save some, however. His team "optimised" the virus by placing the IL-4 gene in a different part of the viral genome and adding a promoter sequence to maximise production of the IL-4 protein, he told a biosecurity conference in Geneva last week. Buller has also constructed a cowpox virus containing the mouse IL-4 gene, which is about to be tested on mice at the US Army Medical Research Institute of Infectious Diseases at Fort Detrick, Maryland.

Cowpox infects people, but Buller says the IL-4 protein is species-specific and would not affect the human immune system. The experiments are being done at the second-highest level of biological containment. Ramshaw says there is no reason to do the cowpox experiments, as his group's work on rabbits has already shown the method works for other pox viruses. While viruses containing mouse IL-4 should not be lethal to humans, recombinant viruses can have unexpected effects, he says. "You'd hope the combination remains mouse-specific." Why his group's engineered viruses are not contagious is a mystery, he says. It is not, for instance, because the host dies faster than usual, taking the virus with it. But his findings could explain why pox viruses containing IL-4 have never evolved naturally, even though the viruses frequently pick up genes that affect their host's immunity.

Despite the concerns, work on lethal new pox viruses seems likely to continue in the US. When members of the audience in Geneva questioned the need for such experiments, an American voice in the back boomed out: "Nine-eleven". There were murmurs of agreement. Debora MacKenzie, Geneva

[32] The True Origin and Nature of AIDS
http://www.whale.to/v/cantwell3.html
The Secret Origin of AIDS and HIV: How scientists produced the most horrifying plague of all time - and then covered it up.
by Alan Cantwell, Jr. M.D. (Written in 2000)

The Green Monkey Theory

Many people have heard the theory that AIDS is man-made. Thirty percent of New York City blacks polled by The New York Times (October 29, 1990) actually believe AIDS is an "ethnic weapon" designed in a laboratory to infect and kill black people. Some people even think the AIDS conspiracy theory is more plausible than the African Green monkey theory promoted by the leading AIDS scientists. Actually, the monkey theory was proven wrong by researchers as far back as 1988, but most AIDS educators continued to promote it to the public until recently. In a media blitz in 1999, the green monkey theory was totally replaced by the chimpanzee "out of Africa" theory, and the chimp origin of AIDS was fully accepted by the scientific community.

A phylogenetic "family tree" of primate viruses (which few people could understand) was presented to prove that HIV was descended from a primate virus in the African bush. Analysis of virus genetic data performed by the "supercomputer" at Los Alamos in New Mexico indicated that HIV had "jumped species" from a chimp to a human around the year 1930 in Africa. (Los Alamos is the official home of nuclear bomb-building, alleged Chinese spies, and the laboratory which directed secret human radiation experiments on unsuspecting civilians from the 1940s up to the beginning of the AIDS epidemic.) At the international AIDS conference held in 2000 in South Africa, one scientist claimed the chimpanzee virus (SIVcpz) was "ancient" and jumped species as early as 1675 but didn't establish itself in the human population until 1930. This was dutifully reported by science writer Laurie Garrett, who give all the time-honored reasons for the rapid spread of AIDS in Africa: non-sterile needles, non-sterile blood products and widespread promiscuous sexual behavior.

The Special Virus Cancer Program (1962-1977)

Conveniently forgotten by scientists and medical journalists was the fact that surgeons had been transplanting chimpanzee parts into human beings for decades. When Keith Reemtsma died in June 2000, at age 74, he was hailed as a pioneer in cross-species organ transplants (now known as xenotransplantation). By 1964 he had already placed six chimpanzee kidneys into six patients. All his patients died, but eventually Reemtsma succeeded in many successful human-to-human organ transplants.

Much more likely to have spread animal viruses to human beings is the largely forgotten Special Virus Cancer Program (SVCP). This research program was responsible for the development, the seeding, and the deployment of various animal viruses, which were capable of producing cancer and immune system damage when transferred between animal species and into human cells and tissue.

The SVCP began in 1964 as a government-funded program of the National Cancer Institute (NCI) in Bethesda, Maryland. Originally designed to study leukemia and lymphoma forms of cancer, the program was soon enlarged to study all forms of cancer. The SVCP marshalled many of the nation's finest virologists, biochemists, immunologists, molecular biologists, and epidemiologists, at the most prestigious institutions in a coordinated attempt to assess the role of viruses in causing human cancer. Many of the top AIDS scientists, including Dr. Robert Gallo (the co-discoverer of HIV), Myron (Max) Essex (of "cat AIDS" fame), and Peter Duesberg (who claims HIV is not the cause of AIDS), were connected with the Program.

The scope of the program was international and included scientists from Japan, Sweden, Italy, the Netherlands, Israel, and even Uganda, Africa. A main mission of the SVCP was to collect various human and animal cancers from around the world and to grow large amounts of cancer-causing viruses. In the process, many animal viruses were adapted to human cells. These cultured viruses would then be shipped to researchers throughout the world.

An annual report of the accomplishments of the SVCP was published by the NCI. The 1971 SVCR report indicates a mouse leukemia virus had been adapted to grow in human cells. A "hybrid virus" - a mixture of a mouse sarcoma and a cat (feline) leukemia virus - was engineered and grown in cat cells. Chicken and feline retroviruses produced cancer in monkeys. Mouse-cat virus hybrids and feline leukemia virus were adapted to human cells in tissue culture. Thus, "species jumping" was a common occurrence in these experiments.

Biological Warfare, Primate Research and the SVCP

Also joining forces with the SVCP at the NCI were the military's biological warfare researchers. On October 18, 1971, President Richard Nixon announced that the army's biowarfare laboratories at nearby Fort Detrick, Maryland, would be converted to research on the cause, prevention, and treatment of cancer. As part of Nixon's so-called War on Cancer, the military biowarfare unit was renamed the new Frederick Cancer Research Center. Litton Bionetics was named as the military's prime contractor for this project.

The 1971 annual report noted that one of the primary tasks of the now jointly connected National Cancer Institute-Frederick Cancer Research Center was "the large scale production of oncogenic (cancer-causing) and suspected oncogenic viruses to meet research needs on a continuing basis." Special attention was given to primate viruses (the alleged African source of HIV) and "the successful propagation of significant amounts of human candidate viruses." Candidate viruses were animal or human viruses that might be capable of initiating human cancers. And primate cancer-causing viruses were adapted to 'normal' human cells. A steady supply of research animals (monkeys, chimpanzees, mice, and cats) was necessary, which resulted in the establishment of breeding colonies for the SVCP. Healthy animals were shipped in from various parts of the world for breeding purposes and experimentation; and virus-infected animals were shipped out again to various labs.

By 1971, a total of 2,274 primates had been inoculated at Bionetics Research Laboratories, under contract to Fort Detrick. Over 1000 of these monkeys had already died or had been transferred to other primate centers. (Some animals were eventually released back into the wild). By this time, experimenters had spread lymphoma-producing viruses into several species of monkeys, and had also isolated a monkey virus (Herpesvirus saimiri) that would have a close genetic relationship to a new Kaposi's sarcoma virus that produced the "gay cancer" of AIDS a few years later.

In order to prime primates and other research animals to acquire cancer, their immune system was deliberately suppressed by drugs, radiation, or cancer-causing chemicals or substances. The thymus gland and/or the spleen was removed, and viruses were injected into newborn animals or into the womb of pregnant animals. Some animals were also injected with malaria to keep them chronically sick and immunodepressed.

Primates (especially newborn and baby chimpanzees) were the most favored lab animals because they were most similar biochemically and immunologically to human beings, and because there would be no official testing of these lab viruses on humans. An irradiated rhesus monkey colony supplied animals for transplantation experiments.

Robert Gallo was a project officer of a primate study contracted by Bionetics that pumped cancerous human tissue, as well as a variety of chicken and monkeys viruses into newborn macaques (a small species of monkey). This 1971 SVCP report (NIH-71-2025) declared: "Inasmuch as tests for the biological activity of candidate human viruses will not be tested in the human species, it is imperative that another system be developed for these determinations and, subsequently for the evaluation of vaccines or other measure of control. The close phylogenetic relationship of the lower primates of man justifies utilization of these animals for these purposes." Researchers at Bionetics evaluated the long-term cancer effects of injecting human and animal cancer material into various species of monkeys. Newborn monkeys, irradiated monkeys, and monkeys primed with cancer-causing chemicals, were injected with blood ("using multiple sites and volumes as large as possible") taken from various forms of human leukemia. In other studies, tissue cultures infected with various animal viruses were inoculated into primates. Many kinds of human cancer tissue were injected into the animals. How many "new" and "emerging" viruses were created and adapted by the SVCP is not known. And it is unlikely that complete records of this animal cancer virus experimentation will ever be examined.

Cats were also bred for leukemia and sarcoma cancer studies. An inbred germ free colony of mice was established. Mouse cancer viruses were manipulated to produce resistant and non-resistant strains. These adapted viruses would be employed in the 1980s in human gene replacement experiments. Such experiments utilized a weakened strain of the mouse leukemia virus to infect and "taxi-in" the missing genes to genetically-defective human cells.

The End of the SVCP and the Birth of AIDS

By 1977 the SVCP came to a inglorious end. According to Gallo, "Scientifically, the problem was that no one could supply clear evidence of any kind of human tumor virus, not even a DNA virus, and most researchers refused to concede that viruses played any role in human cancers. Politically, the Virus Cancer Program was vulnerable because it attracted a great deal of money and attention and had failed to produce dramatic, visible results."

Despite all this, the SCVP was the birthplace of genetic engineering, molecular biology, and the human genome project. More than any other program it built up the field of animal retrovirology, which led to the vital understanding of cancer and immunosuppressive retroviruses in humans. Like manna from heaven, AIDS in gays put the virologists back in business. And HIV, a cancer-causing and immunosuppressive retrovirus, would make Robert Gallo the most famous scientist in the world.

Few people understand clearly that AIDS is a new form of cancer, and this aspect of AIDS has not been publicized for obvious reasons. Physicians have always told their patients that cancer is not contagious or sexually transmitted. Virologists wanted AIDS and "gay cancer" to be a new disease because HIV was supposedly brand new. It was easier to blame gays for initiating this new disease with their sexual lifestyle than it was to point the finger at scientists. And if AIDS was connected to animal cancer research, some people might wonder if the new disease had anything to do with all those species jumping experiments in the 1970s. Making people understand that AIDS is cancer would only confuse them. And so, instead of looking for the source of HIV in the thousands of animal cancer experiments performed throughout the world, the virologists insisted on looking for the source of the virus in primates in the African rainforest.

The Pre-AIDS Gay Hepatitis B Experiments (1978-1981)

As the SVCP was winding down, thousands of gay men were signing up as guinea pigs for government-sponsored hepatitis B vaccine experiments in New York, Los Angeles, and San Francisco. In a few years these cities would become the epicenters for "gay-related immune deficiency syndrome," later known as AIDS. Could virus-contaminated vaccines lie at the root of AIDS? In the early 1970s the hepatitis B vaccine was developed in chimpanzees, now widely accepted as the animal from which HIV supposedly evolved. To this day, some people are fearful about taking the hepatitis B vaccine because of its original connection to gay men and AIDS; and older physicians remember the original experimental hepatitis vaccine was made from the pooled blood serum of hepatitis-infected homosexuals.

Was HIV "introduced" into gays during these vaccine trials when thousands of homosexuals were injected in New York beginning in 1978, and in the West Coast cities in 1980-1981? AIDS first erupted in gays living in New York City in 1979 a few months after the experiment began in Manhattan. The astounding and statistically significant fact is that 20% of the gay men who volunteered for the hepatitis B experiment in New York were discovered to be HIV-positive in 1980 (a year before AIDS became "official" in 1981). This would mean that Manhattan men had the highest incidence of HIV anywhere in the world, including Africa, the supposed birthplace of HIV and AIDS. The fact is that definite, proven cases of AIDS in Africa would not appear until 1982.

Some researchers are convinced that these vaccine experiments served as the vehicle through which HIV was "introduced" into the gay population in America. Nevertheless, AIDS scientists have downplayed any connection of AIDS with the vaccine. My own extensive research into the hepatitis B experiments is presented in AIDS and the Doctors of Death: An Inquiry into the Origin of the AIDS Epidemic, published in 1988. Also included in this book is evidence suggesting "patient Zero" story of 1987, which claimed a promiscuous gay Canadian airline steward brought AIDS to America. Montagnier "is doubtful that the American epidemic could have developed from a single patient." Montagnier admits that he stands apart from Robert Gallo on many matters. In a mind-blowing statement he declares "Gallo was not a medical doctor, but rather a biochemist by training. His limited experience with viruses at the time perhaps explains his misinterpretations and the contaminations that occurred in his laboratory." (Gallo has always declared himself as a physician. If he is not, then we certainly do have a conspiracy problem on our hands.) What is obvious from their authored books is that while the continent of Africa dies, these two top scientists in AIDS research continue their vendetta in print, and continue to promote their own pet theories on the origin of HIV and AIDS to an adoring scientific community.

"Gay and Straight" Strains of HIV and Sexual Preference

It is common knowledge that AIDS is a heterosexual disease in Africa, and that AIDS started exclusively as a gay disease in the United States. Although the public was told early on that "no one is immune from AIDS", the fact remains that even now (20 years after the first AIDS cases) 80% of the new AIDS cases in America are gay men, IV drug addicts, and their sexual partners. Why is this? Certainly HIV does not discriminate between sexual preference and race! Or does it?

In the mid-1990s molecular biologists identified at least 8 different subtypes (or "clades" or "strains") of HIV that were infecting various people around the world. Remarkably, it turns out that the "B" strain is the predominant strain infecting gays in the U.S. Even more remarkable is that this strain of HIV has an "affinity" to infect rectal tissue, thus explaining why gays are more likely to get AIDS than straights. In contrast, the HIV strains common in Africa have an affinity for vaginal and cervical cells, as well as for cells of the foreskin of the penis. Thus, HIV is more likely to infect heterosexuals in Africa.

How do we know this? Max Essex (a Harvard veterinarian who performed pre-AIDS experiments transferring feline leukemia virus between cat populations) tested subtype E strains of HIV from Thailand. He discovered that this Asian strain readily infected women's genital cells of the vagina and cervix. But the "gay" B strain of HIV did not infect them as easily. AIDS experts tell us American AIDS came from Africa, but the strain of HIV prevalent in gay men is almost never seen in Africa! How is this possible? Were strains of HIV engineered to adapt easily to cells likely to be infected in gay sex? Or adapted to genital cells involved in vaginal sex? We know scientists in the SVCP were able to adapt certain retroviruses to infect specific kinds of cells. As early as 1970 biowarfare scientists were learning to design certain infectious agents (particularly viruses) that would attack the cells of certain racial groups.

More recently, in 1997, Stephen O'Brien and Michael Dean of the Laboratory of Genomic Diversity at the National Cancer Institute have shown that one out of ten white people have AIDS-resistant genes, whereas blacks in Africa have none. Is this simply another peculiarity of a virus that jumped species in the African bush? Or is HIV a designer virus, specifically adapted in its subtypes to infect certain racial groups and gay people?

When AIDS appeared in 1981, health officials assured the "general public" that there was nothing to fear. "AIDS is a gay disease" was the phrase repeated over and over again in a media blitz. As late as 1987, Robert Gallo told Playboy reporter David Black, "I personally don't know of a single case (in America) of a man getting the (AIDS) virus from a woman through heterosexual intercourse."

In Africa, where AIDS affects men and women in equal numbers, Gallo's explanation to Black was: "It happens, but that may be due to differences in sexual practices, more promiscuity or to a greater incidence of venereal disease." Gallo give Playboy his reassurance of the future of heterosexual AIDS in America: "AIDS will never become an overwhelming danger to the general public."

Solving the Mystery of the Origin of AIDS

The pre-AIDS species jumping experiments of the Special Virus Cancer Program (SVCP) have been largely expunged from the history of HIV and AIDS. The viral contamination problems inherent in viral research have also been downplayed. As a result, the origin of HIV and AIDS has been distorted and obscured.

A serious examination of the SVCP provides "missing links" to the possible laboratory origin of HIV. The ability of SVCP scientists to produce "new" diseases with cancer-causing animal viruses is a matter of record. The ability of animal viruses to easily contaminate laboratory experiments and vaccine manufacture is also well known. All these factors make the man-made theory of AIDS rational and compelling.

Some areas of HIV/AIDS history that require further analysis are:

The connection between AIDS and cancer

The connection of HIV to known (pre-AIDS) animal cancer lab viruses

The connection of the SVCP to the outbreak of AIDS

The connection of vaccine programs to the outbreak of AIDS

The connection of biological warfare research to the outbreak of AIDS

The disinformation surrounding the origin of AIDS

The disinformation blaming the "victims" of AIDS for the disease

The total secrecy of biological warfare and its implications for science

The wedding of cancer and AIDS scientists to biological warfare scientists

The "sworn to secrecy" problem of the government/military scientists

The wedding of government to medical science for military b/w purposes

The long history of secret medical experiments on unsuspecting citizens

All these factors need to be explored more fully and impartially in order to more fully elucidate the man-made, laboratory origin of HIV and AIDS. To continue to ignore these issues is to ignore the fate of countless millions who will die from AIDS and other "emerging viruses" in the future. The Special Virus Cancer Program (and biowarfare experimentation worldwide) has forever changed the course of history of medical science, resulting in the current dangers of biological terrorism and the fear of newly emerging man-made viruses and other infectious agents. To study the theories of origin of HIV/AIDS and to ignore the SVCP with its biowarfare implications is like studying the Holocaust and failing to mention the Nazis. Some readers may find this analogy offensive, but in light of the close connection of the SVCP with the outbreak of HIV and AIDS, it is suggested that final judgement be reserved until all the pertinent facts are ascertained.

The SVCP and "the hand of man" lie at the root of HIV. The flowering of the worldwide epidemic of AIDS is proof that the seeds were well planted.

REFERENCES:

Butel JS: Simian virus 40, poliovirus vaccines, and human cancer: research progress versus media and public interests. Bulletin World Health Organization 78:195-198, 2000.

Cantwell Jr, A: AIDS & The Doctors of Death: An Inquiry into the Origin of the AIDS Epidemic. Los Angeles: Aries Rising Press, 1988.

Cantwell Jr, A: Queer Blood: The Secret AIDS Genocide Plot. Los Angeles: Aries Rising Press, 1993.

Cantwell AR Jr: Bacteriologic investigation and histologic observations of variably acid-fast bacteria in three cases of Kaposi's sarcoma. Growth 45: 79-89, 1981.

Cantwell AR Jr: Kaposi's sarcoma and variably acid-fast bacteria in vivo in two homosexual men. Cutis 32: 58-64,68, 1983.

Cantwell AR Jr: The Cancer Microbe. Los Angeles: Aries Rising Press, 1990.

Cantwell AR Jr: "Gay cancer, emerging viruses, and AIDS." New Dawn (Melbourne), Sept 1998.

Connor S: "AIDS science on trial." New Scientist, February 12, 1987, pp 49-58.

Faden RR (Chair): The Human Radiation Experiments: Final Report of the President's Advisory Committee. New York: Oxford University Press, 1996.

Gallo R: Virus Hunting: AIDS, Cancer and the Human Retrovirus. New York: Basic Books, 1991.

Garrett L: "AIDS virus traced to 1675." Newsday, July 11,2000.

Gold M: A Conspiracy of Cells. Albany, NY: State University of New York Press, 1986

Hatch R: Cancer Warfare. Covert Action Bulletin 39, Winter, 1991.

"HIV sub-types showing signs of spreading differently," All Things Considered (NPR), 10-02-1995.

Hooper E: The River: A Journey to the Source of HIV and AIDS. Boston, MA: Little, Brown and Company, 1999

Horowitz LG: Emerging Viruses: AIDS & Ebola. Rockport, MA: Tetrahedron Publishing Group, 1996.

Larson CA: Ethnic weapons. Military Review, Nov 1970, pp 3-11.

Ljungqvist KI: AIDS Tabu. Stockholm: Carlssons Bokforlag, 1992.

Mathew A, Ennis FA, Rothman AL: Transient decreases in human T cell proliferative responses following vaccinia immunization. Clin Immunol 96: 100-107, 2000.

Montagnier L: Virus. New York: WW Norton Co, Inc, 2000.

O'Brien SJ, Dean M: In search of AIDS-resistence genes. Scientific American, September 1997, pp 28-35.

O'Brien TR, Kedes D, Gamem D, et al: Evidence for concurrent epidemics of human herpesvirus 8, and human immunodeficiency virus type I in US homosexual men: rates, risk factors, and relationship to Kaposi's sarcoma. J Infectious Disease 180: 1010-1017, 1999.

Special Virus Cancer Program (Progress Report #8). Bethesda, MD: National Institutes of Health, July 1971.

Special Virus Cancer Program (Progress Report #9). Bethesda, MD: National Institutes of Health, July 1972.

Stevens CE, Taylor PE, Zang EA, et al: Human T-cell lymphotropic virus type III infection in a cohort of homosexual men in New York City. JAMA 255; 2167-2172, 1986.

Quinnan GV Jr (Ed): Vaccinia Viruses as Vectors for Vaccine Antigens. New York: Elsevier, 1985.

Related Websites:

http://www.bhc.edu/EastCampus/leeb/aids/index.html

http://aidsbiowar.com

Acknowledgement: I am grateful to Robert E Lee, Vincent Gammill, Billi Goldberg, and Boyd "Ed" Graves, for their contributions of research material for this study.

[Dr. Cantwell is a medical researcher and author of AIDS & The Doctors of Death, and Queer Blood, both published by Aries Rising Press, PO Box 29532, Los Angeles, CA 90029, USA. These books are available on the Internet at Amazon.com, Barnes & Noble, or through mail order at Book Clearing House @ 1-800-431-1579.]

[33] Bio-Weapons Labs and the Fight To Prevent Them

BACKYARD BIOWEAPONS: BIOLABS, BIODEFENSE, BIOTECH, & $ BILLIONS will be one of the major themes at Biodevastation 7: A Forum on Environmental Racism, World Agriculture and Biowarfare

May 16 - 18, 2003, St. Louis, Missouri, www.biodev.org

After sabotaging a UN inspection system for biological weapons research facilities, the Bush Administration is spending billions in a massive expansion of America's biodefense program. Communities across the country are confronting bioweapons in their backyards. With biological weapons, offense and defense are virtually inseparable. From Boston to Honolulu, more than three dozen new "hot zones" have been proposed. These labs are said to be necessary to defend the US from biological terrorists; but the biodefense program itself is the bigger threat to peace, health, and the environment. These labs will store and grow the world's most dangerous organisms and genetically engineered diseases. They will train hundreds, perhaps thousands, in the perverted science of making biological weapons. Few of the priority diseases pose a significant health threat in the US. But as public health systems crumble, federal money has been found to genetically engineer anthrax. Secrecy at the labs threatens biological weapons control and surrounding communities. Government agencies with atrocious records of public accountability will finance and operate them, including the Departments of Defense, Energy, and Homeland Security. When you mix biotech, the military, and billions of dollars you get profound dangers to people, the environment, and peace. You can hear from those opposing this new military-biotech frontier at the panel on "Backyard Bioweapons." This Biodevastation 7 panel will bring together activists resisting the out-of-control expansion of research on bioweapons. Speakers will discuss:

* the US Army's plans for Dugway Proving Ground in Utah,
* how nuclear weapons maker Lawrence Livermore National Lab wants to go biological,
* Boston University's big secret—a $1.6 billion lab plan for Boston's South End,
* the University of Texas' monster facility in Galveston, and
* how a five pound primate may have sunk a $200 million University of California scheme.

[34] Lab Accident Explained As Outbreak Of Rare Disease
http://www.organicconsumers.org/meat/hoofspreading.cfm
English Hoof-and-Mouth Disease Spreading
Published Monday, February 26, 2001

Livestock Disease Spreads in Britain
By LAURA KING / Associated Press Writer

LONDON (AP)—Racehorses stayed in their stables. Soldiers stood down from a military maneuver. Zoo-goers who hoped to see an elephant or a giraffe went away disappointed. The ripple effects of Britain' s week-old outbreak of foot-and-mouth disease spread far beyond the farm Monday, as all sorts of everyday activities were curtailed in the struggle to stem the virulent livestock ailment. More new cases cropped up, bringing to 12 the number of farms or slaughterhouses where the highly contagious infection has been found. More than 7, 000 animals—mainly pigs, cows and sheep—have been slaughtered in Britain, and another 3, 500 killed in continental Europe, where no cases have been found but authorities fear the disease could spread. " This is a nightmare for the whole farming community, " said farm leader Ben Gill, who met Monday with Prime Minister Tony Blair. "People are scared out of their wits."

[35] It is highly possible that this refers to the SARS virus which emerged in 2003.

[36] Sanctioned or Organized Acts Of Aggression

1. The World Trade Centre on September 11, 2001
2. The Bali Bombings in October, 2002
3. The Second Gulf War in 2003
4. The weekly incidents of terrorism in the Middle East and Far East

[37] Media Control

" I have the greatest admiration for your propaganda. Propaganda in the West is carried out by experts who have had the best training in the world—in the field of advertizing—and have mastered the techniques with exceptional proficiency ... Yours are subtle and persuasive; ours are crude and obvious ... I think that the fundamental

difference between our worlds, with respect to propaganda, is quite simple. You tend to believe yours ... and we tend to disbelieve ours. "

a Soviet correspondent based five years in the U.S.

The site below has a list of timely books and articles regarding the manipulation of the truth by the world's media sources. http://www.thirdworldtraveler.com/Media_control_propaganda/Media_Control.html

[38] Loss of Personal Freedom By Government Mandate
The USA Patriot Act passed October 25, 2001
http://www.eff.org/Privacy/Surveillance/Terrorism/20011025_hr3162_usa_patriot_bill.html

[39] Genocide in Rwanda
http://edition.cnn.com/WORLD/

Extract from CNN Online: June 4, 1998

UNITED NATIONS (CNN)—CNN has learned a report submitted by a human rights team investigating massacres in the former Zaire uses the term "genocide" in concluding what happened to thousands of Rwandan refugees as they were forced back into Rwanda in 1994. The report, still under review by senior U.N. officials, was seen by a source before it was turned over to U.N. Secretary-General Kofi Annan.

Following the Rwanda genocide of 1994, in which an estimated 500,000 minority Tutsi and Hutu moderates were killed, surviving refugees were forced into the former Zaire and neighboring countries. The human rights team has been investigating the massacres that resulted when the refugees were forced out of Zaire. The report says forces loyal to Democratic Republic of the Congo President Laurent Kabila may have committed serious human rights violations and that there may have been serious "crimes against humanity". Investigators also told the U.N. the real investigation has not begun yet.

[40] Rwanda: Four In Five Deaths Aids-related

May 2, 2000. More than four out of every five deaths in Rwanda are now Aids-related, according to government officials. The figure - which covers the past three months - was given at an international conference on Aids by Rwandan health minister Ezechias Rwabuhihi. He told delegates that 70% of patients in the main hospital in Kigali were suffering from illnesses related to HIV - the virus which causes Aids. The startling figures add to a picture of devastation caused by Aids in Africa. In Tanzania, President Benjamin Mkapa said on Monday that Aids was ravaging the country's economy and government - leading to a shortage of trained workers. These latest developments follow a recent warning by the United States that the spread of the Aids epidemic throughout the world had become so serious that it was a threat to international security.

Around 500,000 Rwandans, more than 6% of the population, are infected with HIV, the country's health minister announced on Tuesday. As a poor country, Minister Rwabuhihi said, Rwanda simply cannot cope with the devastation caused by the disease. "We are facing a silent and devastating epidemic which threatens national security," Mr Rwabuhihi told a conference attended by delegates from Rwanda, Burundi and Uganda. In some areas, hospitals were so overcrowded that Aids patients were often kept two to a bed. "Our hospitals are overwhelmed, the staff is overwhelmed, some services of the internal medicine are overwhelmed," the minister said. "This is not a bearable situation."

In his May Day address, Tanzanian President Mkapa's said that the country was losing large numbers of trained workers to Aids. Some ministries were losing up to 20 employees a month. Mr Mkapa urged religious leaders to drop their opposition to even discussing the issue. "I pray that religious leaders consider the stark reality in the light of the current situation and the given statistics," the president said. An estimated 20% of Tanzanians are infected with the HIV virus. The World Bank has estimated that if Aids continues to spread at its current rate, the Tanzanian economy will shrink by up to 25% by 2015.

[41] California Earthquake Rang Planet Like A Bell
December 23, 2002 11:30 AM PST
http://fddp.theage.com.au/articles/2003/12/23/1071941725870.html?from=storyrhs

California's largest earthquake in four years struck today, causing Planet Earth to ring "like a bell" and mountains to grow 30cm taller, geologists said. The magnitude 6.5 quake hit near the coastal city of San Simeon almost exactly half way between San Francisco and Los Angeles, setting high-rise buildings swaying in both cities. Earthquakes relieve pressure between clashing continental plates. The plates float on the earth's mantle, which has a putty like consistency and moves as the earth's core heats it. Today one piece of crust shoved beneath another about 7.6km beneath the surface of the earth and at the intersection of the Pacific and North American plates, US Geological Survey seismologists said. That sent tremors along America's west coast and beyond.

"For an earthquake this size, every single sand grain on the planet dances to the music of those seismic waves," the Geological Survey spokesman Ross Stein said at a news conference. "You may not be able to feel them, but the entire planet is rung like a bell."

[42] Lasers Uncover Stonehenge Secrets
High-tech lasers have been used to unlock the secrets of Stonehenge.
http://news.bbc.co.uk/go/pr/fr/-/2/hi/uk_news/england/wiltshire/3196284.stm

Story from BBC NEWS: Published: 2003/10/16 The work at the ancient site in Wiltshire has already found two carvings which are invisible to the naked eye. The markings left by bronze axe heads are between four and six inches long. Similar carvings were found at the site in the 1950s, but archaeologists say these are now too badly eroded to be seen. The research by Wessex Archaeology and 3D laser scan firm Archaeoptics began in the summer of 2002. They used a low-powered laser beam to scan the stones without causing damage to the rock's structure. Three stones have been scanned to date, and the investigating team insists a full survey of all 83 would probably reveal more carvings. "The laser scanning has opened up a whole new way of seeing Stonehenge," said Tom Goskar of Wessex Archaeology. "With more time we could uncover many more and make plainer the outline of some known carvings that are difficult to see. "This would give us a much better idea of the extent of the carvings and help us achieve a greater understanding of the monument."

[43] New discoveries in Xihetan Ruins in NW China, Oct.9, 2003 http://english.peopledaily.com.cn/200310/09/eng20031009_125622.shtml

Household items, including stone and bone vessels, dating back 4,000 years have been unearthed at the Xihetan Ruins, in northwest China's Gansu Province. Prof. Zhao Congcang with the Archaeology Department of the Northwest China University announced that the first phase dig at the Xihetan Ruins had been completed. Within the excavated area of 11,000 square meters, 53 household items, 536 pits in a variety of shapes and sizes, and many stone and bone vessels had been discovered. The Xihetan Ruins are an important prehistoric site, located along the route of China's west-east natural gas pipeline project as well as at the famous "Gansu Corridor", an important communication channel in ancient northwest China.

Archaeologists say the Xihetan Ruins may cover more than 500,000 square meters, and prove invaluable in the research of ethnic groups along the corridor.

[44] Chariot From 400 BC Found In UK

http://www.cbsnews.com/stories/2003/12/03/world/main586686.shtml

LONDON, Dec. 3, 2003

After 2,500 years, the chariot's wheels remain intact, complete with their iron tires. Inside lie the remains of a man in his 30s, believed to be a tribal chief. Workers constructing a highway through northern England have unearthed a "rare and nationally significant" Iron Age burial chamber containing a two-wheeled chariot and its owner, archaeologists said Wednesday. Oxford Archaeology, an independent archaeological practice investigating the find, said it was the first chariot burial to be found so far inland. The similarity to contemporary French burials "indicates some form of contact and exchange between the continent (of Europe) and Britain during the middle Iron Age," about which little is known.

"Insights gained will make a significant addition to our understanding of the burial rites of the period, and help us to understand a wide range of other elements of cultural exchange," the group said on its Web site.

The remains were discovered by workers constructing the new A1 motorway at Ferrybridge in West Yorkshire, northern England. Archaeologists are now excavating the chariot´s wheels, complete with iron tires, which are in a good condition. The wooden axle has completely decayed, but its position has been identified as a long narrow stain in the soil.

Inside the chariot, a man lies on his back, his legs flexed. He is surrounded by a number of well-preserved bronze and iron objects, some of which are likely to be horse harnesses. Surrounding the grave are the remains of at least 250 cattle, which archaeologists say were probably slaughtered for a funeral feast. Oxford Archaeology said from 500 B.C. to 400 B.C., chariot burial was practiced by a tribe known as the Arras, who came to England from France. The practice was reserved for high-ranking figures. The chariot was placed in a large oval pit in the center of a square ditch, which would originally have been covered by a low earth mound. Archaeologists say square ditches were more popular in continental Europe and the latest find is most similar to others found in France´s Champagne-Ardennes region and the Mosel regionofGermany.

[45] Viking Long Ship Found At Loch Ness-Dec.2003
http://www.lochness.co.uk/exhibition/viking.html

The Loch Ness Free Press has received this exclusive press release from Professor Svenson and his Loch Ness research project: Professor Svenson and Dr. Theo Valdivik announce the discovery of the remains of a Viking long ship at the bottom of Loch Ness. Using their NAVRAD remote bottom probing submarine, the two eminent academics scanned an area of the loch they had carefully selected using their exclusive mathematical formula and a little luck. Professor Svenson, who has previously discovered many new wonders in Loch Ness, said "we are very excited about this find. Initially we thought we had just come across a few rotting old fence posts but it soon became clear that we were looking at the oldest surviving remains of the Viking presence in Scotland."

The pair were even more amazed to discover preserved coffee grounds in the timbers. All previous data indicates that the Vikings did not have access to coffee and this find may cause a whole chapter of their history to be re-written as it now appears that they may have sailed as far afield as South America before heading for the ancient cultural capital of Loch Ness, Drumnadrochit. The remains will now be sent to a mineral processing unit at NASA where they will be carbon dated and injected with fleuron, a special substance that glows if the material around it is more than 1000 years old.

Professor Svenson denied that his find was simply a cheap PR exercise to try and boost the flagging tourist season or a vain attempt to get a plaque erected with his name on it. "That's quite ridiculous. Eminent researchers like me are only devoted to the science and research of Loch Ness and would never issue statements unless we thought they were true. The fact that this is the holiday or silly season has absolutely nothing to do with anything".

[46] Tombs From Egypt's Golden Age Found
http://www.cbsnews.com/stories/2002/10/02/world/main523989.shtml

CAIRO, Egypt, June 6, 2002

*Quote: "Archaeologists have unearthed six 3,500-year-old tombs they believe reveal important details about the structure of government in a period considered Egypt's golden age, the nation's top archaeologist said Thursday."

[47] Would A Microchip Keep Your Child Safe?
http://news.bbc.co.uk/go/pr/fr/-/2/hi/uk_news/magazine/3307471.stm

Transmitter chips and GPS trackers are devices designed to help to trace a child's whereabouts. But do hi-tech solutions raise more problems than they solve? A month after the bodies of Holly Wells and Jessica Chapman were found in a remote ditch, a cybernetics professor known for his headline-grabbing stunts came up with a plan to microchip children to prevent them being abducted.

Professor Kevin Warwick, of Reading University, convinced the Duval family that a microchip implanted in their 11-year-old daughter Danielle's arm would ease their fears. The youngster was nervous about going out alone, following media coverage of the Soham case. If she went missing with a chip installed, it would send a signal via mobile phone networks to a computer, which would pinpoint her location on an electronic map. In the past five years, dozens of murderers have been convicted partly as a result of evidence from mobile phones

But 15 months on, Danielle remains unchipped. "We never heard nothing more about it," Mrs Duval told BBC News Online. "Danielle is still nervous about going out alone. If she does go out, myself or my husband goes with her. She always carries her mobile around now." Professor Warwick says the backlash against the scheme - numerous children's charities came out against the plan - forced him to reconsider. "I was perceived to be an ogre trying to do nasty things to children. The opposition to it made me think that ethically, this is something not deemed to be appropriate."
The Duvals are not alone in their interest in child surveillance technologies. "Every week I get someone e-mailing me to ask if I can do something for their child," says Professor Warwick.

Research by nVision, the online database of the think tank Future Foundation, found that 75% of British parents would buy a device to trace their child's movements. Just such a gadget is on sale in the United States - a GPS locator which can be locked onto a child's wrist - and the company, Wherify Wireless, is now eying up the UK market.

BBC NEWS: Published: 2003/12/18

[48] Bio-chips in Human Bodies - Sierra Times.com

If homeland security's extreme precautions against terrorists haven't gotten under your skin, look again. That's just what they're about to do with VeriChips. A VeriChip is a rice-sized radio frequency identification microchip designed for tracking everything from products to people. The company who created the chip Applied Digital Solutions (ADS) has announced that organizations in Brazil and Mexico have begun implanting the chips in children. And, the Department of Defense announced Oct. 23 that the government will begin using Radio Frequency Identification (RFID) devices throughout the military and the U.S. for product inventory beginning in 2005. U.S. companies such as Wal-Mart also expect to be using RFID tags in 2005.

Depending on the public's response, some American's can expect to find VeriChips being offered in the U.S. as part of a child-identification program very soon. DoD claims RFID technology greatly improves the management of inventory by providing hands-off processing for everything from ordnance to office supplies.

The RFID tags will be applied to everything in the military except sand, gravel, liquids and similar items. Dod expects the system to not only speed up the inventory process, but make it more accurate and less susceptible to human error. Soldiers won't be chipped yet. At least not in the United States. However, the VeriChip is now being used to track people outside the United States. ADS has a program called VeriKid. Under the program children are implanted with a VeriChip an RFID device, using a large needle which injects the device under the skin. The chip gives off a 125-kilohertz radio frequency signal which is transmitted to a nearby scanner or hand held wand. Scanners read the transmitted ID number and use it to identify the child through a database. When a "chipped" child is abducted or missing, authorities place scanners in areas where the child might turn up such as shopping malls, bus stations, airports and other areas. If the child goes by the scanner, the chip triggers the scanner and alerts authorities to the location.

Both Brazil and Mexico have implemented the program for "security purposes" and to track abducted and missing children. Mexico's National Foundation of Investigations of Robbed and Missing Children estimates that 133,000 children in Mexico have been kidnapped over the past five years. According to VeriChip, Mexico launched their VeriKid program earlier this month to protect children from abduction. The company claims the chip will alert whether the child is unconscious, asleep, silenced or even dead.

Brazil has ordered 10 wall-mounted VeriGuard scanning devices to be used as part of their security system which will be launched in Brazil in mid-November. That program, VeriChip claims, will be the first in which implantable chips will be used as part of a building access security system for adults. VeriChip claims their original purpose for the program was medically focused not for security. The company wanted to be able to identify people with specific medical needs, even if they were brought into a hospital unconscious. But VeriChip claims the chip goes far beyond medical uses the company claims.

Parolees could be chipped to make sure they do not break parole. Sex offenders could be tracked even if they did not register with the city as required by law.

It sounds good to some, but opponents to the chips claim that while the RFID's provide some measure of security, they do so at the severe expense of personal privacy. The chip can be linked to any kind of information including financial, medical, criminal history or past convictions, drug use etc. and those with scanners or access to scanners would have access to that information as well.

Law enforcement wouldn't even have to stop a person on the street to question them. A patrol car mounted scanner could relay the person's criminal history faster than a cop could type in a license plate number. If that becomes the case, then the scanners might start popping up anywhere highway overpasses, libraries, schools, or stores.

Those with access to the central database would be able to follow chipped people wherever they went. The chip would easily become an embedded leash and the refrain, "Home of the free," would take on an entirely different meaning.

[49] An ATM Card Under Your Skin
http://www.randyodowd.com/Projects/an_atm_card.htm

Applied Digital Solutions is hoping their 12-by-2.1mm radio frequency identification tag catches on as an under-the-skin alternative to an ATM or credit card.

THE SURGICAL PROCEDURE, which is performed with local anesthetic, embeds a 12-by-2.1mm RFID tag in the flesh of a human arm. ADS Chief Executive Scott Silverman, in a speech at the ID World 2003 conference in Paris last Friday, said his company had developed a "VeriPay" RFID technology and was hoping to find partners in financial services firms. Matthew Cossolotto, a spokesman for ADS who says he's been "chipped," argues that competing proposals to embed RFID tags in key fobs or cards were flawed. "If you lose the RFID key fob or if it's stolen, someone else could use it and have access to your important accounts," Cossolotto said. "VeriPay solves that problem. It's subdermal and very difficult to lose. You don't leave it sitting in the backseat of the taxi."

RFID tags are miniscule microchips, which some manufacturers have managed to shrink to half the size of a grain of sand. They listen for a radio query and respond by transmitting a unique ID code, typically a 64-bit identifier yielding about 18 thousand trillion possible values. Most RFID tags have no batteries. They use the power from the initial radio signal to transmit their response. When embedded in human bodies, RFID tags raise unique security concerns. First, because they broadcast their ID number, a thief could rig up his or her own device to intercept and then rebroadcast the signal to an ATM. Second, sufficiently dedicated thieves may try to slice the tags out of their victims.

"We do hear concerns about this from a privacy point of view," Cossolotto said. "Obviously the company wants to do all it can to protect privacy. If you don't want it anymore ... you can go to a doctor and have it removed. It's not something I would recommend people do at home. I call it an opt-out feature." Chris Hoofnagle, a lawyer at the Electronic Privacy Information Center said implanted RFID tags cause an additional worry. "When your bank card is compromised, all you have to do is make a call to the issuer," Hoofnagle said. "In this case, you have to make a call to a surgeon. "It doesn't make sense to go from a card, which is controlled by an individual, to a chip, which you cannot control."

[50] Chemtrails April 28, 2003
http://educate-yourself.org/ct/index.shtml

The subject of immune suppressing EM signals ties directly into the chemtrail phenomenon. In 2000 I wrote *Chemtrails: Suppressing Human Evolution* which hypothesized that chemtrails contained viral vectors engineered to infect and genetically alter targeted populations to prevent their DNA from activating into a higher evolved form. This may sound like science fiction to you, but read the article and decide for yourself. I still stand by this hypothesis as nothing has yet disproved it.

At the time of the article's publication, there was no evidence of barium or aluminum salts in chemtrail fallout because no one had tested for it, and only shortly thereafter was barium titanate first found in samples. Barium titanate is an incredible dielectric, meaning it holds charge very well. It seemed to me at the time that this substance was used to hold charge on chemtrail fibers so that they would not clump but rather repel and spread out. Today, it is known fact that various barium and aluminum salts and particles are present in chemtrails, some of which are better radar and microwave reflectors than charge holders. This indicates additional reasons for their presence besides homogenizing chemtrail cover.

Various excuses have emerged to explain the chemtrail phenomenon away as benign or benevolent government projects. I already refuted the three main theories in 2000 that chemtrails were part of a mass inoculation program, severe population reduction project, or weather modification, but a couple new ones have emerged since then. One example is a report posted anonymously at carnicom.com (http://www.carnicom.com/report1.htm). It proposed two theories, that chemtrails contain metal particles which reflect sunlight away from earth in order to combat global warming, and that they also create conductive atmospheric ducts to be used in a military 3d terrain mapping project. The global warming theory is clearly false, because biological materials such as various pathogens and dried human blood cells have been found in chemtrail fallout, and also because chemtrails are regularly seen during the night. Where is the sunlight to reflect at night? William Thomas has adopted and popularized this theory, and I must call into question his intentions or sources. The second theory is an actual technological application within the military known as Radio Frequency Mission Planner (RFMP) and Variable Terrain Radio Parabolic Equation (VTRPE). Read about these at the carnicom.com link above. These are used to map enemy territory and more easily monitor their communications. While this may be true, radar and microwave reflective particles such as barium and titanium salts can serve much more sinister purposes. Also, this theory does not explain the presence of biological components in chemtrail fallout, the immune-suppressing nature of chemtrails, nor the fact that thousands of cities across America have been weekly sprayed by chemtrails since at least 1998—if this is a military project, how much testing is needed, and why only over populated areas? Clearly, this theory is being used as disinformation.

Now, it is absolute fact that disease rates spike several days after any particular chemtrail spraying in any given community. Pathogenic materials have been found in multiple chemtrail samples from multiple locations. People tend to get sick with similar symptoms simultaneously in separate towns whose only common factor is that they were sprayed in the same day. Here is a generic list of ingredients I strongly believe are present in chemtrails:

1) immune suppressing chemicals, such as ethylene dibromide (EDB)
2) radar and microwave reflective metallic substance, like barium or aluminum
3) dielectric hollow polymer fibers
4) viral and bacterial vectors remnants of genetic engineering and replication procedures used to construct the pathogenic vectors

With the preceding information in mind, here is an educated guess as to the purpose of metal particles in chemtrails: The purpose of the chemtrail project is indeed to suppress human evolution on a physical, mental, and spiritual level. Its primary goal is to perform aerosol 'gene therapy' upon targeted populations by spraying them with viral vectors capable of shutting down the DNA activation process in those infected. But because viruses themselves are quite weak, several enhancements are needed:

1) the encasing of viral vectors in a hollow polymer fiber to protect them from destructive effects of UV radiation from the sun and to help the agent spread out via electrostatic repulsion of the charged fibers
2) the accompaniment of chemical immune suppressants to weaken and prep the body for reception of the virus
3) the use of microwave reflective substances to help amplify beamed mind programming and disease-signature signals upon the population in order to disarm their metaphysical immunity mechanisms.
4) Secondary objectives are to mind program the masses and modify their collective behavior in conformity with some agenda.

Using HAARP in conjunction with electromagnetic 'ducts' consisting of conductive channels formed in the atmosphere by metal chemtrail particles, focused beaming of mind programming microwave signals upon the population below is possible. As suggested by Laura Knight-Jadczyk, the resonant cavity formed between a conductive chemtrail sheet and the ionosphere can support induced oscillations in the ELF range. Televisions and microwave cell phone towers, two other control methods, are not capable of generating ELF waves as easily as chemtrails in conjunction with HAARP would.

So to recap, because viruses are often disallowed by the metaphysical protection mechanism, an electromagnetic method of disarming that defense is required, hence the microwave amplification. This is not the only reason for manipulative EM signals - such signals can also muddle the mind, implant thoughts, agitate emotions, and induce docility.

Thorough and all-encompassing as these control methods are, they still fail to achieve their aim of suppression and control in cases of individuals with healthy states of being consisting of high levels of awareness, emotional well-being, and reasonably fit physical immune systems. SARS is a good example to illustrate how diseases function in a political, biological, psychological, commercial, and metaphysical contexts. Both SARS and chemtrails are simply part of a hostile agenda implemented by the world's political and military elite to keep earth's population locked down and under control. Fortunately, their methods are imperfect and with each passing day more individuals awaken and empower themselves. It was the intent of this article to help contribute toward this end. Montalk

[51] Chemtrails: A vast online resource site
http://www.carnicom.com/contrails.htm

[52] People Are Robots, Too - Almost
http://www.spacedaily.com/news/robot-03t.html

Pasadena (JPL) Oct 29, 2003 (EXTRACT)

Popular culture has long pondered the question, "If it looks like a human, walks like a human and talks like a human, is it human?" So far the answer has been no. Robots can't cry, bleed or feel like humans, and that's part of what makes them different. But what if they could think like humans?

Biologically inspired robots aren't just an ongoing fascination in movies and comic books; they are being realized by engineers and scientists all over the world. While much emphasis is placed on developing physical characteristics for robots, like functioning human-like faces or artificial muscles, engineers in the Telerobotics Research and Applications Group at NASA's Jet Propulsion Laboratory, Pasadena, Calif., are among those working to program robots with forms of artificial intelligence similar to human thinking processes.

[53] Embryo Made Using Lab Built Sperm
http://news.bbc.co.uk/2/hi/health/3307523.stm

Scientists believe they have been able to produce working "sperm" from cells taken from another part of the body. The cells were able to "fertilise" a mouse egg and begin the process of making an embryo. If proved safe, stem cells could be a source of viable sperm for infertile men, although scientists say that this is many years away. British experts say that there is no guarantee that an embryo created this way would develop normally. A large number of men either cannot produce sperm, or have lost the ability to do so following medical treatment. For many, the only chance of having a child is to use donor sperm - there is no hope of fathering a child themselves. One potential answer is to use "stem cells" - these are the body's "master cells", which, in the right conditions, can turn into every tissue the developing foetus needs. The richest source of these currently is the embryo, although some may persist into adulthood in the body. In theory, scientists believe that certain specialised types of stem cell could be turned into sperm cells.

The latest research, from the Whitehead Institute for Biomedical Research in Cambridge, Massachusetts, in conjunction with hospitals in Boston and Harvard University, took stem cells from a region of the early mouse embryo known to the be source of "primordial germ cells". These cells will eventually prove the source of the fully-formed sperm cells needed for sexual reproduction. The researchers isolated the right type of embryonic cells, and were able to produce a continuously renewing "line" of germ cells in the laboratory - as would be found in the testes of the mouse. In addition, they found a way of encouraging these cells to turn into sperm cells.

These were injected into mouse eggs - and the first stages of fertilisation took place. In half the experiments, a first cell division took place, while in one fifth, the embryo progressed to the "blastocyst" stage, forming a ball of cells ready to implant into the womb. However, no live births have yet been achieved, and some experts believe that the sperm cells produced this way may not carry all the information needed to produce a viable foetus.

Professor Azim Surani, from Cambridge University, told BBC News Online that, as well as the genetic code carried by sperm cell, each one also carried information which regulated which genes worked at which vital point in development. He said: "There is no evidence from any study involving these sperm-like cells that this 'tag' is present - yet it is very important. "Without it, the function of the cell will not be normal."

"It may well be possible to make germ cells - the problem is that at the moment the details are missing. We don't have full control over the system right now. "All this is a long way from being used in humans."

Contacting the Author

There are several ways of contacting me
and I have listed them below.

E-MAIL
This is actually the easiest method of contact
and my primary address is
dkhthedreamkeeper@yahoo.com.au

THE DREAMKEEPER WEBSITE
will ALWAYS have my current email
address as a click on link at
http://thedreamkeeper.com

Deborah Harmes, Ph.D.
My personal website contains the latest information on
all of my published work, book signings, and lectures.
http://www.deborahharmes.com

www.ingramcontent.com/pod-product-compliance
Lightning Source LLC
Chambersburg PA
CBHW022052160426
43198CB00008B/210
9780975198841